Software from

High Performance Systems, Inc.
The Systems Thinking Company™

An Introduction to Systems Thinking

ithink®
Software

High Performance Systems, Inc. • 45 Lyme Road, Suite 300 • Hanover, NH 03755
Phone: 603.643.9636 • Toll Free: 800.332.1202 • Fax: 603.643.9502
Technical Support: support@hps-inc.com • Pricing & Sales: sales@hps-inc.com
Workshop Info: workshops@hps-inc.com • To Order: orders@hps-inc.com
Visit us on the Web at: http://www.hps-inc.com
ISBN 0-9704921-0-3

Acknowledgements

This Guide was written by Barry Richmond. He received great support of various kinds from various people.

Nancy Maville was the principal source of feedback on content, and also provided invaluable editing suggestions. Useful feedback also came from Nancy Cloud, Steve Peterson, and Peter Welles. Steve also readied all of the models associated with the Guide. Working with Debra Gonzales, he also helped create the Index. Debra formatted the text and also helped with rendering the Figures. Jeremy Wallis and Karim Chichakly programmed the features in the wonderful new 7.0 version of the ithink software upon which the Guide is based.

We hope you enjoy the fruits of our labor.

May 2001

Contents

Part 1

Setting the Stage

The two chapters in this Part of the Guide provide context for what follows in the remainder of the Guide.

Chapter 1 surfaces a pressing challenge that virtually all organizations face: *How to create performance-improvement initiatives capable of achieving their intended impacts.* A look at the record suggests that...be it reengineering a set of processes, seeking to realize synergies inherent in a merger or acquisition, developing a successful growth strategy, implementing a change effort capable of sustaining change, creating an effective set of operating policies, or devising a useful Balanced Scorecard, the "fixes" too often fail—frequently, in fact, often exacerbating the very situations they were intended to improve!

The Chapter argues that the cause of our disappointing record within the performance-improvement arena is the poor quality of our underlying mental models, and the unreliability of the associated mental simulations. The conclusion is that finding ways to improve both is the key to meeting the performance improvement challenges we face.

Chapter 2 offers Systems Thinking as a framework, and the *ithink®* software as an associated key tool, that can significantly contribute to improving the quality of our mental models and the reliability of the associated simulations. In Chapter 2, a core set of eight Systems Thinking skills is identified. Each of the chapters in Parts 2 and 3 of the Guide then focuses on helping you develop one or more of these skills in the context of learning to use the *ithink* language to construct progressively better mental models.

Chapter 1

A Pressing Need:

Improving Performance

It is estimated that more than 75% of reengineering efforts do not produce targeted performance improvements. The collapse of the dot.com boom bears vivid testimony to the fact that growth strategies often fail to yield real growth. The great majority of large-scale projects overrun both schedule and budget by very wide margins. Among the avalanche of mergers and acquisitions that has unfolded over the last decade, those that have realized anticipated synergies, number in the small handfuls. Stories abound of costly organizational change efforts that either have fizzled, or worse, exacerbated the situations they aimed at improving. The number of organizations with Balanced Scorecards—replete with metrics that no one understands how to use to improve performance—is approaching epidemic proportions.

How come? Why do so many well-intentioned performance-improvement efforts, conceived by so many smart people, so often miss the mark? And, perhaps more importantly, what can we do about it? What will it take to significantly increase the likelihood that the initiatives we design can achieve the results we intend? These are the questions we'll explore in this Chapter.

Getting to Root Cause

The first step in "fixing" *anything* is to understand why it's broken. If, in general, our performance improvement initiatives too often fall short, a good place to start looking for "why" is at the process by which these initiatives come into being. So how *do* our performance initiatives come into being? The simple answer is: *We think 'em up*! That is, they arise out of the process of thinking. So, let's take a closer look at *that* process.

The first thing to note about thinking is that when we ponder something, we do not actually have that "something" in our head. Think about it...You're trying to figure out whether you should let your kid drive to the party. You're struggling to decide whether to quit your steady, but relatively unchallenging day job, to pursue the wild and wooly challenges of a start-up. You're wondering about the best way it is you are thinking about, you do not have it in your head.

Then, what do you have in there? What are you working with when you're "thinking?"

You're working with a "mental model"—which is to say, a "selective abstraction" of the reality about which you are thinking. You've constructed that model using certain assumptions about how reality, in general, works, and also certain specific assumptions about the particular piece of reality you're thinking about. Let's go through a simple example to make these ideas more concrete.

You're at a nice restaurant. You are thinking about what to have for dinner. The mental model you are "working with" probably includes certain *general* assumptions about the reality of eating, such as: eating makes my hunger go away; when I eat too fast I get indigestion; if I eat dinner with my hands, people will think I'm a slob; and so forth. I'll refer to such general assumptions as "meta assumptions," because they transcend the specifics of any given eating situation. As you'll see, the "meta assumptions" we use when constructing our mental models will play an important role in explaining why our performance-improvement initiatives often don't fare so well. Your dinner-related model also will include some assumptions *specific* to the particular eating situation: the beef here is superb; I'll have a dry, red with dinner, and so forth.

Once you've assembled a preliminary set of assumptions into a mental model, you then "think" with them. I'll use a more operational term to describe what you are doing with them. I'll call it "mental simulation." You are *simulating* your mental model; you're "running what if's"..."Yah, the beef is good here, but what about my cholesterol? I can already taste the wine, but the roads are icy and I don't want to chance it." And so on. You run these simulations in an effort to predict what outcomes in reality are likely to occur.

So, let's review the bidding...When we create any sort of performance-improvement initiative, we think. And, when we think, we construct, and then simulate, a mental model. Therefore, if our performance- improvement initiatives come up short of the mark, it is reasonable to suspect that something is awry in the processes by which we construct and simulate our mental models.

"What's up" with our Mental Model Construction & Simulation Processes?

Each of us has been constructing and simulating mental models for virtually our entire lifetime. And, since practice makes perfect, we ought to be pretty good at doing so! Let's test this plausible conjecture...

What follows is a passage that describes a very simple supply chain. Use it to construct a mental model. Then, simulate the model in order to predict how the system will perform in response to the "disturbance" to which it will be exposed.

A retailer maintains an inventory of product that is shipped to customers on demand. Upon shipping, the retailer orders more product (to re-stock inventory) from the firm that supplies it. The retailer always emails an order to the supplier for an amount of product exactly equal to what was shipped in a given day. If ten units go out in a day, the retailer emails an order for ten units at the end of the day. The retailer never delays in placing the order, and always orders *exactly* the amount of product that was shipped in a given day.

The supplier also is very regular. The supplier always processes the retailer's order immediately upon receipt, then ships the requested amount of product to the retailer. Product always arrives six days after the retailer places the order. The supplier has never been out-of-stock (and never will be!), and has always (and will always) be able to get product to the retailer exactly six days after the retailer's order is placed. Furthermore, no product shipped by the supplier is ever, or will ever be, defective, damaged or lost in transit.

This simple supply chain has been in steady-state for some time. This means that the volume of product being demanded at retail by customers has been constant at some level for a long time, as has therefore the volume of product the retailer has been ordering from the supplier, as well as the amount the supplier has been shipping to the retailer. Everything is in perfect, constant balance. Now suppose, all of a sudden, the volume of demand from customers coming into the retailer steps up to a new higher level, and then remains there (i.e., a one-time, step-increase occurs). On the axes provided in Figure 1-1, sketch the *pattern* you think will be traced by the level of the retailer's inventory, over time, following the one-time step-increase in customer demand.

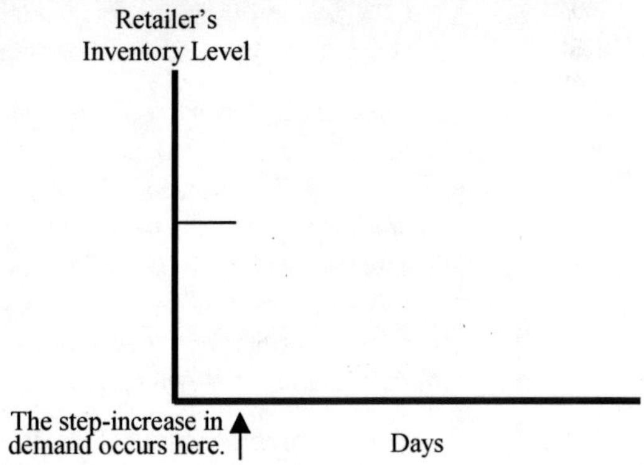

Figure 1-1.
A Sketch of Your Prediction.

Typically, upwards of *80%* of any group who is asked to conduct this type of thought experiment traces an incorrect pattern! The correct pattern is that: *following the step-increase in demand, the Retailer's inventory will decline in a straight-line manner for six days; it then will level off and remain at the new, lower level.* (You'll develop an understanding of why in the next chapter). The relatively small percentage of people who *do* trace the correct pattern has proven to be independent of culture, education level, or experience with supply chains. These results strongly suggest that human beings, in general, either are not very good at constructing mental models (of even very simple systems!), performing mental simulations of these models, or both!

Why Are We Not So Good at Constructing & Simulating Mental Models?

So how come we're not better at constructing and/or simulating mental models—especially given all the experience we've had doing it? I will argue that it's due to a difference in the speed with which biological and socio-cultural systems evolve. The differential speed of evolution has produced a human species whose cognitive machinery is pretty much what it always was, and an operating reality that has become vastly more complex and interdependent. It's this mismatch that's the root of the problem.

Our Simulation Machinery

Simply stated, when our ancestors got thumbs and began to stand up, they unfortunately didn't simultaneously get a huge boost in their cognitive capacities. And, they really didn't need one...at that time. Back when we still lived in caves, our mental simulations served us well. The rules were simple. See bear, whack bear, eat bear...maybe even share. Bear were abundant. Clubs and rocks were "local" weapons. Bear meat wasn't laced with additives, heavy metals, and/or pesticides. We didn't have to trade off time spent hunting, with our day jobs and the kids' soccer practice. Lawyers weren't yet invented. Life was straightforward. Our mental models were very simple. The associated simulations were slam-dunks.

Then came "progress." We created tools, used them to decimate most of the bear, started wearing bear coats and growing our own food, someone invented MTV...and the rest is, as they say, history! Life got complex. It became difficult to do anything without inadvertently causing a bunch of other things to happen—most of which we remained oblivious to. Everything became a "competition." We began competing for resources, people, time, and mind-share. All the free lunches were eaten.

The problem was simply that socio-cultural evolution happened too fast for cognitive evolution to keep pace. To this day, we still can't juggle more than a few variables in our head at a time. And, as far as reliably tracing out the consequences of an action over more than a very limited time horizon...fugeddaboudit! As the little mental simulation exercise you just completed demonstrates, our cognitive machinery limits our ability to conduct reliable mental simulations of even the most elementary sets of relationships.

And, while inadequate mental simulation capability is bad enough, unfortunately, there's *more* bad news! Growing evidence, not the least of which is our record with performance-improvement initiatives, suggests that the mental models we construct do not capture enough of the essence of how reality actually works! There are three reasons why these models don't pass muster: (1) *what's in them*, (2) *how what's in them is represented*, and (3) *the process for honing both content and representation*. We'll examine each...

Reason 1 for Poor Quality Mental Models: Content

Problems with the quality of our mental models begin with what we choose to put in them...and what we choose to leave out—that is, how we choose to "filter" reality for purposes of selecting material for inclusion in our mental models.

The "contents" problem again harkens back to our ancestral past as individual actors in a perilous natural environment. Our neurobiology was honed to respond to what was right in front of us—both in space and time. And for good reason: what was right in front of us could *kill* us—a fact which, unfortunately, remains too true even today! Content-wise, our ancestors' mental models contained lots of detail about what was *immediate,* in both space and time. We knew a lot...about a little. The fact that our weed-level perspective afforded only a limited view of the overall garden was OK, because cause and effect connections were short and direct. Our actions had immediate-in-time, local-in-space, impacts. "Overall garden" impacts just weren't an issue. Our neurobiology was well-adapted for surviving in the primeval garden.

And survive, we did. In fact, we thrived! Our "garden" is now pretty much fully populated—we now number in the billions. And instead of operating as individual actors, we're now members of communities and organizations who operate within a highly-interdependent web. Actions taken by individuals now regularly have "whole garden" impacts. Yet our neurobiological machinery remains essentially the same as when all we had to focus on was immediate! To make matters worse, the structure of many of today's organizations plays to the tendencies toward "localness" inherent in our neurobiology. Manufacturing, Sales, R&D, Finance, IT, HR, and Marketing "silos"—each with its own dialect and culture, each with its well-defined spatial boundaries—encourage the development of highly "local" mental models. Like our ancestors, we continue to know a lot about a little. And, Wall Street does its part to make sure we don't forget about Bears—keeping us locally-focused in time, by making everything ride on *this* quarter's earnings.

So, while almost any action to improve performance taken today has extensive ramifications, both spatial and temporal, the *contents* of our mental models (i.e., the associated boundaries) do not allow us to "think through" these ramifications! As a result, we get "surprised" a lot—and usually the surprises are not pleasant. In addition, because we don't capture the ramifications, it's not possible to *learn* from them! Hence, we are destined to re-live past mistakes. Figure 1-2 depicts the situation…

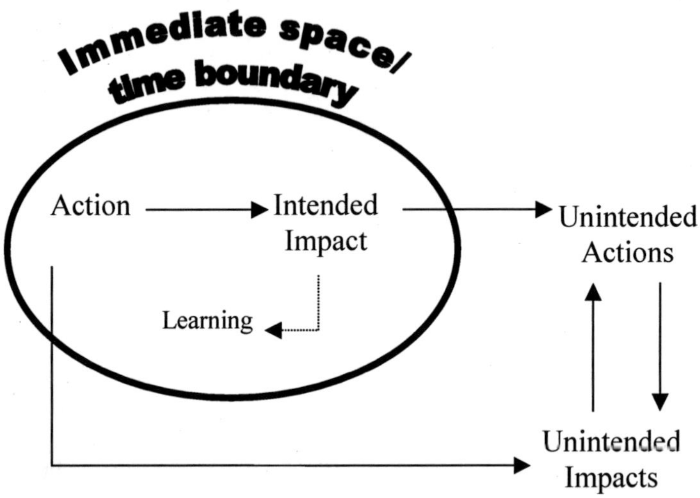

Figure 1-2.
Deep, Narrow Content Undermines the Reliability of Mental Simulation and Limits Learning.

Thus, the first step in improving the quality of our mental models is to improve their content. To do that, we need a better "filter." We need a perspective that allows us to capture content that will enable us to "see" beyond the immediate in space and time, and that will prevent us from getting so bogged down in the weeds that we can't appreciate the "whole garden." As we'll see in Chapter 2, Systems Thinking offers one such perspective.

Reason 2 for Poor Quality Mental Models: Representation of Content

Even if we were able to improve the filter we use for selecting content for our mental models, we'd still need to improve the way we *represent* that content. Simply stated, the "meta assumptions" we use to structure our mental models are not sufficiently congruent with reality. As a result, the "structure" of our mental models does not mirror reality closely enough to yield reliable inferences when simulating them.

Because we make such extensive use of "meta assumptions," they submerge…outright disappear from consciousness! They become so "obviously true," they're no longer subject to scrutiny or question. But if we are to have any hope of improving upon these assumptions, we must first bring them back into view. One way to surface them is to identify conceptual frameworks and analytical tools that are in widespread use in diverse arenas. The fact that they are widely used suggests they mask a set of commonly embraced "meta assumptions."

A popular candidate on the conceptual framework front is what we might label "Critical Success Factors Thinking." Most organizations have identified a set of *critical success factors*. The set most often manifests as a list of "drivers of the business." You see them tacked up on cubicle partitions, taped to conference room walls, and on little laminated cards that people carry around in their wallets. From service delivery to heavy manufacturing to educational institutions, all sorts of organizations have them. And, individuals also have embraced the critical success factors framework. One of best-selling popular books of all time is Steven Covey's *The Seven Habits of Highly Effective People*—critical success factors for individuals seeking to live the "right life." Numerous other best-sellers offer similar success factor recipes for "prevailing" in our complex, fast-paced times.

If we were to diagram the generic structure that underlies a "critical success factor" (CSF) model, it would look like what you see in Figure 1-3.

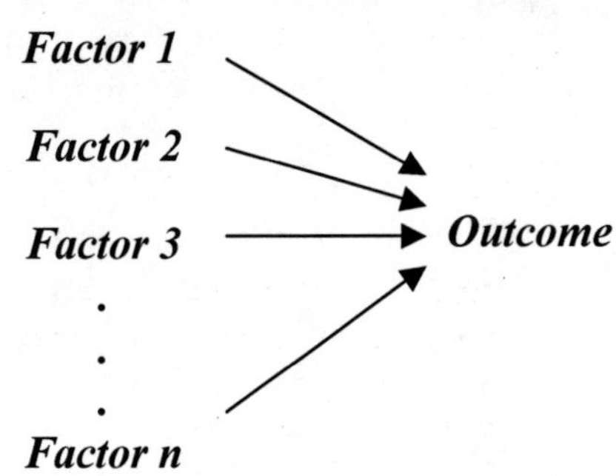

Figure 1-3.
The Generic Structure of a "Critical Success Factor" Model.

Okay, so what "meta assumptions" does this structure reveal? Two obvious ones suggest themselves. The first is that the "Factors" operate *independently*. Each "impacts" the outcome, but it does so, independently. The second is that the "Outcome" does not *cycle back* to influence any of the Factors. That is, *causality is assumed to run one-way*—from Factor to Outcome, but not back again.

Both "meta assumptions" are highly suspect! In today's highly-interdependent world, it's difficult to find *any* "factor" that doesn't influence, and isn't influenced by, multiple other factors. Consider an example from an organizational context. A firm might list, say, technology, good people, and learning as three "drivers" of success. But is it not the case that, top-quality people create good technology, and that good technology is part of what enables people to remain "top-quality?" And further, isn't it "learning" that drives technological advance, and technological advance that, in turn, drives learning? Don't top-quality people learn more effectively than lower-quality people? And isn't the opportunity to learn a key to attracting and retaining top-quality people? So much for the *independence* of "factors" assumption!

The other "meta assumption"—that causality runs one-way, from driver to outcome (and not back again)—is equally easy to dispatch. Certainly it's true that top-quality people help to create successful organizations. But is not the opposite equally true? Isn't the following storyline more congruent with reality as you know it? An organization is spawned by some top-quality people who, if everything comes together, begin to have some success. The success, in turn, attracts other high-quality people to the expanding organization. More success results, and more top-quality people are attracted…and we're off to the *reciprocal causality* races. At some point, the organization will encounter some type of "limits to growth" (nothing can spiral forever!). How the organization addresses these limits will determine whether the spiral continues upward, reverses direction producing a nosedive, or settles into some sort of steady-state.

And so, isn't there really a reciprocal, or closed-loop, causal relationship between top-quality people (or any of the other "factors") and organizational success? Success is not just an *outcome*, something that is "driven" by a set of factors. Success is, itself, a driver! Causality runs *both* ways, not *one-way*! That's "meta assumption" number two you hear landing with a thud!

If we look a little more closely at "Critical Success Factors" models, we can infer the existence of other "meta assumptions." The assumptions also are clearly evident in some of the highly popular analytical tools in use today. So, let's use them for our examples.

One of these tools is the spreadsheet. Another is *The Balanced Scorecard* bubble diagram. A third is "root cause" or "fishbone" diagrams. In the artifacts created by each tool, like the CSF framework, we find "logic trees" with associated causality running only one way. We also often find more independent than interdependent factors. But these popular tools also generally reflect two other "meta assumptions," as well. The first of these is that impacts are felt *instantaneously* (i.e., delays are largely ignored). The second is that impacts are *linear* and *constant* (i.e., an x% change in input always results in a y% change in output).

Looking at "instantaneous impacts," virtually every system/process known to humankind has some inertia in it. Almost nothing responds instantly—at least not the *total* response! There may be some immediate reactions to things, but these usually set in motion other reactions that take time to play out. Delays are a ubiquitous fact of life! They're an important attribute of both organizational and individual reality. Similarly, looking at the second assumption (impacts are linear), what makes life interesting, and impacts so difficult to predict, is that sometimes you can push "a ton" and get an ounce, while other times the tickle of a feather brings down the house! Like delays, non-linear relationships are an essential characteristic of operating reality. The validity of two more popular "meta assumptions" are thus called into question.

If we are to improve the quality of the representations of content within our mental models, we need a better set of "meta assumptions!" In place of the assumptions of independence, one-way causality, and impacts that are instantaneous and linear, we need assumptions that celebrate interdependence, closed-loop causality, delays and non-linearities! Only when the representations in our mental models commonly bear these characteristics, will we increase the likelihood that the initiatives we design will create the outcomes we intend.

Reason 3 for Poor Quality Mental Models: The Honing Process

So, fine... our biology and modern-day organizational structures encourage us to form narrow "filters" that restrict the content of our mental models. And, the "meta assumptions" we employ destine us to represent that content in ways that do not mirror how reality actually works. But, as a result, after "getting it wrong" so many times, why haven't we figured it out and improved our mental models? We continue to lack a process for systematically improving the quality of the content, the representation of content, and the simulation of our mental models. In short, neither our individual, nor organizational, learning processes are very effective. We're pretty good at Knowledge Management (collecting, storing and retrieving knowledge), but we're *very* poor at Understanding Management (collecting, storing and retrieving understanding). Why? First, we don't have a sharable language for integrating our "piece understanding" into a coherent picture of "the whole." And second, we don't have tools for then testing the validity of that understanding. I'll take them one at a time...

On the sharable language score, as already noted, most organizations are collections of functional, divisional, and/or geographic fiefdoms. People who understand "the whole" are rare. Those who understand a "piece" are abundant. If it were possible to somehow *knit together* the "piece understanding" into a *manageable* picture of the whole, we'd all be working with a fundamentally better mental model of the reality within which we are operating. So, what stands in our way? Two things. The first is the absence of an *Esperanto*, a universal language that offers a common set of symbols for accomplishing the "knitting together." The second is a framework that provides a "filter" that passes just what's essential about the way the whole works, without admitting all of the piece detail. This gives us the "manageable" part. Systems Thinking, as you'll discover in Chapter 2, can provide *both.*

On the tools front, assuming we succeed in knitting together piece understanding into a manageable picture of the "whole," we'd then need a way to rigorously test the assumptions that constitute this understanding against reality. We need to test our assumptions both *before* implementing our initiatives, and we also need to be able to double-back to re-visit them *after* reality has performed *its* simulation! Pre-implementation tests give us the opportunity to ferret out internal inconsistencies and to surface "blind spots" (places where we need further information and understanding). Tools, here, are serving as "practice fields"—no risk, rapid-turnaround opportunities to learn before having to do it for real. Post-implementation tests provide opportunities to discover how and why model-projected outcomes differed from what reality actually served up. When discrepancies arise, model assumptions can be modified to better reflect how reality actually works. As a result, over time, the organization's collective understanding can be continuously and systematically improved.

As you'll see in Chapter 2, the *ithink* software is a tool that has been designed to play the aforedescribed role. Used in conjunction with Systems Thinking, it can serve as a powerful resource for meeting the challenge of creating effective performance-improvement initiatives.

What's Next

In this Chapter, I've teed up the challenge: *improving our ability to create effective performance-improvement initiatives.* I've argued that the reason the record of success is not very distinguished is that the quality of the mental models underlying our performance-improvement initiatives is poor, and that the simulation of these models is unreliable. I've also asserted that Systems Thinking and the *ithink* software constitute a powerful tandem for supporting our efforts to improve this situation. Chapter 2 takes on the task of supporting this assertion.

Chapter 2

Systems Thinking & the *ithink* Software

Better Mental Models, Simulated More Reliably

In Chapter 1, I began by reeling off data indicating that a wide variety of performance-improvement initiatives fail to achieve their intended impacts, and in many cases actually fuel the very fires they were seeking to extinguish. I then offered an explanation: the quality of the mental models underlying the improvement initiatives was not sufficiently high, and the simulations of these models were not reliable enough. The prescription I offered was to embrace a conceptual framework and tools capable of yielding both higher quality mental models *and* more reliable simulations. I claimed that Systems Thinking and the *ithink* software were one such framework and tool.

This Chapter is devoted to supporting these claims. To do so, it systematically revisits Chapter 1's "framework of shortcomings" associated with current paradigms (like Critical Success Factors Thinking) and tools (like regression analysis), discussing how Systems Thinking and the *ithink* software can address each shortcoming.

In the "framework of shortcomings," I took current mental models to task for: (1) their content, (2) their representation of content, and (3) for the process used for honing the quality of both. I also averred that our limited mental simulation capacity wasn't up to the challenges posed by the highly interdependent systems within which we must now operate. I will address each shortcoming in turn.

Improving the *Content* of Our Mental Models

The issue with the *content* of our mental models stems from the "filter" we employ to sift from reality the essential raw materials with which to construct our representations of that reality. As you may recall from Chapter 1, the "shortcoming" I identified was that our "filters" tend to be too narrow. As a result, our mental models end up being filled with narrowly-focused detail. We know a lot, about a little.

There really are *two* problems here: not enough breadth, too much depth. Systems Thinking offers "filtering" thinking skills that address both issues. "10,000 Meter Thinking" inspires breadth while moderating depth. "System as Cause Thinking" primarily focuses on breadth.

10,000 Meter Thinking

Imagine you're in a plane at 33,000 feet on a bright, clear day looking down at the earth beneath you. Look at all those cars lining the freeway...Poor suckers! Say, what kind of car is that over there? Can't really tell the make, can you? Could be a Ford, might be a Mazda. Actually you can't even tell what color it is! All you can be sure of is that it is some kind of automobile...it could even be a light truck. That's the view from 10,000 meters. You get a big picture, but you lose discriminations at the details level. You focus more on *categories* than on differences between individual members of a given category. It's "doctors," rather than the 43 medical specialties. Things take on a "generic" character. You can't afford to include all the detail because you are expanding the *breadth* of what you're taking in, and there's a limit to how much content you can structure into a useful mental model.

Figure 2-1 illustrates the difference in the nature of mental model content when a conventional, narrow filter is employed versus a "10,000 Meter" perspective.

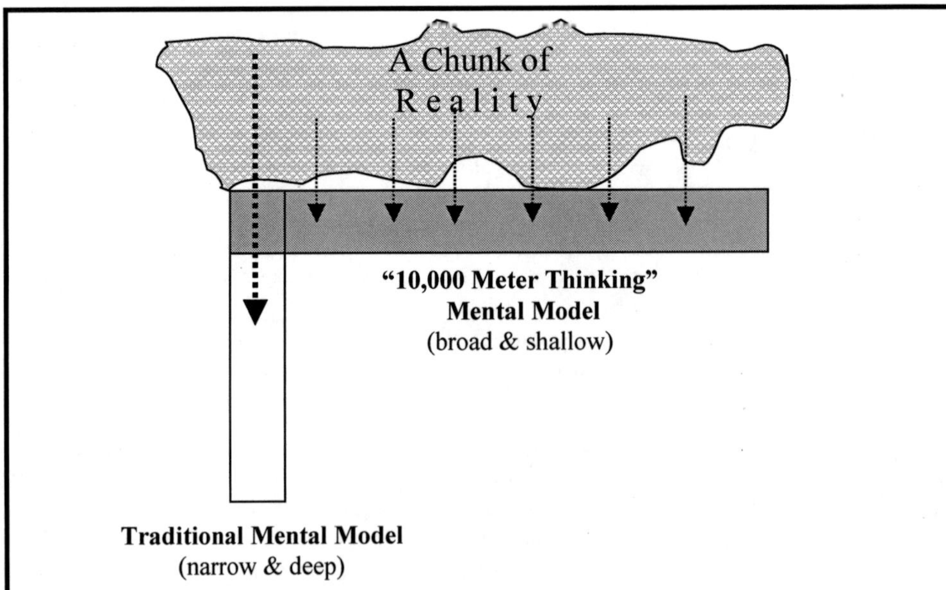

Figure 2-1.
The Content in a Traditional, versus a "10,000 Meter Thinking," Mental Model.

It's important to note that as you "push back" spatially from the reality you're examining, you also are able to take in a broader sweep of time. Compare the breadth of time inherent in the view from your airplane seat relative to your automobile seat. When you are actually down there in all that morning rush hour traffic, all you can perceive is *events* at points in time! A police car speeds by in the breakdown lane. An ambulance follows soon thereafter. Next, a fire truck. By contrast, from your seat at 10,000 meters, you can see the whole *pattern* of traffic backup in both directions, the overturned vehicle, the parade of emergency vehicles making their way to the scene of the accident. You get the big picture in time, as well as space—something vital to successfully anticipating the full ramifications of any initiative you may design.

The other "filtering" skill offered by Systems Thinking is called "Systems as Cause Thinking." We often use a simple physical demonstration to convey what this thinking skill does for you. The demonstration involves supporting a slinky from underneath with one hand, while grasping the top couple of rings with the other, as illustrated in the first frame of Figure 2-2.

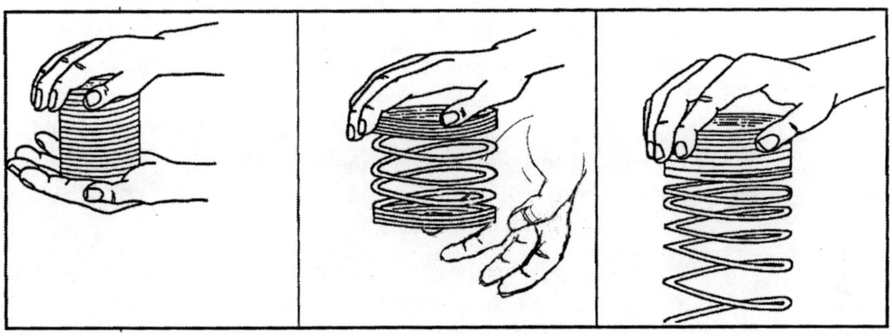

Figure 2-2.
The Slinky Demo.

Next, the supporting hand is withdrawn (the middle frame of Figure 2-2). The question then posed, is: *What is the cause of the resulting oscillation?*

Were you thinking…removal of the supporting hand? Or, perhaps… gravity? Well, congratulations if you were! Those are the two answers we've gotten from 90% of the people to whom we've put the question over the last 20 years or so.

Sure, it's true that had the supporting hand not been removed, the slinky *never* would have oscillated. And, it's also true that even if you *did* remove the hand, had there been no gravitational field, the slinky wouldn't have oscillated. *However*, suppose that the identical experiment were repeated, but this time with, say, a cup! No oscillation, huh? Same removal of the hand...same gravitational field...but no oscillation!

As the experiment makes clear, another way to look at why the slinky did what it did is to consider that its behavior is caused by its *internal structure*. Seen from this perspective, the slinky is an "oscillation waiting to happen." When the right stimulus comes along, the slinky oscillates in response. It's in its nature to do so. Oscillation is "its thing." Not so for the cup.

It's important to note that we are not talking here about a "right" and a "wrong" way to view phenomena. We are talking about two *different* ways to view them. Each has implications for the amount and nature of content that is included in mental models. Briefly, if you embrace a "System as Cause" viewpoint, you will include only those things over which the actors *within the system* can exert some influence. In the slinky example, the slinky *is* the system. So, options for influence center on its design—perhaps we could increase its damping characteristics; make it less of an oscillator. Relatively little attention would be paid to the usually very much larger number of factors (such as removal of the hand and gravity, in the slinky example) over which *no* influence can be exerted. It's not that those embracing "System as Cause Thinking" would completely ignore such factors. But, rather than clutter the mental model with details about them, they'd be lumped into an undifferentiated category called "shocks," things that can "call forth" the dynamics inherent within a system. Little, if any, attention would be paid to their details.

Improving Content, In Summary

"10,000 Meter Thinking" and "Systems as Cause Thinking" work in determining the content that "makes it through the filter" to become the raw materials for constructing your mental models. Embracing these "filtering perspectives" will help to ensure that the mental models you construct will be sufficiently broad in scope, and that their detail will focus on relationships over which you can exert some influence. These thinking skills "get you in the ball park." How well you do, once inside, depends upon mastery of the content-representation skills: *Operational*, *Closed-loop*, and *Non-linear* Thinking.

Improving the Representation of Content Within Our Mental Models

Thinking back to Chapter 1, I asserted that the quality of the representation of content within our mental models depends upon the set of "meta assumptions" we choose to employ. I identified the four most important of these, currently in widespread use. They are: (1) causal factors act independently, (2) causality runs one-way, (3) impacts are felt instantaneously, and (4) impacts are linear. Systems Thinking offers a diametric alternative to each.

Causal Factors Act Interdependently and Causality Runs Two Ways

I've combined the first two "meta assumptions" because they really are two sides of the same coin. That "coin" is *interdependency.* The relevant Systems Thinking skill here is called "Closed-loop Thinking."

In Chapter 1, using the example of key factors driving an organization's success, I hope I dispelled the notion that causal factors act *independently*, and that "outcomes" are "driven." The viewpoint offered by Systems Thinking is essentially that mostly reality is interdependent. Not that it's prudent to try to represent all the linkages in a mental model, but rarely do elements work as independent agents. And, "outcomes" virtually *always* feed back to influence "drivers." As such, it makes no sense to even recognize such a distinction! Rather than a list of independent "causes" running down the left-hand side of the page, with arrows—all of which point to an "effect"—on the right, we instead arrive at a picture that looks more like Figure 2-3…

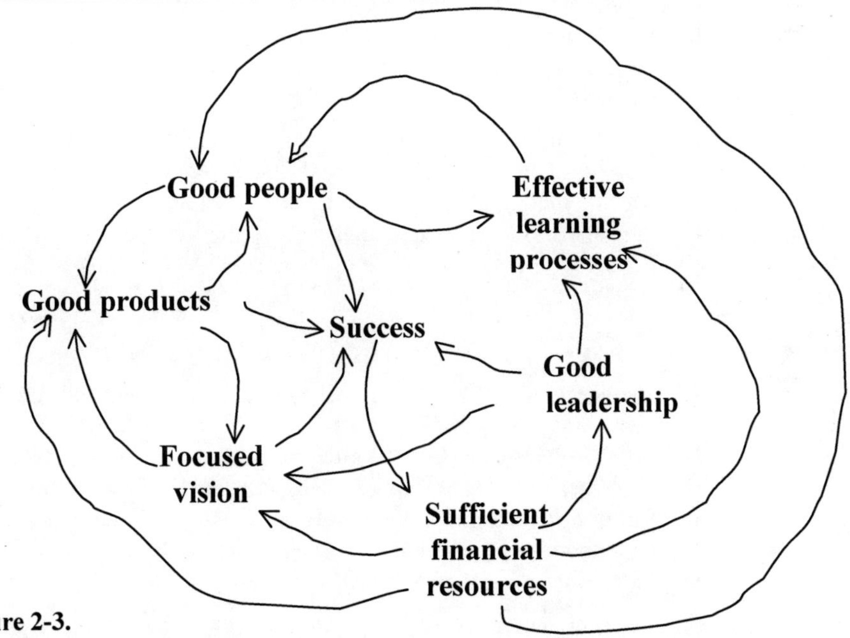

Figure 2-3.
A Reciprocal-causality View.

In this picture, it's virtually impossible to distinguish "factors" from "outcomes." And given the reciprocal-causality, or *feedback loop* view, represented in the picture, it's not clear why doing so would be useful! Representing the content within mental models as existing within a network of feedback loops casts that content in a *dynamic* perspective. Feedback loops, as you'll learn more about in Chapter 6, *self-generate* dynamics! Kick a feedback loop into motion, and like a slinky, it will take it from there! It is being able to divine how a web

Impacts Are Delayed, and "Impact" Should Become "Cause"

of loops is likely to perform that will help us to identify high-leverage initiatives capable of achieving intended outcomes with minimal resource expenditure.

Notice here that I have added something to the description of the *Impacts Are Delayed* "meta assumption." The addition—"Impact" should become "Cause"—is important and necessary because the conventional "meta assumption" that "impacts are instantaneous" belies a much broader assumption about the nature of relationships—an assumption that Systems Thinking disputes. That assumption is that it's okay to think in terms of "impacts" or "influences." A more direct way to say this is that, mental models based on *correlational* relationships are sufficient for underlying reliable mental simulation.

Most Systems Thinkers would say correlational relationships are *not* okay, when the purpose to which you will put your mental model is *improving performance*. A soon-to-be immortal Systems Thinking jingle succinctly expresses the counter notion: "When improving performance is your aim, *causation* must be your game!" Let's look at a simple example that will help to solidify the argument...

Many years ago, while toiling as an economist, I came across an article in a prestigious economic journal that described a model whose aim was to predict milk production in the United States. The model was of the standard "regression analysis" form, expressed mathematically as...

$$Y = (a_1X_1 + a_2X_2 + a_3X_3 + \ldots)$$

milk production = *f* (GNP, feed prices, interest rates, ...)

In plain English, the model posited that milk production in any given year was "impacted" by a set of macroeconomic variables. Specifically, it held that: milk production could be predicted by movements in variables like GNP, feed prices, interest rates, and so forth. For economists, the proof was in the pudding! The model did an extremely good job of "tracking history"—"goodness of fit" being the traditional way such models are "validated."

Later in life, having abandoned the reckless ways of my youth, I returned to reflect on this model, asking myself, and now you, a commonsensical question. Is there a variable, which is left out of consideration when focusing on macroeconomic factors, that's absolutely essential to milk production? By "absolutely essential," I mean in the absence of which there would be NO milk production? Not a single drop!

If you said, perhaps somewhat sheepishly, "Cows"... first, keep your animals straight... and second, welcome to the world of *Operational Thinking*! Operational and Closed-loop Thinking are the two most important Systems Thinking skills associated with *representing content* in mental models. Chapters 3-5 of this Guide are devoted exclusively to Operational Thinking. Only one other thinking skill gets even *one* full chapter's attention (and that's Closed-loop Thinking, Chapter 6). In short, Operational Thinking is a big deal! It's a big deal because, like Closed-loop Thinking, it has to do with how you structure the relationships between the elements you include in your mental models. Specifically, Operational Thinking says that neither "correlation," nor "impact," nor "influence" is good enough for describing how things are related. Only *causation* will do!

In our milk production example, *cows* would be the very first variable included in a model guided by operational thinking. No cows, no milk produced...as simple as that! But why *isn't* correlation good enough, especially since models based on it often yield quite accurate tracking of the past?

Correlation *is* good enough if your purpose is forecasting...and you're lucky (meaning that the relationships that have existed in the past, and from which the correlations have been derived, persist). But, when your purpose is to *change* performance, you are explicitly seeking to *alter* relationships that have prevailed in the past, and to create new relationships in their place. You are trying to identify levers that you can pull to effect change. For this, you *must* understand the associated *causality*!

Let's continue with the milk production example to make these points more concretely. Figure 2-4 shows a simple *ithink* map that paints an operational picture of milk production...

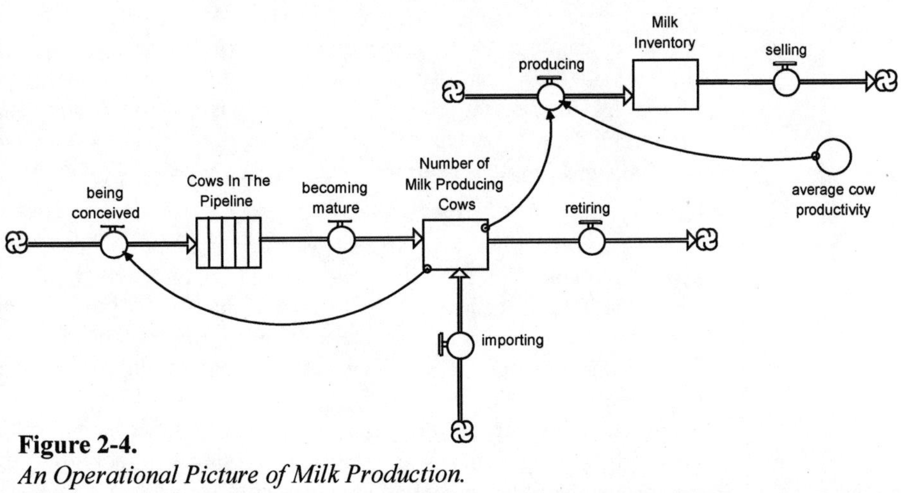

Figure 2-4.
An Operational Picture of Milk Production.

Briefly, the nouns and verbs in the *ithink* language, as you'll discover in Chapter 3, are represented as "rectangles" and "directed pipes with regulators," respectively. The rectangles, two varieties of which are shown in the Figure, represent "accumulations." The directed pipes represent activities. Activities feed and drain accumulations, changing their magnitudes. So, for example, as the volume of milk producing increases, milk inventory will fill—unless the volume of selling activity exceeds the producing volume. The two cow-related accumulations, Cows in the Pipeline and Number of Milk-Producing Cows, are depicted as "conveyors"—think of them as like moving sidewalks—to reflect "maturing and aging" processes. That is, it takes awhile (after being conceived) for calves to become mature enough to join the milk-producing herd. After they do, they remain productive for some average amount of time before aging into retirement.

Given such a picture, we can now "get operational" about levers that can be pulled to increase milk production. "Producing" is *caused* by the number of cows that are producing milk, and how much milk, on average, each of these cows produces in a given period of time (i.e., "average cow productivity"). I did not develop the logic underlying cow productivity for this example. Instead, I focused on making explicit the levers for change on the "number of cows" side. Four such levers are shown in the diagram. Take a moment to see if you can identify them.

To boost producing we must boost the producing herd size. One way to do this is to import mature dairy cows from somewhere outside the US. The diagram does not show all of the "non-instantaneous" transactions that would have to occur in order to bring this about, but you can be pretty sure there would be several. A second lever is the "being conceived" flow. That's right, cow aphrodisiacs and fertility drugs! Want more milk-producing cows? Engineer more cow conceptions! But note that even if you were to succeed, you would have to endure a gestation delay while embryos developed, and then a maturation delay for calves to reach lactating age. Voila a classic *non-instantaneous* impact! Pull the lever now...wait several years for the impact.

The other two levers are a bit less obvious. The first of these is to accelerate maturation (i.e., shorten the length of time calves spend in the Cows in the Pipeline conveyor). Not being a "cow boy," I'm not sure how possible it is to exercise this lever. But in concept, if you *could* reduce the maturation delay, other things equal, you'd have a larger milk-producing cow population. The final lever, for many people, is all but invisible. It is to *reduce* the volume of the retiring flow! In practice, this would mean increasing the retirement age. Exercising this lever is analogous to seeking to grow your customer base by reducing "churn," rather than, say, increasing the inflow of *new* customers. Several companies have found this outflow-based lever to be an extremely useful one to pull. However, growing an accumulation by *reducing* its outflow, as opposed to *increasing* its inflow, continues to remain a counterintuitive notion to many people (*especially* Americans!).

I hope this extended illustration has made clear both what Operational Thinking is, and why the associated "meta assumption" (impacts are non-instantaneous, and more broadly, relationships must be expressed *causally*) is important to embrace when deploying your mental models in service of performance-improvement efforts. You will hear a lot more about Operational Thinking in subsequent chapters. Honing this skill is the key to mastering the practical application of Systems Thinking.

Impacts Are Non-linear

The final "meta assumption" identified in Chapter 1 is that impacts are "linear." This means that if a particular "input" is tweaked by, say, X%, we should expect to see a mX% impact on outcomes—where "m" is a *constant*. So, for example, one might assume that a 10% increase in spending on training will yield a 2.5% increase in productivity, or that a 25% increase in advertising will boost sales by 15%.

In reality, such linear relationships between inputs and resulting outcomes seldom exist! Markets saturate, customers acclimate to product discounts, technology advances, and top-of-mind awareness fades. As a result, sometimes a tweak of a given magnitude will be reciprocated in kind. Other times, it will take an enormous tug just to produce a muted whisper. And still other times, a small piece of straw will be enough to break the camel's back. In short, the "elasticity" of any particular linkage within a web of closed-loop causal relationships is highly dynamic! That's how feedback loops work! Their strength waxes and wanes. Thus, assuming such strengths remain constant, as "linear impact" mental models do, is very likely to earn you a "surprise." That's why Systems Thinkers have identified "Non-linear Thinking" as one of the important thinking skills to be mastered. Much of Chapter 7 is devoted to developing this skill. And, as you'll discover in that Chapter, one of the real powers of the *ithink* software is that it enables you to represent non-linear relationships without the need for any complex mathematics!

In Summary, Improving the Representation of Content

How we represent what we decide to include in our mental models depends upon the "meta assumptions" we embrace. There are four such assumptions in widespread use today. They are: (1) factors act independently, (2) causality runs one-way, (3) impacts are instantaneous (and correlation is "good enough"), and (4) impacts are linear. Mental models that are structured using these assumptions are unfit for underwriting the design of effective performance-improvement initiatives. Systems Thinking offers four counter-assumptions: (1) factors act interdependently, (2) causality runs both ways (there are no "factors!"), (3) impacts are non-instantaneous (only causal relationships will do), and (4) impacts are non-linear. Embracing this set of assumptions yields models that are far more congruent with how reality actually works, and hence stand a much greater chance of underwriting initiatives capable of achieving their intended impacts.

In Chapter 1, I asserted that most organizations (and individuals, for that matter!) lack a process for systematically improving the quality of the content, and representation of content, in their mental models. I cited two reasons why this is the case. First, we don't have a *sharable language* for integrating "piece understanding" into a coherent picture of "the whole." And second, we don't have tools for testing the validity of that understanding. Systems Thinking, and the *ithink* software, can help in addressing both.

An important part of what makes "Operational Thinking" operational is having an icon-based language to create "here's how it works" portraits. The language consists of only four simple icons (each with a few variations), yet it has been used to represent everything from very tangible bottom-line variables (like Accounts Payable, Cash and Inventory) to the squishiest of the squishy (Trust, Commitment, and Morale). The language truly constitutes an organizational *Esperanto*. And this has some very practical importance in terms of honing the quality of our mental models.

Having a language that everyone across the organization can "read" and understand means that "blind spots"—both in content, and representation of content—can be brought to light and discussed. "Oh, *now* I see what you are thinking. I like that part, but this piece over here doesn't square with my experience!" Such comments are typical of the kind generated when a well-written *ithink* map is circulated around an organization. It is obvious from the comment that a "blind spot" has been identified. Less obvious, is something that's very important for the process of honing mental model quality. Because the comment is directed *at the ithink map*, and *not* at the person who authored it, *defensive responses* are much less likely. Such responses literally shut off learning. Thus, by serving as a "third-party object," an *ithink* map can facilitate discussions that enable everyone to share their "piece expertise," and, as a result, work together to *build shared understanding*—the holy grail of any good organizational learning process!

But, an *ithink* map is much more than just a "pretty picture" that facilitates cross-organizational discussion. They can be simulated on a computer to determine whether the relationships people agree are operating, can in fact generate the dynamics being exhibited! In other words, *ithink* models offer an opportunity to "sanity check" a group's thinking—in scientific terms, a way to test whether a model constitutes an "entertainable hypothesis." And, if a model cannot produce the dynamics being exhibited, there's much learning to be had in exploring what changes to content and/or representation of content must be made to enable it to do so? Updating the *ithink* model updates the mental models around the organization. Everyone learns together. The quality of mental model content and representation of content is systematically ratcheted upward.

Before implementing a performance-improvement initiative, the *ithink* software enables people from across the organization to literally "get onto the same page," as well as to ensure that the page everyone has gotten onto is indeed an "entertainable" one. Once this matter is settled, quickly adding an interface, transforms the *ithink* model into a "practice field." People can use a Dashboard to test-fly strategies, new process designs, merger & acquisition possibilities, alternative Balanced Scorecard metrics, and so forth. Organizations can build an understanding of what works, what doesn't, and why—thereby increasing the likelihood that when real "flights" occur, a crash-and-burn (or even an in-flight "turbulence") scenario can be avoided.

Thus far, I've discussed only *pre-implementation* honing of mental models. A huge honing opportunity exists in the post-implementation period as well! Unfortunately, it's an opportunity that too often goes untapped because mental models are not re-visited after reality has spoken. One of the most important reasons re-visiting doesn't happen is that mental models are rarely made explicit. In cases where they are, frequently the job falls to a "back-room analyst." The resulting model is then usually both abstract and complex—often enshrined in a large, multi-sheet spreadsheet. Frequently, such models omit the rich set of *qualitative* assumptions contained in most mental models. The combination of single-person-authorship, analytical complexity, and the absence of qualitative richness, creates low across-the organization ownership for the model. This makes re-visiting an unattractive proposition. And without re-visiting, the enormous potential for learning associated with correcting bad assumptions, filling in the missing pieces, and deleting what's excess, is completely lost!

By contrast, rendering mental models using the *ithink* software is a multi-author, across-the-organization activity. Resulting *ithink* maps are easily "readable" by *anyone* in the organization. In addition, the software elevates "qualitative" variables to full-citizen status, so the full richness in peoples' mental models can be captured. As a result, *ithink*-based models engender a sense of *collective* ownership. And, if the portfolio of various *ithink* models is maintained in an easy-access, on-line database, people from around the organization can "re-visit" at will to compare model-generated to actual outcomes. Anyone then can offer suggestions for improving the content, and/or the representation of content, within a model. Everyone can review the suggestions, posting their reactions to a Listserve, or other electronic forum. In this way, the collective understanding, as reflected in the current state of the *ithink*-based "library," can be systematically ratcheted upward over time. Anyone has instant access to that understanding. With such an *ithink*-based *organizational learning infrastructure* in place, everyone can contribute to helping everyone else to get smarter.

It's also important to note that the previously-described organizational learning infrastructure is robust with respect to people movement. That is, when people leave the organization, they won't "take away" their understanding because it also exists within the collection of *ithink* models. And, when new people join the organization, they can visit the "Library" to quickly come up to speed on the best available current understanding within a range of arenas.

The *ithink* software can play an important role in the process of honing our mental models at both the level of the individual and the organization. The opportunity awaits!

Improving Our Inherent Simulation Capabilities

The final shortcoming (identified in Chapter 1), which undermines our efforts to design effective performance-improvement initiatives, is the inherent limitations of our mental simulation capabilities. There's not a lot anyone can do about the neurobiological portion of these limitations. But there is something Systems Thinking and the *ithink* software can do to help us realize more of the capability that we do have, and "cover our backs" for what we don't.

Systems Thinking, as argued throughout this Chapter, can help by improving the quality of the mental models you construct. Higher-quality mental models—broader spatial and temporal boundaries, just-what's-needed detail, and more congruent representation of content—yield more reliable mental simulations. In addition, used judiciously, the *ithink* software can help strengthen your mental simulation "muscles" by providing rigorous feedback on your mental simulations. To benefit from this feedback, it is essential that you make predictions about simulation outcomes explicit *prior to* initiating an ithink simulation! Then, by checking to see if you were right, and for the right reason (or were you just lucky?), you can progressively hone your capacity for intuiting dynamics. Used in this manner, you can think of the software as a kind of aerobics studio for the mind.

To illustrate how the *ithink* software can be used to hone your intuition for dynamics, let's return to the mental simulation exercise you did in Chapter 1. Recall you were asked to predict how a simple supply chain would respond to a "disturbance" by charting the pattern you thought would be traced over time by the level of a retailer's inventory. I've created an *ithink* map from the description provided in Chapter 1. I'll use it to rekindle your memory of that description. The map appears in Figure 2-5.

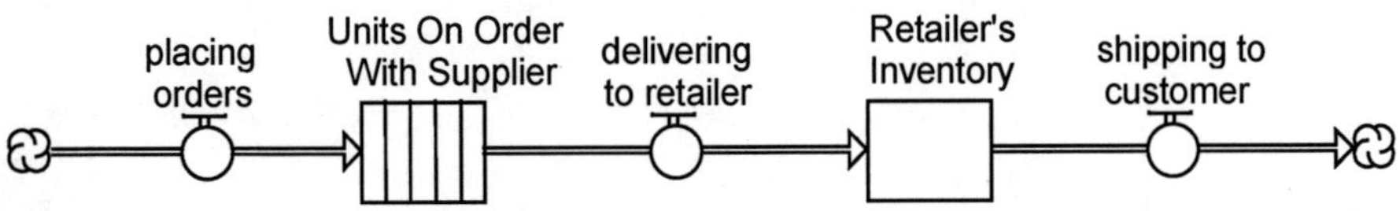

Figure 2-5.
An ithink Map of the Simple Supply Chain.

There are two general things to note about the diagram in Figure 2-5. First, several paragraphs of text have been replaced by a simple picture. An economy of communication has been realized. Second, the same set of icons that was used in Figure 2-4 to represent cows, and the associated milk production, is now being used to depict a supply chain. Holy *Esperanto*, Batman!

From the diagram, it should be clear that the retailer ships product out of inventory to customers, using information about the shipping volume to determine the ordering volume. The final salient detail in the diagram is the delay that exists between the time an order is placed, and its subsequent delivery to the retailer. With this brief description, let's now use the diagram to facilitate a mental simulation of this system...

The system as described is initially in "steady-state," a condition that's easy to visualize by looking at the map. It means, in this case, that the three *flows* in the chain are equal and constant, and hence the two *stocks* are unchanging in magnitude. Note that, in order for the delivering flow to equal the ordering flow, each of the six "slats" (one for each day of the delay) in the conveyor (only five "slats" are shown in the conveyor icon!) must contain an amount exactly equal in volume to the ordering flow. This will be the case because the system has been in "steady-state" for more than six days. Look at the diagram and make sure you can visualize this.

Suddenly, a step-increase occurs in the volume of shipping to customers. What happens? See if you can trace it through using the map. Because you are interested in the pattern traced by the retailer's inventory over time, focus your mental simulation on the inflow to, and outflow from, inventory...

Shipping, the outflow from Retailer Inventory, steps *up*. Does delivering, the inflow to Retailer Inventory, step up at the *same* instant? No! Ordering does, yes. But *not* delivering! Delivering will remain at its pre-step volume for six days, because that's how long it will take to empty the six "slats" carrying the *pre-step-increase* ordering volume. After six days, the new, stepped-up ordering volume will have made its way through the pipeline and begin being delivered into inventory! Hence, delivering will again equal shipping, and the retailer's inventory will again remain constant.

So, in summary: Inventory will continue to decline for six days by a daily amount equal to the difference between the new, higher shipping volume and the pre-step delivering volume. After six days, the delivering flow will step up to once again equal the shipping flow, and the system will be back in steady-state—but the retailer's inventory will be at a permanently *lower* level!

This example is intended to illustrate that *ithink* maps are useful for facilitating mental simulation, and can help in developing your capacity for intuiting dynamics. Computer simulation then can be used as a check on mental simulation, to ensure you were "thinking it through" correctly. If we simulated the supply chain system using the *ithink* software, and graphed the retailer's inventory level and the three flows in the system, we'd get something that looks like Figure 2-6. As predicted, the retailer's inventory traces a straight line downward for six time periods following the step-increase in shipping that occurs at Day four. Note that ordering also steps up at exactly the same time. However, as the graph clearly shows, delivering does not follow suit until Day ten—*six* days later! If the inflow volume to a "bathtub" is less, by a constant amount, than the outflow volume, the level of water in the tub will decline at a constant rate. The *ithink*-based simulation helps to concretize the intuition.

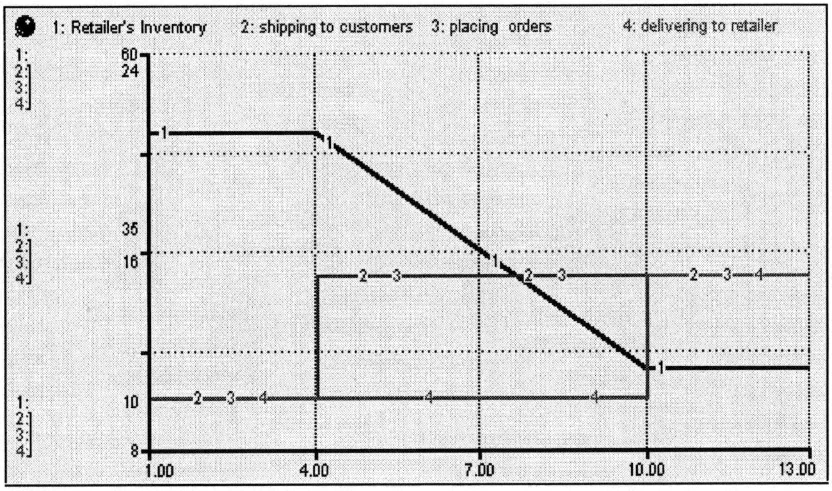

Figure 2-6.
A Graph of Key Supply Chain Variables.

Summary & What's Next

This Chapter has sought to support the claim that Systems Thinking and the *ithink* software offer a powerful combination for improving the quality of our mental models, and increasing the reliability of the simulation of these models. Without them, or some equally powerful alternative, we will continue to create poor quality mental models and to generate unreliable simulation results from these models. This means we will continue to risk missing the mark with our strategies, policies, processes, change efforts, and other performance improvement initiatives.

By embracing Systems Thinking, and leveraging its application through judicious use of the *ithink* software, we have a much greater chance of *constructing* mental models that better reflect the reality whose performance we are seeking to improve, and also of *simulating* these models more reliably. The result of doing so is an increased likelihood of creating performance improvement initiatives capable of achieving their intended impacts.

In the Chapters that follow, you will build your Systems Thinking skills, and gain a thorough grounding in the language of the *ithink* software. You will learn how to use these thinking skills and language to render your (and others') mental models. *Congratulations* on your purchase of the software! You have taken an important step toward thinking more clearly, learning more productively, and communicating more effectively.

Part 2

Learning to "Write" Using the Language of Systems Thinking

The purpose of Systems Thinking is to offer a better conceptual framework for underwriting construction and subsequent simulation of our mental models. All mental models are "written" in some language. Usually it's a word-based language, and often the words are "specialized," in that they reflect a dialect specific to a particular realm—be it a functional, geographic, or generational domain.

The language of Systems Thinking, as reflected in the *ithink* software, integrates words with a simple set of icons. The icons are *generic* in nature, the purpose being to create an *Esperanto* (a universal language). Such a language enables people with diverse viewpoints and specialized expertise to jointly contribute to building a collective, systemic understanding. Without such an understanding, designing effective performance initiatives becomes a hit or (more likely) miss proposition.

As in learning any language, there is a logical progression to follow. It begins with the basic parts of speech, moves on to constructing sentences, then building paragraphs, and finally to writing short stories and more elaborate forms of composition. The Chapters in this Part of the Guide are organized in accordance with this progression. Each chapter also targets development of one of the key Systems Thinking skills. Chapters 3 thru 5 target *Operational Thinking*. Chapter 3 discusses the nouns and verbs of the Systems Thinking language. Chapter 4 treats the grammar for constructing good *basic ithink* "sentences." Chapter 5 shows how to link sentences together, introducing "adverbs" in the process. Chapter 6 targets development of *Closed-loop Thinking* skills. In this Chapter, you'll learn to construct paragraphs—or, in the parlance of Systems Thinking, "feedback loops." Finally, Chapter 7 will develop your *Non-linear Thinking* skills.

Chapters 8 and 9 really are more like an Appendix to Part 2. They present a portfolio of classic "storylines." These simple generic infrastructures can serve as nuclei for the short stories, and even full-length novels, you choose to write with the software.

Viewed within a language context, the *ithink* software is analogous to a word processing package. That is, it facilitates the *rendering* of what you wish to express (in this case, the assumptions constituting your mental model). However, it does not help you in coming up with *what* to express. And so, just as a great word processing package won't make you a great writer, the wonderful *ithink* software will not make you a great model builder. Something more is needed. Part of that "something" is mastery of the set of Systems Thinking skills, and facility with the associated language. The chapters in Part 2 of the Guide will help you develop both.

Chapter 3

Nouns & Verbs

Operational Thinking

Most languages recognize the fundamental distinction between nouns and verbs. Nouns represent things and states of being; verbs depict actions or activities. The *ithink* language is no different. And, as we'll see in the next chapter, it takes at least one noun and one verb to constitute a grammatically correct "sentence" in the *ithink* language as well. So we're on familiar ground with this language. The big difference is that the *ithink* language is icon-based, and the icons are *operational* in nature. This means that when you tell a story using the *ithink* language, you can see it not only in your mind's eye, but also with your *real* eyes! And everyone else can see it with his or her real eyes, too. As a result, both opportunities for ambiguity, and chances for miscommunication, are greatly reduced. The *ithink* language is super-literal. You wouldn't want to compose sonnets for your loved one with it. But if you're trying to make explicit your mental model of how something works, it's tough to beat!

Nouns

As already noted, nouns represent things and states of being. The "things" are usually physical in nature, like: Inventory, Headcount, Cash, Debt, and Pollution. The "states of being." are usually non-physical in nature, like: Quality, Anger, Hunger, Thirst, Self-esteem, Customer Satisfaction, Commitment, and Trust.

A theme that emerges early on in Systems Thinking is the *full-citizen status* accorded non-physical variables. That is, Systems Thinking recognizes that non-physical variables play just as important (and in many cases *more* important) a role in determining the behavior of many systems as physical variables do. It's true that organizations don't function very well without cash or people. But it is equally true that they don't function very well without commitment or trust. Leaving such variables out of consideration when constructing explanations for why a particular pattern of dynamic behavior is being exhibited often makes no sense! But people do it. And it's usually because they feel such "intangibles" can't be measured. And they're right! But they can always be *quantified*! And once they are, they look just like any other quantity to the *ithink* software. They then can be treated rigorously.

A full discussion of these weighty issues awaits you in Chapter 13. For now, recognize that the nouns in the *ithink* language—even though it's a computer-simulatable language—include all those squishy things that really make the world go 'round. After all, where we would be without lust, jealousy, greed and anger?

Nouns in the *ithink* language are represented by rectangles. The rectangle was chosen because it looks like a bathtub viewed from the side. And bathtubs turn out to be a good physically-intuitive metaphor for what all nouns represent: i.e., *accumulation.* That's right, accumulation! Inventory accumulates on store shelves, in transport trucks, and in warehouses. Cash builds up in pockets, wallets, and bank accounts. Anger builds up all over your body, in circulating adrenalin, in blood pressure, in the tightness in your muscles. Love swells over the course of a relationship. So, when you think about nouns in the *ithink* language, think rectangles. See them as bathtubs that fill and drain. The difference is that these tubs will only rarely contain water.

Nouns, in the *ithink* language, are called "stocks." The convention in naming stocks is to designate them with first-letter capitalization. As you'll see, this will help in visually distinguishing them from flows—which typically are scripted in all lower-case letters.

There are four varieties of stocks: *reservoirs, conveyors, queues, and ovens.* The *Help Files* do an exquisite job of documenting the functioning of each. Here, our task will be to help you distinguish the four types, and to determine when each is the most appropriate one to use.

By far, the most frequently used type of stock is the *reservoir.* You can use a reservoir to perform essentially all of the functions of any of the other types of stock. A distant second in frequency of use is the *conveyor.* And way back there, almost in total obscurity, are the *queue* and *oven* (which is why these two are not included in the *Strategy* version, and appear only in the *Analyst* version). The lineup of stocks appears in Figure 3-1.

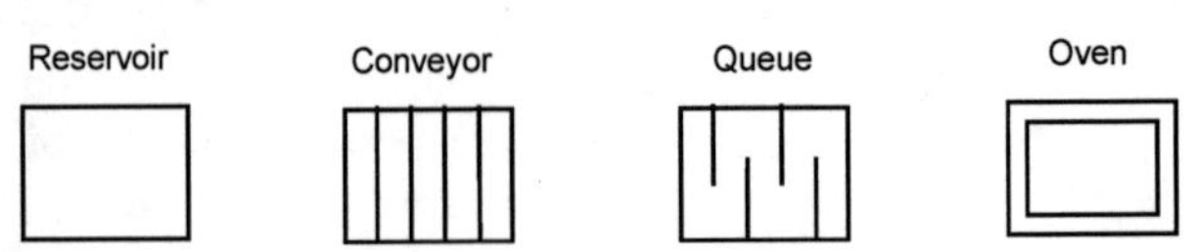

Figure 3-1.
The Four Types of Stock.

The Reservoir

Reservoir

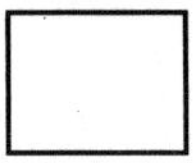

The reservoir operates most like the bathtub. Stuff flows into a reservoir, and once it does, individual entities become indistinguishable. So, for example, looking at a bathtub full of water, it is impossible to distinguish which molecule arrived first, which 10th, and which came in last. Instead, the molecules blend together; all arrival time discipline and size-chunking are lost. You've simply got a certain number of liters of water in the tub. The same is true when you use a reservoir to represent, say, headcount or cash. You can't distinguish Jamal from Janice in a reservoir labeled Headcount. You just have a total number of people. And the $100 bills are indistinguishable from the $1,000 bills in a reservoir named Cash. You just have a total amount of money. You can't tell which bill came in when, nor can you distinguish bills of different denomination. Reservoirs blur distinctions between the individual chunks of stuff that flow into and out of them. Instead, they collect whatever *total* volume of stuff flows in, and give up whatever *total* volume flows out. At any point in time, they house the net of that which has flowed in, minus that which has flowed out.

The Conveyor

Conveyor

Think of conveyors as like those "moving sidewalks" you see in airports, or like an escalator at your favorite mall or department store. You step on, you stand and ride for some distance, you get off—unless you're one of those Type A's who has to walk at full stride (while being transported), so as to *double* your unassisted ground speed. That's how conveyors work. Whatever quantity arrives at the "front door" gets on. That quantity takes up a "slot" on the conveyor. Nothing else can occupy that slot. The quantity "rides" until the conveyor deposits it "at the other end." The "trip" will take a certain amount of time to complete (known as the transit time). Conveyors are great for representing "pipeline delays." Such delays exist, for example, in all value chains, and in all "processes" in general. Indeed, conveyors often are used to provide a "quick and dirty" representation of process—stripping the process to its bare essentials: i.e., it takes "this long" to complete the activity, and x% of the stuff doesn't make it all the way through (i.e., is defective, is lost to waste, quits, etc.).

Unlike reservoirs, then, conveyors maintain arrival integrity and, sometimes, also batch size. If one $100 bill arrives at time 3, and one $500 bill arrives at time 5, and both "get onto" the same conveyor, you'd be able to continue to distinguish the bills while they're on the conveyor, and the $500 bill will arrive two time units after the $100 bill—assuming the transit time of the conveyor remains constant (an assumption that can be relaxed—see *Help Files* for details). Batch size is *not* retained in situations where, say, two $100 bills arrive at the *same* time (you'd then have a quantity of $200 "riding along").

Queues and Ovens

Queue

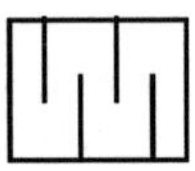

Oven

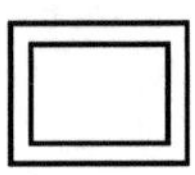

The danger in relying too heavily on conveyors (or queues and ovens), is loss of "the view from 10,000 meters"—one of the key filtering skills needed to do effective Systems Thinking. When you begin distinguishing between individual trucks, and worrying about whether that particular package (the red one over there) was delivered at 9:15 or 9:17, you have descended into the weeds. You are no longer seeing "the big picture." You're looking for specific answers, not general insights. And you're also pushing the boundaries of what the *ithink* software is best suited for doing. As a general rule, try to capture accumulations with a reservoir. If that really doesn't work, go with a conveyor. If you find yourself using a lot of conveyors, call us (we'll schedule you a plane flight).

I've disparaged queues and ovens pretty thoroughly, so you're probably wondering if you should even bother reading this section. You can skip it with no loss of continuity. Frankly, we included them in the software because the very technical end of the population using ithink asked for them. These elements are pretty important for doing what's called "discrete event" simulations. Don't worry if this term is foreign to you. Suffice it to say that the *ithink* software emanates out of a "continuous" viewpoint on reality—again, we are talking the "view from 10,000 meters." Queues and ovens are instruments in service to the "discrete" worldview. Including them in the software represents our attempt to do what physicists have been trying to do for 150 years—resolve the wave/particle duality issue! We figured, "No problem guys, here's the answer you've been looking for!"

With these caveats in place, for certain applications, queues and ovens can be useful. A queue is a "line" like you often see waiting to check-in at an airline ticket counter, or in front of our offices every morning waiting to purchase the *ithink* software. Queues develop when things arrive at a rate that exceeds the capacity to "absorb" them. Think of cars stacking up at the tollbooths on the George Washington Bridge, waiting to enter New York City. Or, even closer to my own heart... imagine cars amassing at one of the entries to what New Englanders affectionately refer to as a "rotary" (and what I call, "the wheel of death"). Ah, civility at its best!

Queues retain both arrival integrity and batch size. In the *ithink* software, there's no "cutting in line," and there's also no "leaving" once you're in line. When a volume of stuff "arrives," if it can't "enter," it stacks up in the queue (in a unique spot). Stuff that arrives later, "gets in line," behind the stuff that's already there, and it stays there! Again, the *Help Files* provide more information on Queues.

If conveyors are escalators, ovens are elevators. People arrive at an elevator and if the doors happen to be open, they enter and then ride.

In the much more likely event that the doors are closed…people queue up, the car arrives, the doors open, people exit, the mob enters, the person with the bad breath stands next to you, the doors close (no one else can get on), and you ride. It's the same in the *ithink* software—minus the bad breath! Stuff arrives at an oven. If it is currently "baking," the stuff waits (in a queue, or a reservoir). When the "baking cycle" is complete, what's inside exits, and the stuff that's waiting, enters (up to the capacity of the oven, or until the "doors open" time expires). That stuff then "bakes" for the length of the oven's "bake time." It's then disgorged and the cycle begins anew. The *Help Files* are once again your authoritative source for detail on oven operation.

Verbs

Nouns are wonderful things, but sans verbs…no sentences! Verbs represent actions or activities. Unlike nouns, which exist *at a point in time*, verbs exist *over time*. The distinction is the same as that recognized by Balance Sheets and Income Statements. The former reports on the state of a business *at a point in time*, say, December 31, 2002. The latter reports on what has happened *over a period of time*, say between, January 1, 2002 and December 31, 2002. So, if stocks tell you how things *are* in a system, flows indicate how things *are going*! As flows occur, they *update* the values of stocks. The only way for the water level in a bathtub to change is for new water to flow in, or for water that's in the tub to flow out. Without flows, conditions within a system would remain *unchanged*. So, it's flows that give us dynamics!

Like stocks, flows can be physical or non-physical in nature. On the physical side we have things like: hiring, quitting, delivering, dying, producing, in-migrating, selling, and ordering. On the non-physical side we have things like: getting angry, building self-confidence, becoming frustrated, praising, cajoling, discussing, arguing, and learning. Notice all the "ing" endings! It is good practice when naming your flows to use the gerund ("ing") form of the verb. Doing so eliminates ambiguity (in particular confusion with stock concepts) and also better connotes movement.

Consider for example the difference between the words "hiring" and "new hires." In conversation, both are used to refer to the volume of people who have recently joined an organization. But the former is a rate, or "per time," concept, while the latter is an "at a point in time" (i.e., stock) concept. For example, someone might say we have 10 "new hires." Those "new hires" could have flowed into the company over, say, a 6-month period. In that sense, they constitute an accumulation of people, a stock! But if someone were using the term "hiring," they'd necessarily be talking about an action. We're hiring

10 new people between now and the end of the year. So, in naming your flows, in general, try to use the gerund form wherever possible.

Frequently, exceptions to the "ing" naming convention occur in the financial domain. And it is because of these exceptions, in my opinion, that there is so much confusion about financial variables among the relatively financially uninitiated. So, it's on the income statement (the document dedicated to reporting "flow" volumes) that we find things like revenue, expense and profit—not an "ing" in the bunch! And it's because of the absence of "ing's" that people, for example, often want to make revenue and profit *stocks* in their *ithink* models. They're not! They're flows. Cumulative revenue (e.g., revenue *for* the quarter, as opposed to *over* the quarter) is a stock, but not revenue itself. So watch yourself with financial variables, and in general, try to make your flow names end in "ing." "Sales," by the way, is another one of these frequently misconstrued concepts. It is often represented as a stock in *ithink* models—and it isn't! To compound the confusion, when people say "sales," and then use a stock to represent it, they frequently are meaning "sales revenue," which has the units $/time, and as you now know, is also a flow.

One of the real benefits that come from being careful to recognize the distinction between stocks and flows is that the accuracy and clarity of your verbal communications will increase. Ambiguities, which cause people to talk right past each other, will disappear. Communication will become much more efficient and effective!

Flows come in fewer flavors than stocks. There are two varieties, and one "wrinkle." Pictures of all three appear in Figure 3-2.

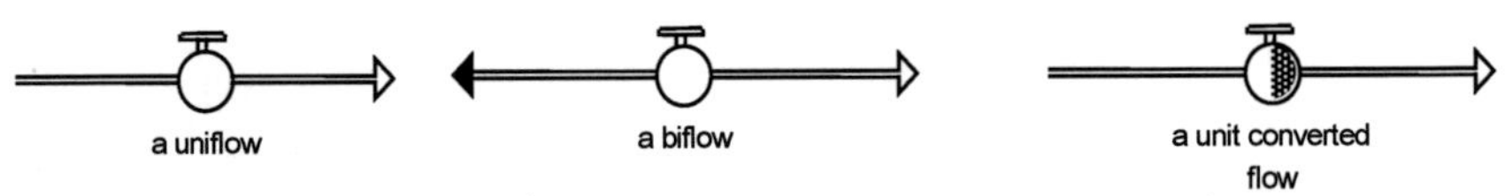

Figure 3-2.
Two Flow Types and One "Wrinkle."

The Uniflow

The standard type of flow is called a "uniflow," which stands for "unidirectional." The direction of flow is indicated by the arrowhead. If the arrowhead points *into* a stock, the flow can only *fill* the stock—and vice versa. If a uniflow is an *inflow*, and for whatever reason, its magnitude evaluates to a *negative* number (indicating that the flow should be *draining* the stock), the flow will assume a value of *zero*!

That is, inflows cannot operate as outflows! Another way to say this is, what you see in the map is what you get! The diagram doesn't lie.

The Biflow

The other kind of flow is the biflow. It allows flow volume to go in *both* directions, either into or out of a stock. As you discover when you learn how to "write sentences," the general rule is that if the processes governing the inflow and outflow are identical in nature, use a biflow. Otherwise, use a uniflow. A good example of a legitimate biflow is "profit." Suppose you had a stock called Cumulative Profit, which represented the total amount of profit accumulated, say, over a year. The associated flow would be profit (perhaps more accurately named, quarterly, or monthly, profit). If the flow of revenue over a quarter exceeds the flow of expense over that quarter, profit flows *into* Cumulative Profit. If the expense flow exceeds the revenue flow, profit flows *out of* Cumulative Profit. The "accounting process" that defines profit (i.e., revenue – expense) is identical, and therefore the flow of profit is aptly depicted as a biflow. However, if we were to consider the nature of the revenue and expense flows themselves, these would be very different! Hence, both revenue and expense are best depicted as uniflows.

The Unit-converted Flow

We're now up to the "wrinkle:" unit-conversion. In some rare cases, it makes sense to convert the units-of-measure of what's flowing, *while it's flowing*! This would enable you to, for example, pull logs out of a pile and convert them into board-feet before they were deposited into an inventory of lumber, as is illustrated in Figure 3-3.

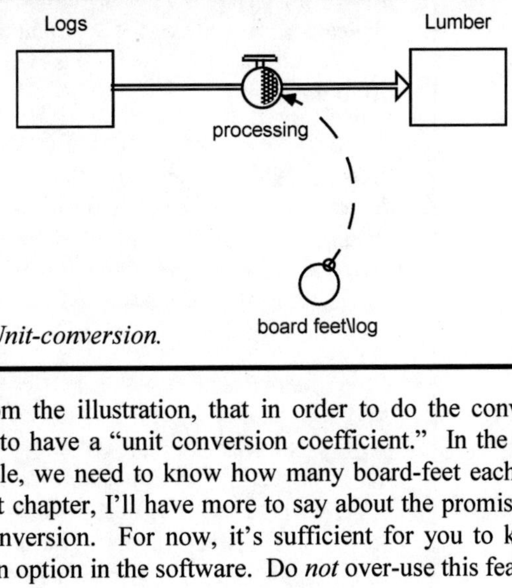

Figure 3-3.
Illustrating Unit-conversion.

Notice from the illustration, that in order to do the conversion, it's necessary to have a "unit conversion coefficient." In the illustration, for example, we need to know how many board-feet each log yields. In the next chapter, I'll have more to say about the promise and perils of unit conversion. For now, it's sufficient for you to know that it exists as an option in the software. Do *not* over-use this feature!

Distinguishing Between Stocks and Flows

We've made a pretty big deal about distinguishing between stocks and flows. But what's all the fuss really about? Why is the distinction so important?

The distinction is so important because stocks and flows constitute the two fundamentally different processes by which reality actually works: *accumulation* and *flow*. If you fail to make the distinction in constructing your mental models, you are virtually assured of making erroneous inferences about dynamics! First, I'll illustrate the distinction. Then, I'll illustrate how failing to recognize it can lead to erroneous inferences—and hence ineffective policies, strategies, processes, and Balanced Scorecards!

Distinguishing Stocks from Flows, a Simple Test

In practice, the best way to distinguish stocks from flows is to perform a simple thought experiment. Imagine instantly "freezing" all activity within a system. This means, in stock and flow terms, that all of the flows instantly go to *zero*. But notice that the stocks do not instantly become zero! Instead, they remain at whatever magnitude they were at, at the instant the "freeze" occurred. The magnitudes of stocks *persist*, even if all activity disappears. Let's take a couple of examples to cement the idea...

If you are scolding a child, when you stop, by definition the scolding activity goes to zero. But the child's level of self-esteem, anger, chagrin, or whatever other non-physical stock the scolding activity may have been impacting, does not go to zero when the scolding stops! In fact, often the dynamics will only begin to unfold *after the scolding flow has ceased.* The accumulations that have built up, or been depleted, as a result of the scolding activity will, in turn, set in motion new activities. These activities will impact other stocks. And we're off to the races!

To give an example in more of a business context...Say you shipped a defective product, and you then fix the process responsible for the defect. Doing so doesn't cause the level of Customer Satisfaction to instantly shoot back up to pre-defective levels! The defect-generation flow has gone to zero, but the magnitude of the stock (Customer Satisfaction) that was impacted by the flow, persists. And because its magnitude persists, new dynamics are set in motion.

Accumulation and flow are, hence, fundamentally different in nature. And, viva la differènce! It is the existence of stocks that enable flows to vary, sometimes wildly, without causing major disruptions to our lives. Water reservoirs enable communities to withstand droughts. Food reserves guard against poor growing seasons. Cash reserves and debt enable businesses to survive despite negative profits. Inventories permit supply to not always equal demand. Without stocks, we'd be living hand-to-mouth. We'd have no buffers or "shock absorbers" to protect against the inevitable "slings and arrows of outrageous fortune."

The fact that accumulation and flow constitute two fundamentally different processes by which reality operates is interesting, but so what?

The "So What"

The "so what" comes in the form of erroneous inferences that often result from simulations of models (be they mental or computer-based) that do not recognize this important distinction. To illustrate, consider the following…a friend calls and suggests that you invest in a Company that she's just "discovered." The company is, and has been, profitable. Its cash reserves are huge, and growing. In addition, the friend has seen the firm's Customer Satisfaction ratings, and Customer Satisfaction levels are among the highest ever recorded within the firm's industry! Your friend is beside herself with excitement because the firm has yet to be widely "discovered," and hence its stock price, given its financial and customer satisfaction performance, would appear to be seriously under-valued. You've got some discretionary cash. Do you invest?

From the data reported in the previous paragraph, the answer would appear to be a resounding, "yes!" But if you recognize the distinction between stocks and flows, and then look at the resulting data a little more closely, the answer would be an unequivocal, "No way!" Figure 3-4 is useful in explaining why…

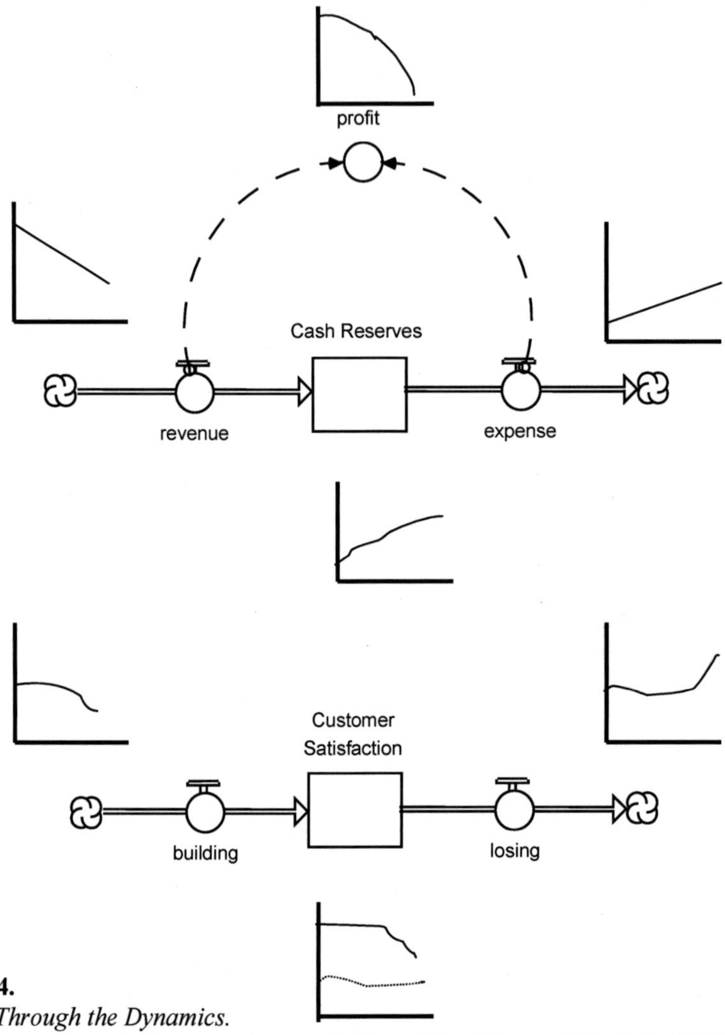

Figure 3-4.
Thinking Through the Dynamics.

The Figure shows graphs over time for each of the stocks and flows in the system. The patterns are consistent with the description of the firm's performance. Cash reserves are high, and growing because cash flow is positive. Profit also is positive. The firm's level of Customer Satisfaction remains at a level well above the industry average! All of these commonly-reported barometers are A-OK!

However, if you study the graphs in Figure 3-4, you'll discover that all of the barometers are just about to become not so good! High *levels* of Customer Satisfaction say nothing about its *rate of change*, just as rising *levels* of Cash say nothing about its *rate of change*. In the case of Customer Satisfaction, it's high, yes. But the rate at which it is currently building is slowing, while the rate at which it is being lost is rising! So the fact that it continues to remain well above the average says little about where it's headed! The opposite is true for Cash. The level of Cash is *increasing*, a good thing, and also *high*, also a good thing. But neither says anything about the rate at which it's *changing*. In fact, as the curves in Figure 3-4 indicate, Cash appears to be just about ready to begin plummeting! As soon as the revenue curve (tracing a downward spiral) crosses the expense curve (on an upward spiral), Cash will begin dropping like a stone!

The bottom line here is, again, that unless the distinction between stocks and flows is recognized, the chances of drawing erroneous conclusions about dynamics are high! Stock magnitudes can be rising while associated rates of inflow (or outflow) can be either rising, or falling! The magnitude of a stock can be falling while associated outflows (or inflows) are either falling, or rising. To accurately assess a dynamic situation, you must have all the information on the time course of both the stocks and the flows. Drawing conclusions about the efficacy of a strategy, policy, or decision based on mental models (or, say, spreadsheet models—to take a conspicuous example) that do not recognize the distinction between stocks and flows can be *very* misleading!

What's Next

Okay, you've now "got" the nouns and verbs. A good way to practice making the distinction between them is to catch the failure to do so that frequently occurs in newspaper articles, memos, and general discussions. In my experience, for example, many an argument has been defused simply by pointing out that one person is focused on the stock, while the other is focused on the flow. Someone will, in effect, be arguing that conditions are really deplorable, while someone else will be saying we've been making a lot of progress on improving them. And, they'll both be right...but ne're the twain shall meet, until the stock/flow distinction is recognized.

You've taken the first step in building your Operational Thinking skills. In the next Chapter, you'll learn how to put stocks and flows together to form "sentences." That's another big step! Good luck with it.

Chapter 4

Writing Sentences

Operational Thinking

To say anything interesting, you really need to put nouns and verbs together to form "sentences." Sentences, in turn, are the building blocks of paragraphs. Paragraphs are *interesting*! So, learning to write sentences is important.

Defining a Sentence

A simple "sentence" is one stock, with its associated flow(s). A compound sentence involves at least two stocks connected by at least one flow. Figure 4-1 shows a picture of a couple of simple, and a couple of compound, sentences.

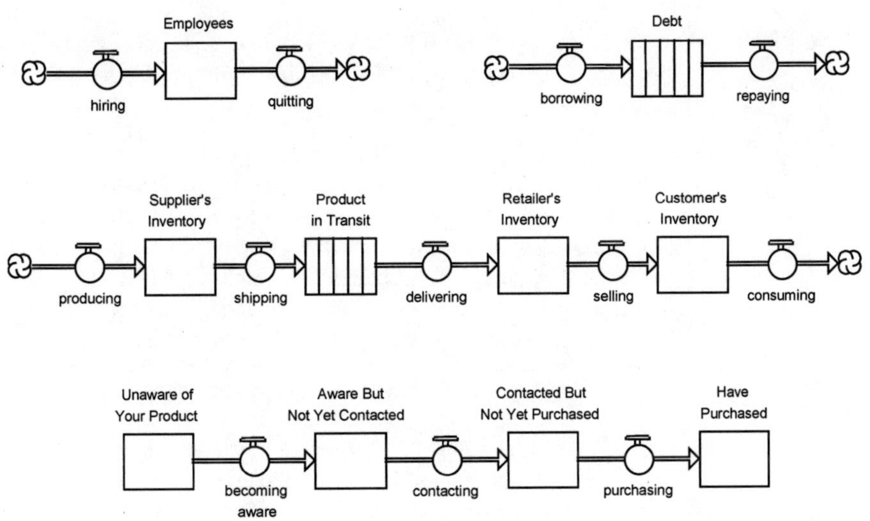

Figure 4-1.
Simple and Compound "Sentences."

Grammar

No, not your father's mother, but rather the rules for composing sentences. The *ithink* language, like any other language has some of these. Fortunately it has a very limited number. Two, to be precise. Learn and abide by these and you'll be a master *ithink* sentence-writer!

Rule 1: Respect Unit Consistency

The first rule is to "respect unit consistency." Simply stated, this means that the units-of-measure of the flows attached to a given stock must be the same as the stock's, except for "per time." This rule gets bent a bit when "unit conversion" is invoked—which is why, in Chapter 3, we cautioned against exercising this option too frequently.

In practical terms what this first rule of grammar means is, don't flow toothpaste into a vat of envy. Don't mix apples and oranges. Once you have decided on a unit-of-measure, a denomination, for a stock, always check to make sure that the stuff flowing into and out of it has the *same* units-of-measure (with the addition of "per time").

The rule seems straightforward enough, but it is surprising how difficult it is to obey for many people. The difficulty stems from both the inherent looseness of common parlance, and the lack of "discipline" inherent in most mapping/diagramming languages. When using typical flowcharting programs and diagramming software, it is not necessary to respect *any* unit-consistency rules. That's because they are not based on *operational* thinking! The result is pictures that do not show how things really work, but rather indicate "what's somehow *connected to* what," and/or "what in, some way, *influences* what."

In Systems Thinking, "somehow connected" and "in some way influences" simply are *not* good enough. Systems Thinkers are striving to capture how things actually work. That's because their intent is usually to *alter* how things work for purposes of *improving* the performance that is being generated. And, it is not possible to make such alterations with any confidence, unless you first understand what is actually *causing* current performance to be what it is.

The first step in "telling it like it is," is recognizing the distinction between stocks and flows. The second step is respecting the unit-consistency relationships that exist between the two. Let's take a look at a couple of examples, so you can get a better feeling for the challenges involved.

Saying that "*salary levels contribute to employee motivation*" wouldn't be perceived as crazy. And, if we were to use the *ithink* software to "draw a literal picture of the statement," it would look like what you see in Figure 4-2.

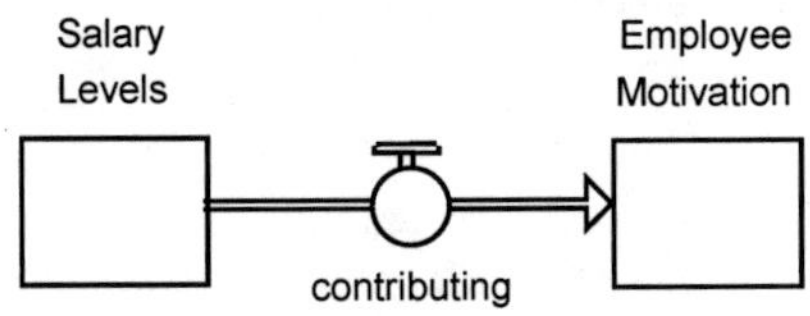

Figure 4-2.
Salary Levels "Contributing to" Motivation.

Though plausible-sounding when spoken or written, if you were to mentally simulate the ithink translation (as depicted in Figure 4-2), you would indeed get a crazy result! You'd discover that in order for Employee Motivation to *increase*, Salary Levels would have to *decrease*! That makes no sense at all! What someone means when they draw a picture like the one shown in Figure 4-2 is that Salary Levels "contribute to," or are an "input to," Employee Motivation. But if you make this kind of "loose" statement with the *ithink* software, you'll get simulation results that are ludicrous! Such results alert you to the fact that your mental model, when simulated, does not produce the results you know it *should* produce—which is to say, it doesn't work the way the real world works! That's important feedback because it helps you to learn; i.e., to improve your mental model!

It's easy to "fix" the *ithink* diagram pictured in Figure 4-2 to make it better describe what is going on between salary and motivation, but that's not the purpose of this chapter. Here, what's important is that *ithink* "sentences" should be accurate descriptions of the relationship between accumulations and the flows that feed and drain them. Flows do not "influence" stocks. Flows do not "have impacts on" stocks. Nor are they "inputs to" stocks. Flows *fill* and *drain* stocks; they make the level of stuff in the bathtub go up and down. If the bathtub happens to have self-confidence in it, then self-confidence better be what's flowing into, and out of, it. For example, it's not "praise" that's flowing in—as one might be led to conclude from the plausible-sounding statement: "praise builds self-confidence." It's okay to say that, just don't draw the *ithink* picture that way! It would be more accurate to say that praising is one of the "activity bases" for building self-confidence.

Bottom line: when constructing "sentences" using the *ithink* software, *always* check to ensure unit consistency between a stock and any flows that fill or drain it. If the units do not match (except for the "per time" associated with the flows), you have not accurately depicted how that aspect of reality works. And, when you violate the rules of grammar, you will pay the price in terms of the unreliability of the associated simulation!

Rule 2: Respect Conservation Laws

The second rule of grammar actually is pretty closely related to the first. There is a famous "Law" in physics that holds that physical stuff is neither created nor destroyed, but only changes form (i.e., matter and energy are "conserved" quantities). That Law pretty well describes how the physical universe works. When you take possession of some chunk of physical stuff, it has "come from" somewhere else. It is now absent from that somewhere else. However, because it has changed its location, doesn't mean there is any less of it in existence. When all is said and done, there's still the same *total quantity* of stuff! That's the Law of conservation of matter and energy.

In your *ithink* models, you will regularly violate this Law. You must, otherwise you'd never be able to bound your model. However, there are legitimate ways to violate it...and illegitimate ways to violate it. Stay "legit" and you'll have no problems with your models. So, what are the legitimate ways to violate the conservation law? There are two.

The first is to make a *conscious decision* to end a particular chain of conserved physical flows. The rationale: what you are leaving out of the model is not germane to the issue you are using your model to address. Consider the *ithink* "simple sentence" depicted in Figure 4-3 as an example...

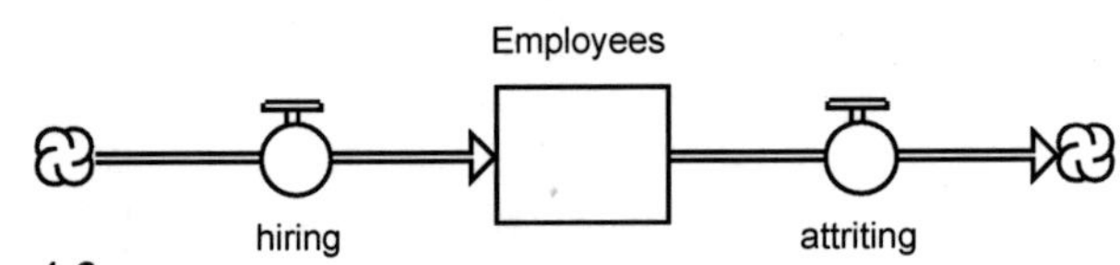

Figure 4-3.
A "Simple Sentence."

The "clouds" at the end of the two flows suggest that employees are being hired "out of thin air" and are attriting into same. Is this "true?" Of course not! We are violating the hallowed Law of conservation of matter and energy. But hopefully, we are doing so *consciously*. For example, we *know* employees actually come from somewhere else. That "somewhere else" is a *stock*, not a "cloud!" But we are willing to live with the assumption that, for the purposes the model is to serve, we can ignore the "issues" associated with where they come from. For example, we'd be assuming an ample supply of people, and that the quality of those people is "not an issue." Making these assumptions may be wrong...but at least: (1) we've made them *explicit*, so that others can see/challenge them, and so that you have a constant *visual* reminder that you've made them, and (2) they've been made *consciously*; you're not violating the Law because you're oblivious to it. That's the first legitimate way to violate the conservation Law.

The second legitimate way to violate this Law is using a stock to represent a non-physical quantity—other than time. This is because non-physical variables do not obey conservation laws! For example, if you ask the question: Where do knowledge, anger, commitment, or morale come from? The correct answer is…out of thin air! That's right, no place (and no one) has any *less* knowledge, anger, commitment or morale, because someone else now has *more*. Everyone can have more of each of these quantities, and no one has to have any less! Non-physical quantities therefore offer a "free lunch!" And therein lies an important realization!

When searching for high-leverage points, a good place to look is in the non-physical domain. That's because, unlike physical stocks, to increase the magnitude of a non-physical stock, it is not necessary that you decrease the magnitude of any other stock. If you re-allocate budget, headcount, or time away from one group within an organization to another, one group now has less, one now has more. But if you boost the commitment of one group within an organization, you do not have to "take" that commitment from any other group! Because non-physical variables do not operate in a zero-sum manner, they are attractive targets for high-leverage interventions.

As was the case with unit consistency, the notion that non-physical variables do not obey conservation laws seems straightforward. However, many people who represent non-physical variables in their models seem to have trouble with the idea. For example, someone will defend "the sentence" depicted in Figure 4-4 by saying that "customer dissatisfaction leads to employee dissatisfaction." It's hard to argue with the words…but it's easy to argue with the *ithink* diagram. And, it's also easy to resolve the argument by simulating the model! When you simulate, you discover that when Customer Dissatisfaction goes *down*, Employee Dissatisfaction goes *up*! That is exactly the opposite of what the verbal description implies.

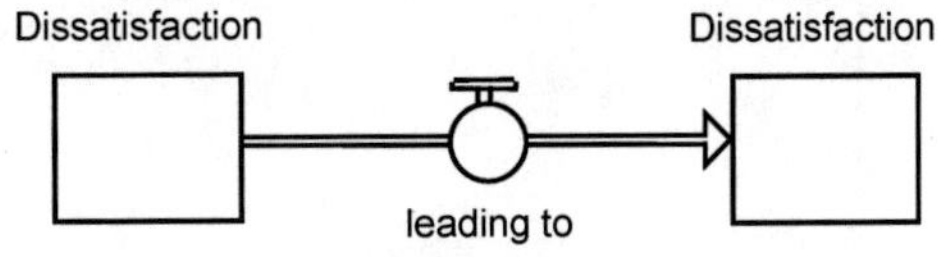

Figure 4-4.
"Customer Dissatisfaction Leads to Employee Dissatisfaction."

You can catch the grammatical error by being careful about the units-of-measure, but in this case, it's a little tricky because both stocks are denominated in units of dissatisfaction. So one could argue that there is no unit-consistency problem here. But, there *is* a unit-consistency problem, and the tip-off is the fact that a non-physical quantity (other than time) is being conserved. That's a no-no! And, the simulation confirms it. Customers do not "give" their dissatisfaction to employees. It's not a communicable disease! Through an expression of dissatisfaction, customers can stimulate employees to produce feelings of dissatisfaction within themselves. But it is the employees who produce the feelings—customers don't "give them" *their* feelings!

And so, the second rule of sentence construction grammar is: *Do not conserve non-physical quantities* (with the exception of "time"). If you find yourself doing it, check the units-of-measure. You should discover a problem there. If not, run a mental simulation. Ask whether the stock being fed goes up when the stock doing the feeding goes down. If both tests check out, call us, we will feature you on our website.

What's Next

You should now know how to distinguish between stocks and flows, and also how to write grammatically correct simple and compound sentences. These two sub-skills constitute 2/3 of what you need to master in order to think *operationally.* In the next Chapter, you'll add the third *Operational Thinking* sub-skill to your armada: *linking sentences*.

Chapter 5

Linking Sentences

Operational Thinking

On the path to writing paragraphs, the next important step is to learn how to join sentences. It turns out there are only two ways to do it. Master the distinction between the two, then learn when to use which, and you'll be well on your way to writing rich paragraphs!

Two Ways to Link Sentences

If you think about how you could go about linking one sentence to another, there are three possibilities...but one of them doesn't work! Figure 5-1 enumerates the possibilities.

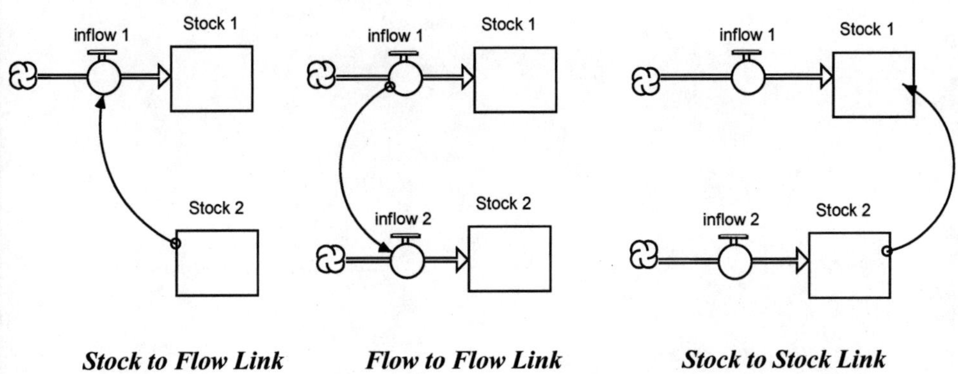

Figure 5-1.
Enumerating Three Possible Ways to Link.

The first possibility, linking one sentence to another via a connection from a stock in one to a flow in the other, is a possibility. The notion here would be that a "condition" (i.e., the current magnitude of a stock) is generating an inspiration to take some action (i.e., cause the volume of a flow to be greater than zero). A good example would be, say, hunger stimulating you to eat...familiar with that one, are you?

The second possibility also is plausible. In this case, one action "carries along" another action. A simple example would be your reading of this text and the associated learning that accompanies it…that *is* happening, right?

The third possibility? Created with smoke and mirrors…the *ithink* software will not allow such a connection! Remember what I said in Chapter 3. The magnitude of stocks can't change by being "influenced by," or "input to." Stock magnitudes change only via filling and draining. Filling and draining are *activities* (i.e., verbs!). And verbs are represented by *flows*, not those skinny little "wires" that you see in Figure 5-1. Only a flow can change a stock. So the only way to link sentences is by linking a stock to a flow, or a flow to a flow. And, as you're about to see, it makes a difference which one of these two possibilities you choose!

Stock-generated versus Flow-generated Flows

Stare at Figure 5-2. Decide which of the two representations makes most sense as a representation of the process of "knowledge transfer" that's occurring with the material you're now reading…

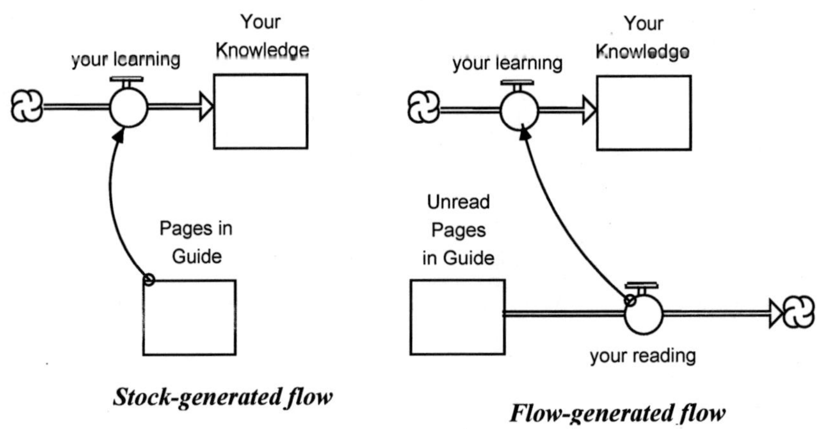

Figure 5-2.
Stock-generated versus Flow-generated Flows.

If you said the flow-generated representation, you were right! If the stock-generated representation were correct, all we'd have to do to enable you to learn more rapidly is add pages to the Guide. You wouldn't have to take any *action* to learn the material contained in those pages, you'd learn simply because the material was there! According to the representation on the right, reading constitutes an "activity basis" for learning. If you stop reading, you stop learning.

The latter statement may not be completely accurate because you certainly can learn the material contained in this Guide in ways other than reading it! But, if you were reading, it is true that you would stop learning from *that* source when you stopped reading.

Introducing the Connector

In the preceding example, we resolved the issue of which is the better representation by conducting a mental simulation—always a good thing to do, and something the visual nature of the *ithink* language facilitates. However, we also could have simulated the two representations on a computer using the *ithink* software, and we'd have quickly discovered the problem with the first of the two representations. However you choose to conduct your thought experiments, the first step in linking sentences together is to determine whether it makes most sense to link stock to flow, or flow to flow. And after you've made that determination, you will use "the connector" (the thin wire) to do the linking. Connectors, by virtue of their role as "linkers," become the *conjunctions* in the *ithink* language.

As you may already have noticed, there are two types of connectors in the *ithink* language. The one we used in Figure 5-2, the solid wire, is called an "action connector." That's because the wire is transmitting an "action," as opposed to transmitting "information." To make the distinction clear, examine Figure 5-3…

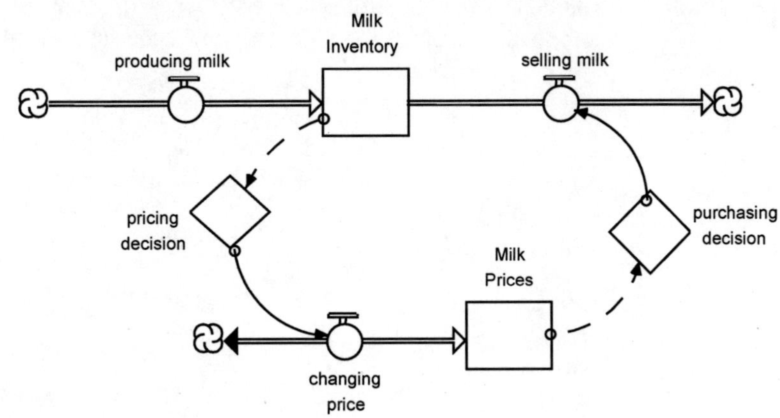

Figure 5-3.
The Supply & Demand for Milk.

This example is a downstream extension of the "cows and milk-producing" illustration from Chapter 2. Remember, we determined that it was more "operational" to think in terms of *cows* producing milk, than having it be a "function of" things like GNP and interest rates! The example shows pretty clearly the distinction between the two types of connector.

Information (represented by the dashed connector) radiates off Milk Inventory levels and serves as one of the inputs to the pricing decision. The full "logic" of the decision is not visible in the picture because it is embedded within the space-compressed Decision-Process Diamond (DPD). However, out of that decision process comes a decision! The decision is, say, to cut price by 10%, or raise it by 20%, or hold it constant. But the point is that the information leads to a decision, and the decision leads to an *action*! Hence, the dashed wire begins the process, and the solid wire finishes it.

The same is true on the demand side. Information about milk prices radiates to consumers. It's part of what influences how much milk they will purchase, and hence how much milk producers will sell. Consumers make their purchasing decisions, and then take *action*—i.e., they purchase a certain quantity of milk that day/week/month.

Information connectors thus carry the information that's used to arrive at decisions. Action wires then transmit the action resulting from the decision. The action manifests as a change in the volume of a flow. The distinct difference in purpose between the two types of connector explains why only information connectors can "stick into" DPD's. However, both types of wire can "come out" of a DPD because, in addition to the action that will be taken as a result of the decision, information about the decision, or about the inputs to that decision, also can be transmitted.

Information and Action connectors are similar in that neither can be used to represent a conserved-flow linkage. That is to say, no "stuff" flows through either type of wire! When information is "radiated" there isn't any less of it left to radiate! Thus, for example, when you step on the bathroom scale, and information about your body weight radiates off the dial, no actual pounds are being lost through that radiation (dern!). It's not pounds that are radiating, it's *information about* body weight that is radiating! Similarly, if you think back to the "cows producing milk" example, the action wire that runs from the stock of cows to the flow "producing milk" isn't transmitting cows! Just as body weight isn't radiating through the information connector, cows are not radiating through the action wire! At the end of a milking day, milk has been produced, but the stock of cows has not been depleted in the process. The milk inventories residing within the cows were indeed depleted, but that dynamic is below the level of aggregation of the representation. The action wire is thus, in effect, playing the role of an aggregation device in this (and in many other) instance.

And so, flows transport. Wires transmit. Connectors serve as "inputs" and "outputs," not "inflows" and "outflows." Being able to grasp these distinctions is another of the *Operational Thinking* sub-skills.

Introducing the Converter

The astute observer would have noticed a little problem way back in Figure 5-2. If you'd like, mosey on back there and see if something about the representations in that Figure bother you. I'll wait.

Were you bothered by the fact that all of that unit-consistency brouhaha that I threw at you back in Chapter 4 seemed to fly out the window?! Well, you should have been. Let's focus on the second representation in Figure 5-2—the one we said was the more accurate of the two depictions. What are the units-of-measure of the "your reading" flow? If you're having trouble with the question, remember that the units of a flow must be the same units as the stock to which it's attached, except for "per time." The stock is denominated in "pages." Therefore the "your reading" flow must be dimensioned as "pages per time."

There's an action wire that runs from the "your reading" flow to the "your learning" flow. What are the units of this latter flow? Again, you may wish to begin with the stock to which the "your learning" flow is attached and work backward. Hopefully, you concluded that the units of the flow must be "knowledge per time" (or "understanding per time," or some such). But how can that be, if the wire coming *into* the "your learning" flow from the "your reading" flow has the units-of-measure "pages per time?" The answer is: *it can't*!

We need another concept here, folks. And it's not just so we can make the units work out right. It's so we can make the representation more accurately reflect the way reality works! Insisting upon unit-consistency is not just an anal-compulsive behavioral trait that Systems Thinkers have somehow gotten attached to. It's a way to ensure that your representations better reflect how things really work.

In this case, let's discover the missing concept by thinking about the process—rather than backing into it by figuring out what "units" need to be factored in, in order to cause the "your learning" flow to have the correct units-of-measure.

See if the following thought experiment helps...If a three year-old child were to read these pages, would they be learning as much as you are? Unlikely. Why? Because, first, learning experiences have made you a better reader. Second, you know more (i.e., have more "hooks") and can use it to cull understanding from the words and pictures on the pages you're turning. In addition, you are likely to be more motivated to learn this material than the average three year-old. All of these factors will combine to cause you to learn more per page turned than a three year-old. Operationally speaking, your "learning productivity" (dimensioned as "learning per page") is higher! If we add "learning productivity" to the picture, we end up with Figure 5-4.

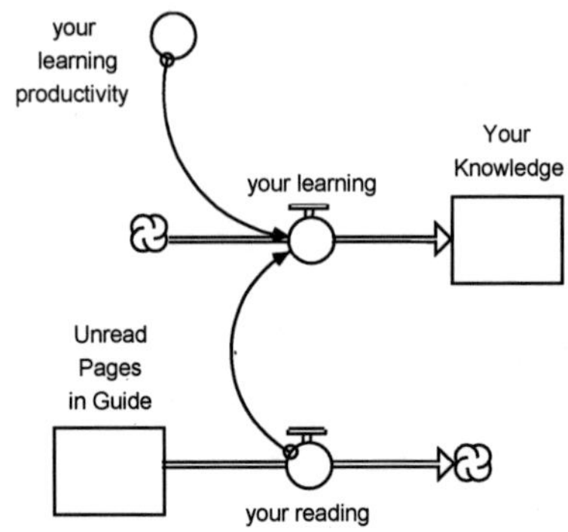

Figure 5-4.
Correcting Figure 5-2.

The *ithink* language element that we used to represent "learning productivity," and that often is used to represent "productivity" in one of its infinite variety of incarnations, is called a *converter*. In this context, the converter is playing the role of an "adverb," in that it is modifying the verb "your learning." It tells how much learning occurs for a given unit of the "driving activity" (in this case, "your reading"). From a unit-consistency standpoint, it "converts" the units brought into the learning flow from the reading flow (i.e., pages/time) into the proper units of learning (knowledge/time). If you want to scrutinize the algebra, it would look like this:

your learning = your reading x your learning productivity ***(knowledge/time) (pages/time) (knowledge/page)***

Note: (pages/time) times (knowledge/page) equals (knowledge/time). The units-of-measure on the left-hand side of the equation balance with those on the right-hand side of the equation—this makes life good, physicists smile, and algebra teachers jump for joy. It also yields representations that more accurately mirror how reality works. As a result, when you simulate those representations for purposes of drawing conclusions about what actions you should take, you have a greater chance of having those conclusions make sense!

And so, converters often play the role of "adverbs," modifying flows. In this role, they tell how much of a contribution to an activity is being made per unit of the "driver" of that activity—be that "driver" a flow (as in the example we just examined), or a stock. Let's look at two more examples, just to cement the concept. Examine Figure 5-5...

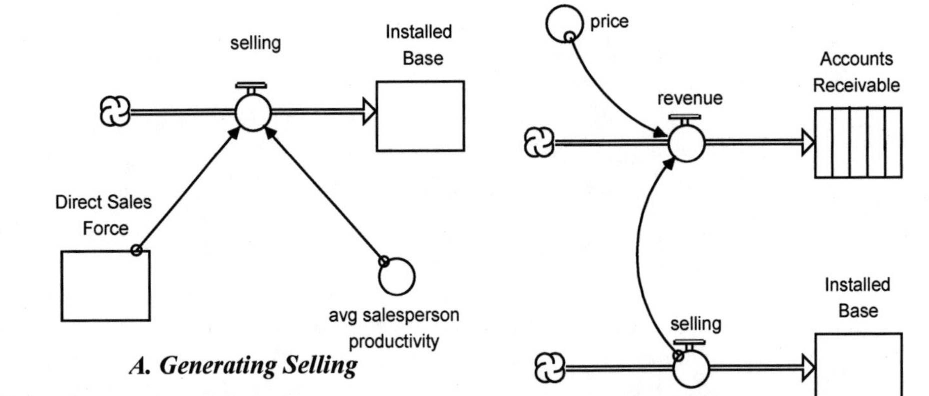

Figure 5-5.
Illustrating Converters as Adverbs.

The first representation in Figure 5-5 depicts the generation of the selling activity. Selling is being represented as a "stock-generated" flow. In the second representation, revenue is a "flow-generated" flow. In both examples, a converter is used to "modify" the flow.

The salesperson "productivity term" converts the number of people in the sales force (i.e., the "driver" of the selling flow) into a flow of sales, whose units-of-measure are "product/time." The productivity term in this case has the units-of-measure, "product/salesperson/time." In the second example, revenue has the units, "$/time." Selling, as we already know, has the units, "units of product/time." Price handles the conversion in this case. It has the units-of-measure, "$/unit of product."

Both converters are functioning as "productivity terms." Average salesperson productivity tells how productive, on average, each salesperson is in selling product. Price tells how productive each unit of product that's sold is in generating revenue.

Hopefully, the preceding examples will drive home the concept of converters as "adverbs"—or in a more substantive context, as "productivity terms." We're on solid ground here, both grammatically and conceptually, in terms of describing how many processes actually work. In fact, the two flow formulations illustrated in Figure 5-5 reoccur so frequently in *ithink* models that we've given them generic names. The *stock-generated* formulation is called an "External

Resource Process," and the *flow-generated* formulation is called a "Co-flow Process." You should study these two formulations. You'll find them to be extremely useful in constructing models using the *ithink* software.

In Chapter 6, we'll introduce three more generic flow templates, bringing the total to five. Here at HPS, we make use of one of these five templates to specify 90% of the flows in the models we construct. Being able to creatively adapt and employ these templates is the hallmark of someone who has mastered Operational Thinking.

The flow templates are things of beauty. But now, we're going to balance all this pulchritude with a dash of "ugliness"...

Converters as Pandora's Box

It turns out that those nice, innocuous-looking little circles we call converters can function as more than just adverbs. They can operate as adjectives, dangling participles,...and about any other dern function you want them to perform! Yep, there's flies in that there ointment. Unfortunately, it ain't all pretty. Converters become a catchall for: doing algebra operations (like summing or dividing two quantities), substituting for either stock or flow concepts that you are choosing (for reasons of simplification) to not represent as such, and representing exogenous inputs. I'll briefly illustrate a few of these practical, and not so beautiful (conceptually, or in terms of the grammatical metaphor), uses of converters here. You then can probably discover even more uses by perusing the various models that come with the *ithink* software.

Several non-adverbial uses of converters are illustrated in Figure 5-6.

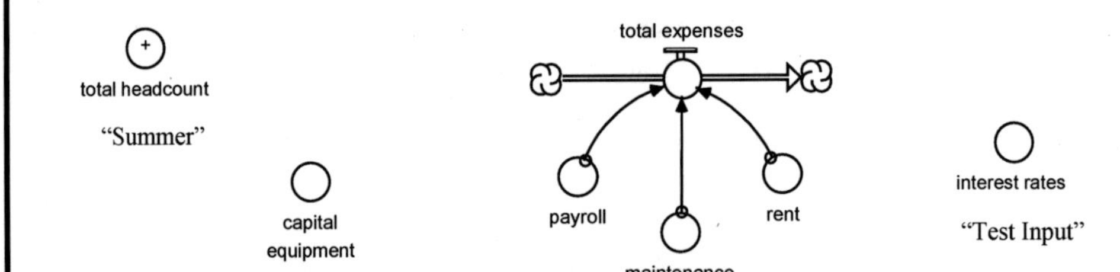

Figure 5-6.
Non-adverbial Uses of Converters.

A Summer Converter

A "Summer," yes, it's something we'd dearly love to have in New Hampshire. So, we added it to the software. The little device is useful for "adding up" quantities without having to "run all the arrows" into some poor hapless converter. Summer converters, a choice within the converter dialog box, allow you to add up any quantities you like just by clicking on them in the Allowable list. Just be careful you click on the right things, because there is no visual feedback!

Stock Substitute

Capital Equipment, the variable chosen to illustrate "stock substitute," is in concept a stock. However, if you are not interested in the inflow to the stock (i.e., investing), or the outflow (i.e., retiring), you may want to simplify things by just representing capital stock as a converter. As we'll see in a later chapter, converters *can* change over time. They are not always just constants! So, using a converter to substitute for something that's a stock in concept, doesn't mean you lose the ability for that variable to change with time. It just means that you will consider those changes as "external inputs," rather than as being generated by relationships within the model. More on all of this when we get to "feedback loops" in the next chapter. For now, suffice it to say that there are instances where simplification dictates that you represent something that is, in concept, a stock, with a converter.

Flow Substitute

The third example in Figure 5-6 illustrates the use of converters to substitute for what are, in concept, flows. No problem. Rather than having every expense category on the income statement represented as a flow, you can represent these flow concepts as converters and then, as in the illustration, sum them into a *single* flow. There is one issue you should be aware of when you do this. Converters are calculated *before* flows. So, when using a converter to represent a flow, you should first click any such converter in the Selected list to select it. Then, click the C → F button (in the Table dialog box). This will shift forward in time the reporting of the calculated values for all such converters, so they will align with the reported values of flows. You can read more about this in the *Help Files*.

Test Input

As you've seen if you've been through the software tutorials, or just played around with the software, in each Converter's dialog box, there is a scrollable list of "Builtin" functions. These "functions" enable you to create various kinds of "patterns" (like ramps, steps, randomness, sinusoids, etc.) that are useful for testing your model, and also for serving as "exogenous inputs." We'll have more to say about these variables in Part 3 of the Guide, where we discuss testing.

What's Next

Over the last couple of chapters, you have been exposed to the essence of what constitutes *Operational* Thinking—a big part of what Systems Thinking is all about. There is a second, really big part. It's called *Closed-loop* Thinking, and it's coming at you in Chapter 6. Master these two "biggees," and you can apply for a Systems Thinker's union card. You'll also be able to write good paragraphs—the building blocks of short stories.

Chapter 6

Constructing "Simple" Paragraphs

Closed-loop Thinking

A "paragraph," in Systems Thinking parlance, is a "feedback loop"—a closed-loop of causality. Previous chapters have alluded to the fact that "paragraphs" are *interesting*. They're interesting because, like those little wind-up toys, you prime them, and they then take off on their own! That is, feedback loops *self-generate* behavior. If you bump into one…get outta the way!

There are only two types of feedback loops: *counteracting* and *reinforcing* (sometimes referred to, in technical terms, as *negative* and *positive*, respectively). We'll begin with a formal definition of a feedback loop, and then discuss counteracting loops, reinforcing loops, and combinations of the two. In this Chapter, we'll deal only with *simple* feedback loops—where "simple" has a technical definition, and is not simply a measure of associated complexity. In Chapter 7, we'll treat "non simple" paragraphs.

Definition of a Feedback Loop

A *feedback loop* exists whenever a "noun" (stock) is linked to a "verb" (flow) in the *same* sentence. The link may be direct, or part of a chain of links passing through other "sentences" first. An example of a direct, and an extended-link, feedback loop appear in figure 6-1.

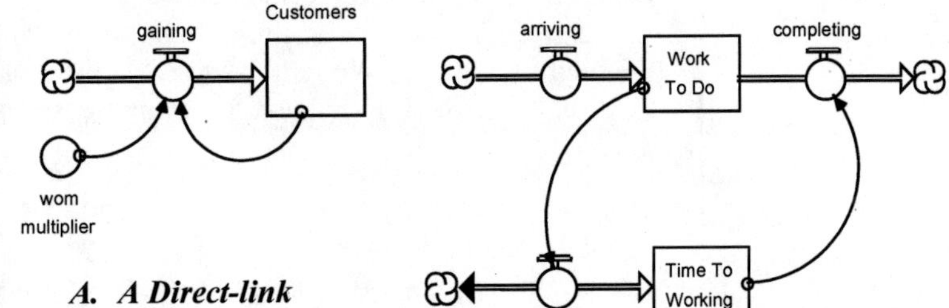

A. A Direct-link Feedback loop

B. An Extended-link Feedback loop

Figure 6-1.
A Direct, and Extended-link, Feedback Loop.

In the "direct-linkexample, customers attract other customers through a word-of-mouth "multiplier." In the "extended-link," when the backlog of things to do swells or shrinks, it causes more or less hours to be allocated to work (a *second* stock). The increase/decrease in hours worked then increases/decreases the rate at which work is completed, thereby bringing the backlog back into balance.

In both cases, the noun connects to its "sentence-mate" verb. Whenever this occurs, we have a "feedback loop." Feedback loops are extremely important to the functioning of *all* natural, physical and social systems. Without them, there would be no life of any kind! It's definitely worth your while to understand more about how they work!

"Simple" Feedback Loops

In building understanding, it usually makes sense to start simple. That's certainly the case with feedback loops, where things can get pretty wild pretty fast. It's important to have a solid grounding in the basics of the structure and behavior of feedback loops before launching off into the ensuing richness. For this reason, I will define here the concept of a "simple" feedback loop.

A "simple" feedback loop is defined as one that has only one *direct* link (i.e., the stock links to its associated inflow or outflow), and in which all parameters (i.e., "productivity terms") are constant. The loop shown in Figure 6-1A is "simple," while that in 6-1B is not.

Counteracting Feedback Loops

Counteracting feedback loops are so-named because they *counteract* change. Try to push something that's being controlled by a counteracting feedback loop, and you'll experience "push back" in the *opposite* direction.

Counteracting feedback loops are everywhere! Each cell in your body uses them to maintain the delicate chemical and electrical balances you need to remain alive. Countries use them to maintain trade and arms balances. And every life form in between uses them to maintain order, to keep things in proper proportion. Counteracting loops act to maintain stability. Without some stability, neither life itself, nor growth, is possible! Here are a few examples of counteracting loops in action…

Implementing change within an organization usually stimulates counter-pressures that resist it. Raising your body temperature by exercising, triggers sweating—a process that works to cool you back down. Falling profits motivate efforts to both cut costs and boost revenues—both of which act to drive profits back up. Committing a faux pas that damages an important relationship stimulates actions to repair that relationship. Losing customers to a competitor inspires efforts to regain those customers.

Figure 6-2 depicts the two incarnations of a *simple* counteracting feedback loop. Like the "external resource" and "co-flow" templates introduced in Chapter 5, the two flow processes shown in Figure 6-2 commonly occur. So, like their predecessors, we have given them names. We call them the "draining" and "stock-adjustment" process, respectively. An Appendix to this Chapter summarizes the five generic flow templates that we have identified in our work (you'll be introduced to the fifth later in this Chapter). We use one of these five templates to specify 80%-90% of the flows in the models we construct. If your intention is to become proficient in applying Systems Thinking, time spent mastering these templates, and when to use each, is time *extremely* well-spent!

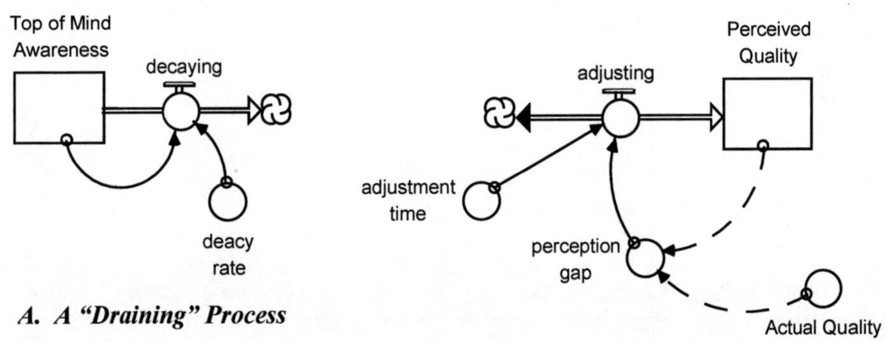

A. A "Draining" Process

B. A "Stock-adjustment" Process

Figure 6-2.
The Two Incarnations of a Simple Counteracting Feedback Loop.

The Draining Process

The "draining" template is used primarily to capture passive decay processes. In the example shown in Figure 6-2, top-of-mind awareness "decays"—which is to say, left to its own doing (i.e., with, for example, no further "spot advertising," awareness simply fades over time). Other examples of common draining processes include any kind of awareness, memory, or perception process. We all remember cramming for those wonderful "content regurgitation" exercises known as multiple-choice tests. Stuff it in, in a frantic all-nighter, dump it out on the ol' "ScanTron." In a week, 30% is gone, faded from memory. In two weeks, 50% is gone. And so forth.

Draining processes are so-named because of how they behave when they have no inflow to offset them. Under these circumstances, draining processes *drain* stocks! And the pattern they exhibit, when the "draining fraction" or "draining time" is constant, looks like what you see in Figure 6-3A.

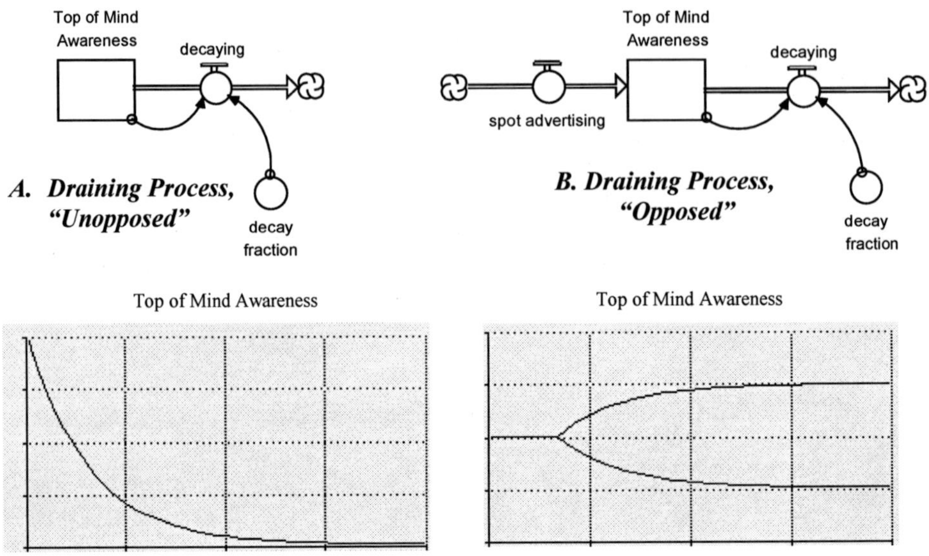

Figure 6-3.
The Behavioral Repertoire of the Draining Process with a Constant Draining Fraction.

The pattern is known mathematically as "negative exponential." But because we believe in remaining "positive," we'll just call it "exponential decay." This pattern also is colloquially referred to as "half the distance to the wall." To see why, imagine that the stock involved is "Distance from the Wall." The draining flow might be called "stepping." The draining parameter might represent the fraction *per time* of the stock that is "drained." Let's assume that fraction to be 0.5 (i.e., 50% of the magnitude of the stock per second—assume you take 1 step per second to keep things simple). Let's say you are initially 3 meters from the wall. In your first step, you'd drain 1.5 meters from the stock—you've gone ½ the distance to the wall. You are now standing 1.5 meters from the wall. On your next step, you will drain ½ of what is left in the stock, or 0.75 meters. And, so on. Each step you take will eliminate ½ of the remaining distance to the wall. Hence, the name.

The astute "calculationist" will recognize that if someone were actually to execute this experiment, they would *never* quite reach the wall. This is true, but it turns out that in "three times the 'time constant'" (the "time constant" being defined as the reciprocal of the "draining fraction"), the magnitude of the stock will be "close enough" to be considered "there" (about 95% of the initial magnitude will have been drained).

Figure 6-3B, shows how a draining process behaves when it is "opposed" by a constant inflow. The two lines on the graph show the results of the two simulations that were conducted. For a brief period at the outset of both simulations, the inflow to, and outflow from, the stock are constant and equal. As a result, the magnitude of the stock is unchanging. That's why the two lines initially are flat and equal (and that's also why you see only *one* line initially). In the first of the two simulations, the inflow steps up to a *higher* constant volume. In the second, the inflow steps down to a *lower* constant volume. The resulting stock magnitude traces symmetrically opposite patterns.

In the step-down case, the draining process manifests in the "classic," exponential decay pattern—except that rather than the magnitude of the stock draining all the way down to zero, it decays toward a *non-zero* level. What that level will be can easily be calculated. The stock will stop falling when the outflow volume has decreased to the point where it is once again equal to the stepped-down inflow volume. The outflow volume is calculated by multiplying the current magnitude of the stock by the draining fraction. When this magnitude has declined to the point where the multiplication produces a value equal to the inflow volume, the decline will cease. When the inflow and outflow volumes become equal, the stock magnitude will once again be constant.

In the step-up case, the draining process doesn't manifest its presence in the classic, exponential decay form. In fact, there's no "decay" at all! But there is a mirror image, exponential process at work. This "half the distance to the wall" pattern is known as "asymptotic growth." What's going on in this case is that because the inflow has been stepped-up (above the initially constant outflow), the magnitude of the stock begins to grow. As it does, the outflow volume (which, again, is calculated by multiplying the magnitude of the stock by the draining fraction) begins to increase. As the outflow volume swells, the magnitude of the stock continues to grow, but ever more slowly. When the outflow volume increases to the point where it just equals the stepped-up inflow volume, the magnitude of the stock ceases increasing, and the system is once again back in steady-state.

So, as you've seen, what is called a "draining process," doesn't always manifest that way. It's more accurate to describe it as a member of the *half the distance to the wall* processes—named for the characteristic pattern of behavior exhibited by *counteracting feedback loops* operating "unopposed." As you are about to see, the draining process is just a special case of the other member of the set of such processes—the *stock-adjustment process*.

The Stock-adjustment Process

Figure 6-4 portrays the Stock-adjustment template and its associated characteristic behavior patterns.

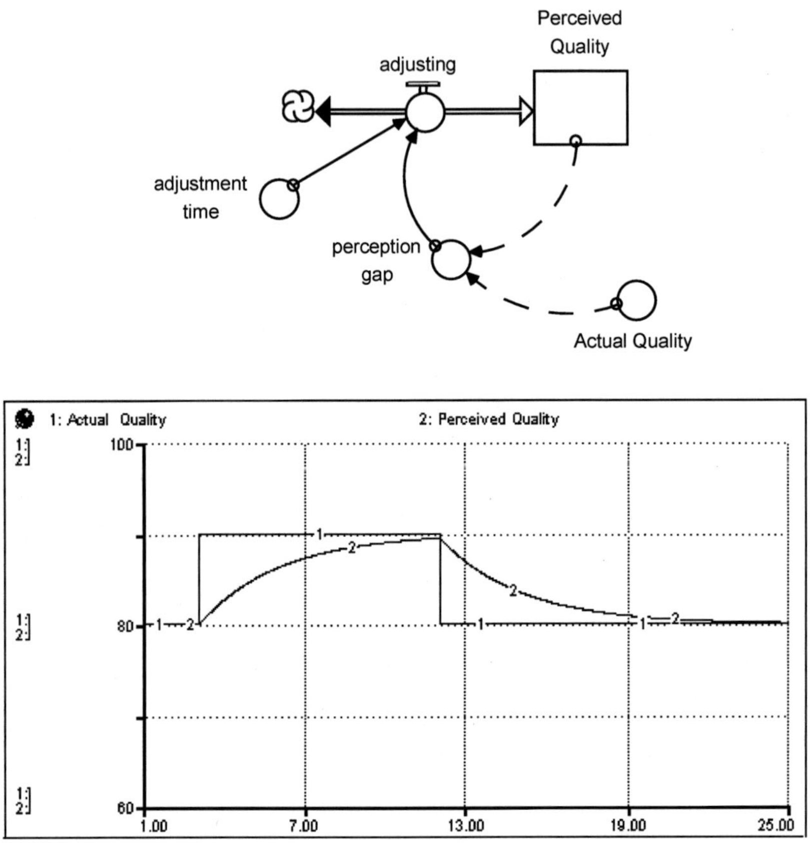

Figure 6-4.
The Stock-adjustment Process and Associated Behavior.

If you take a quick peek back at Figure 6-3B, you will see the similarity in the patterns of behavior generated by an "opposed" draining process and a stock-adjustment process. Both generate "half-the-distance-to-the-wall" patterns. As stated previously, the draining process is simply a "special case" of the stock-adjustment process. It's a stock-adjustment process in which the "goal" toward which the stock is adjusting (in the example, Actual Quality) is *never* larger in magnitude than the stock—which is to say, a stock-adjustment process with the flow only flowing *out* of the stock.

Counteracting Loops: In Summary

The bottom line on "simple" counteracting feedback loops is that they exhibit half-the-distance-to-the-wall behavior. They either decay exponentially toward some goal (or target magnitude), or they increase asymptotically toward same. The story of counteracting feedback loops becomes a lot more interesting when we extend the links to form loops involving more than one "sentence," and also when we allow the associated parameters (draining fractions and perception adjustment times) to vary. But these "more interesting paragraphs" are for Chapter 7. Let's now look at the "simple" *reinforcing* feedback loop...

Reinforcing Feedback Loops

Reinforcing feedback loops are so-named because they *reinforce* change. Push on something that's being controlled by a reinforcing feedback loop, and you'll start an avalanche!

Reinforcing loops are less prevalent, in both natural and human-populated systems, than their counteracting brethren. And that's fortunate. When you mess with a reinforcing loop, you've got a tiger by the tail! Tigers are powerful. Harness the power, and you have a wonderful engine for growth. Lose control of the power, and you have a powerful engine of destruction! Here are a few examples of reinforcing loops in action...

The surge in popularity following the introduction of a new, "hot" website, music CD, or movie. The meteoric run-up, and subsequent free-fall, in stock prices during the dot.com boom/bust. The rapid proliferation of cells in a cancerous tumor. The spread of an infectious disease, or a new fad through a population. Road rage. The "recruiting" of resistors and zealots, against and for, an organizational change initiative. The skyrocketing of free agent salaries in major league sports franchises. The mushrooming of population in US sunbelt cities. All of these examples illustrate reinforcing feedback loops at work. Such loops "feed upon themselves." They are "compounding" in nature. There is nothing inherently "bad" about such loops. But, and this is an important "but," *no* reinforcing process can continue forever! This appears to be something that many people have difficulty grasping. Let me say it again: *No* self-reinforcing process can continue to operate forever!

Anything that compounds must ultimately reach a limit. Either the limit will be "consciously-chosen," or it will be "imposed." The former always yields much prettier pictures.

Consider first, physical stocks. Any such stock experiencing compounding growth will ultimately run out of whatever it is that's "fueling" that growth. So, for example, a word-of-mouth process that brings new customers to a restaurant, or new browsers to a website, will simply exhaust the supply of available new customers/browsers. Ultimately, everyone who is going to try the restaurant, or visit the website, will have done so. That's it! Market saturation. Cancer cells proliferating in a tumor mass actually experience the same sort of saturation—only instead of running out of customers, they exhaust available nutrient flows, and so cells begin dying of malnutrition. Either way, ultimately, enough is enough! Growth *must* cease because fuel is exhausted.

In the case of non-physical stocks, since they do not obey conservation laws, the limits are more subtle, but real nonetheless. Burgeoning confidence tips over into arrogance—something that usually is its own undoing. Spiraling enthusiasm simply cannot be sustained—as reserves of psychic energy ultimately become depleted.

Despite the widespread demonstration of the existence of "limits " to any kind of reinforcing growth process, many people continue to appear surprised when such limits make themselves felt. For example, the dot.com bust seemed to shock many investors. Did they really believe that such meteoric stock price run-ups and IPO valuations could continue forever? Do you suppose that people in Southern California in the 60's believed their sun-drenched "utopia" could continue to experience compounding growth, forever? Do major corporations whose Boards insist that compounding revenue (or earnings) growth be *sustained*, really believe such objectives can be achieved forever?

In each case, and in many more I could cite, the answer appears to be "yes." It is my sincere hope that those of you who are reading these pages, and who know someone in the "our job is to keep this up forever" camp, will share what's here with them. Substantial benefit to the world can result from more people understanding that compound growth *always* has to end, and that it makes a big difference whether the limit is consciously chosen, or whether the limit is imposed it. The latter almost always produces a very painful experience!

"Simple" Reinforcing Loops

Figure 6-5 illustrates the *simple* reinforcing feedback loop structure and its associated characteristic behavior pattern. It's called the "compounding" process, and constitutes the fifth and final generic flow template. The associated pattern of behavior, recognizable to most people, is called "exponential growth." Here, rather than traveling "half the distance to the wall," the wall itself is being pushed away (at an ever-increasing pace). The process is analogous to trying to catch your shadow. The faster you run after it, the faster it recedes from your grasp.

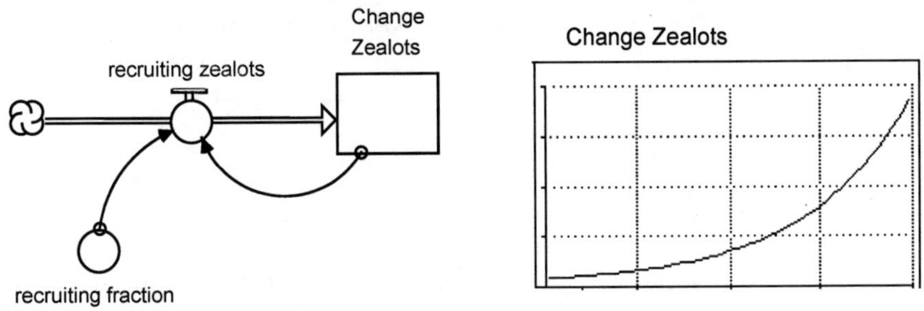

Figure 6-5.
The Structure & Behavior of a Simple Reinforcing Feedback Loop.

The explanation for the pattern of behavior is easy to understand. Stuff flows into a stock, be it money, enthusiasm, or zealots for a change initiative. Once in there, it causes even more of itself to flow in. In the case of money, what you have in your savings account generates an inflow of interest payments whose volume is proportional to the magnitude of money that's already in your account earning the interest. The proportionality constant in this case is called the "interest rate." Similarly, for enthusiasm or change initiative zealots, you get some, and they then bring in still more. Enthusiasm is "infectious," and zealots proselytize. Either way, the stock "feeds upon itself!" The "feeding upon" process produces a pattern of growth in which each increment of inflow is a constant percentage of the preceding magnitude of the associated stock. As a result, as the stock's magnitude grows, so too does the associated inflow volume—by a proportional amount. Hence, the curve of the stock's magnitude (and the flow's volume, as well), literally takes off like a rocket. There's a little story that nicely illustrates the nature of an exponential growth process.

A farmer had a pond that was stocked with catfish. One fine spring morning, he noticed that a lily pad had appeared on the pond. The next day, he noted that a second pad had come into being. On day 3 there were four pads. After 29 days, lily pads covered ½ the pond. The farmer was concerned about allowing the population of Lily plants to grow too much larger, for fear it would endanger the catfish population. He wondered how much longer he ought to wait before taking some action to stem the growth of the lily pad colony. Can you estimate how many more days it would be prudent for the farmer to wait?

The answer is that the farmer has probably already waited too long because on Day 30, the pond will be completely covered with lily pads! That's the nature of exponential growth…it sneaks up on you. And, before you know it, you're toast! Again, fortunately, not many reinforcing loops exist independently of counteracting feedback loops that keep them in check. But because some reinforcing loops are very strong, they can spiral out of control before the consciously-chosen counteracting loops have the opportunity to kick in. When this happens, the "imposed" ones operate, and the picture gets ugly.

Combining a Simple Counteracting and Simple Reinforcing Loop

As already noted, things get considerably more intriguing when we move beyond "simple" loops. But just to complete the "simple" story, and so it will be easier to see what "non-simple" brings us, Figure 6-6 puts a simple counteracting and simple reinforcing loop together. The Figure also shows the behavioral repertoire associated with the combination.

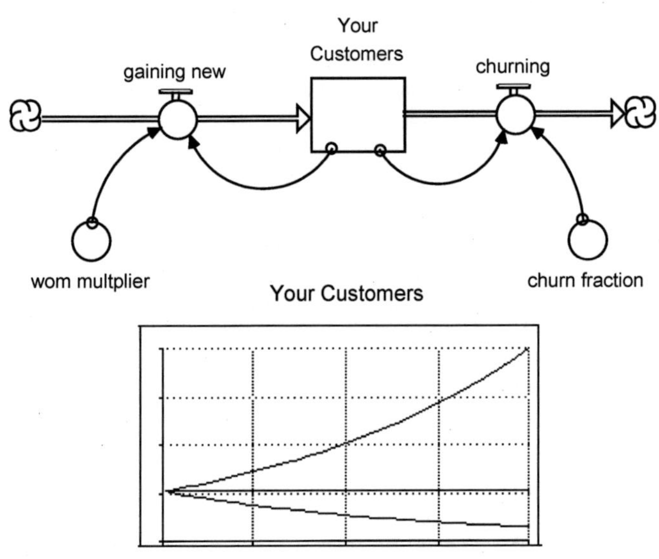

Figure 6-6.
Combining a Simple Counteracting & Reinforcing Loop.

As you can see, when you combine a simple counteracting and simple reinforcing loop, three patterns of dynamic behavior can result. Which pattern is produced depends on the values of the two parameters (generically, the "compounding" and "draining" fractions). When the two parameters are equal, the magnitude of the stock remains unchanged; i.e., *neither* loop dominates, both are exactly equal in strength. When the "compounding fraction" (in the example, the "wom multiplier") exceeds the "draining fraction" (in the example, "churn fraction"), the magnitude of the stock exhibits exponential growth. This means the reinforcing loop is dominant, and (in this simple model) will remain so forever. If the "draining fraction" is larger than the "compounding fraction," the counteracting loop dominates and the magnitude of the stock will decay exponentially (again, forever).

That's it. Not a very elaborate, or very interesting, repertoire of dynamic behavior patterns, is it? Once the two parameters are assigned values, one of three possible patterns of dynamic behavior will result and then persist. Chapter 7 examines the consequences of allowing the parameter values associated with "simple" feedback loops to change dynamically. What we'll discover is that such changes can cause loop dominance to *shift* over time. For example, a reinforcing loop might dominate in the early going, but the strength of an associated counteracting loop could be building all the while. At some point, this may allow the counteracting loop to overpower the reinforcing spiral (cooling it off!). Such shifts in feedback loop dominance are what create the "non-linear behavior" discussed in Chapters 1 and 2, and why "Non-linear Thinking" is such an important Systems Thinking skill to master.

What's Next

Okay, you've come a long way, and you have only one more chapter to process in order to complete the "building blocks of short stories" progression that began in Chapter 3. You've been exposed to Operational Thinking and most of Closed-loop Thinking. In Chapter 7, you'll finish off Closed-loop Thinking and also learn something about Non-linear Thinking. Specifically, you'll learn how to develop feedback loops that involve extended links and have parameters that can vary. Once you have mastered this material, it's only a matter of putting together multiple paragraphs in order to produce an insightful short story.

Appendix:

Generic Flow Templates

External Resource

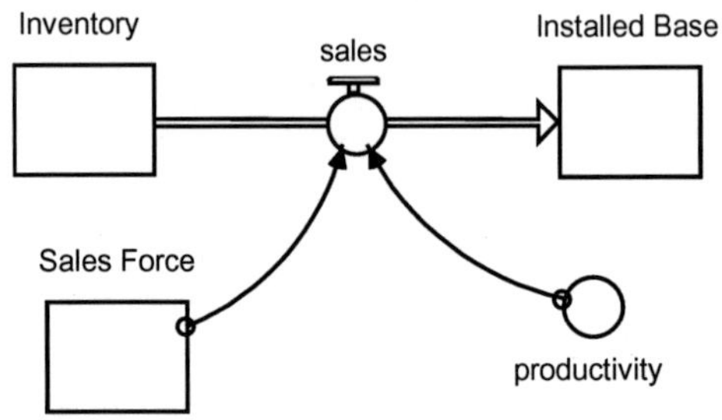

sales = **Sales Force** * **productivity**

units/time = *People* * *units/person/time*

Figure 6-7.
The External Resource Template.

Use the **external resource** template when some resource, other than the stock to which the flow is attached, provides the basis for producing the flow. Usually this resource will be a second stock (an "external resource"), but may also be a converter.

The external resource acts as a catalyst in generating the inflow (i.e., it is not consumed in the process). Below are some examples that fit the External Resource template...

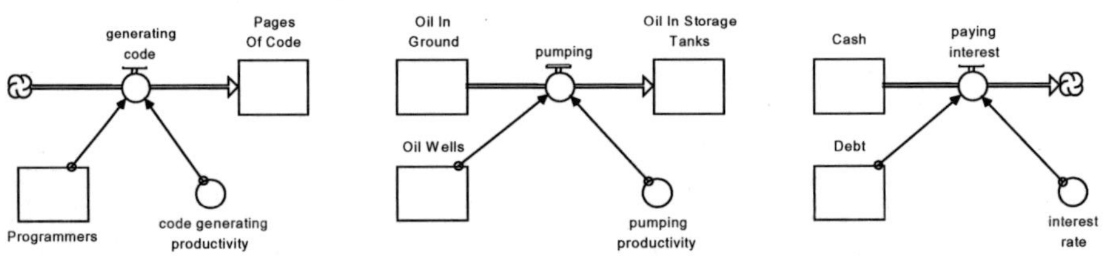

Figure 6-8.
Examples of External Resource Production Templates.

Co-flow

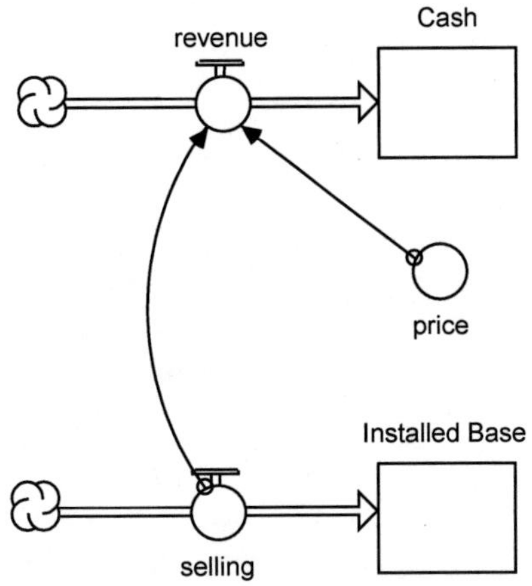

revenue	=	**selling**	*	**price**
\$/time	=	*units/time*	*	*\$/unit*

Figure 6-9.
The Co-flow Template.

"Co-flow" is short for "coincident flow." This template is useful whenever you want to represent a process that has an "activity basis" in a parallel flow. It is also useful when you want to track an attribute associated with a stock.

In a **co-flow** process, the co-flow (*revenue*, above) is linked to some other, primary flow (*selling*). Selling is the activity basis for generating revenue. The inputs to the co-flow process are the primary flow and a conversion coefficient (*price*). The co-flow typically is defined as the product of the two. Thus, the two flows differ only by the conversion coefficient. Some examples…

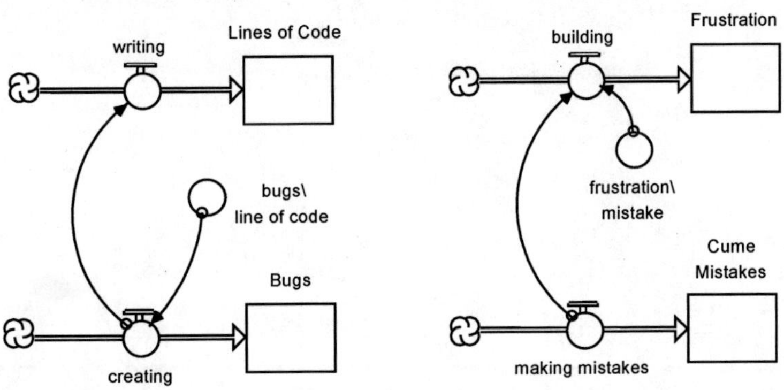

Figure 6-10.
Examples of Co-flow Templates.

Draining

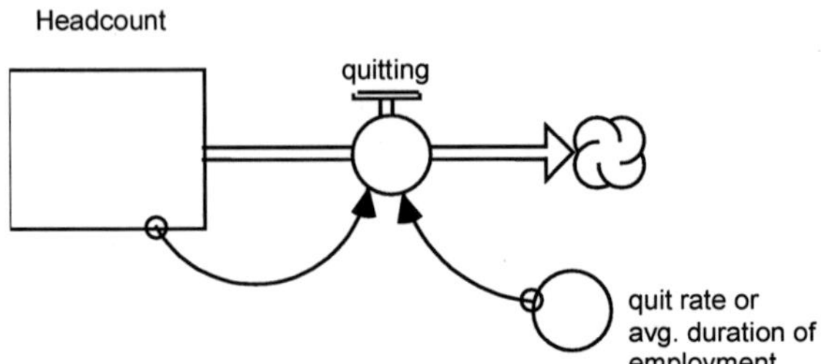

quitting	=	**Headcount**	*	**quit rate**
people/time	=	*People*	*	*fraction/time*

quitting	=	**Headcount**	/	**avg duration of employment**
people/time	=	*People*	/	*time*

Figure 6-11.
The Draining Template.

Use the **draining** template whenever you want to represent the *draining, passive decay*, or *aging* of some stock. In a draining process, the flow is generated by the stock to which it is attached.

The flow (an *outflow* from the stock) is defined as the product of the stock and a draining rate. This rate is the fraction of the stock that is lost or decays per unit of time. In some instances, you may want to substitute the notion of a "time constant" for that of a draining rate. The time constant is the reciprocal of the rate. It indicates the average length of time that it takes a unit to move through the stock, when the stock is in "steady state." Some examples…

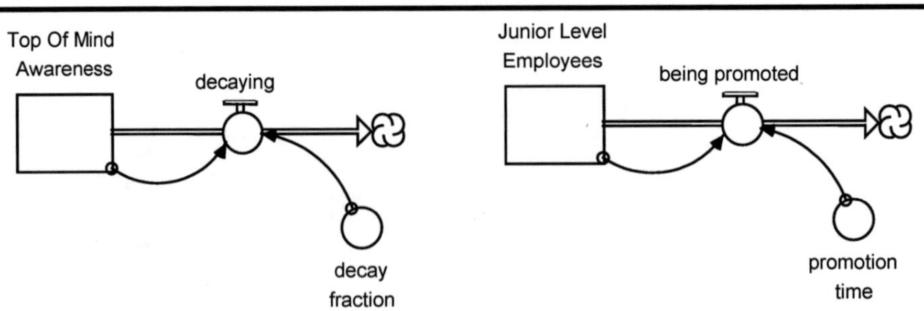

Figure 6-12.
Examples of Draining Templates.

Stock-adjustment

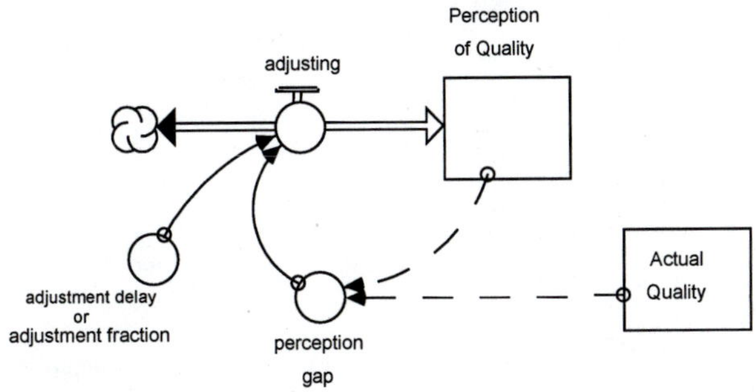

adjusting	=	**perception gap**	/	**adjustment delay**
quality units/time	=	*quality units*	/	*time*
adjusting	=	**perception gap**	*	**adjustment fraction**
quality units/time	=	*quality units*	*	*fraction/time*

Figure 6-13.
The Stock-adjustment Template.

Use the **stock-adjustment** template to represent situations in which a Stock "adjusts to" a target value. This structure often is used to represent the way in which perceptions, opinions, and the like, are adjusted as new "data" become available.

The flow is defined by dividing the *difference* between the stock (*Perception of Quality*) and the target (*Actual Quality*) by the adjustment delay (or multiplying the difference by an adjustment fraction). The flow is a *bi-flow*. Whenever a discrepancy exists between the stock and the target, the flow will *adjust* the stock toward the target level. Both the target and the adjustment fraction can be converters or stocks.

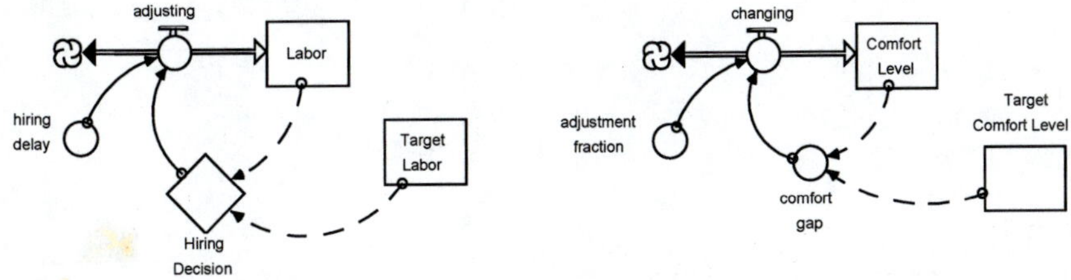

Figure 6-14.
Examples of Stock-adjustment Templates.

Compounding

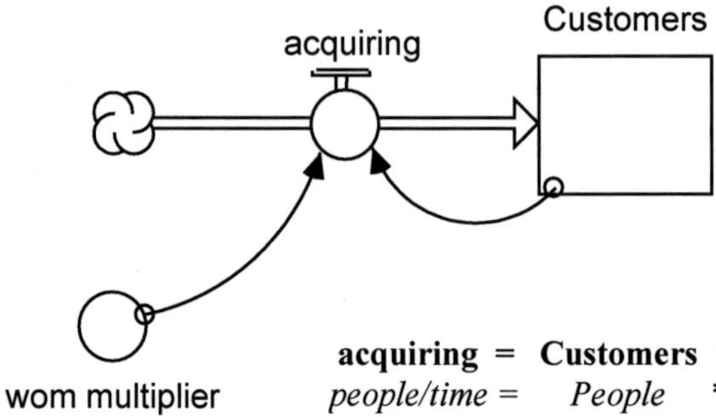

acquiring = **Customers** * **wom multiplier**
people/time = *People* * *people/person/time*

Figure 6-15.
The Compounding Template.

The **compounding** template is appropriate whenever you want to represent a self-reinforcing process. In a compounding process, the flow is generated by the stock into which it is flowing.

The inputs to the flow are the Stock (*Customers*) and a compounding fraction (*wom multiplier*). The flow (an *inflow*) to the stock is defined as the product of the two inputs. The compounding fraction can be either a stock or a converter. Its units-of-measure are “units/unit/time,” where “units” is whatever the stock is measured in. The compounding fraction tells how many new units are produced per unit of time by each existing unit residing within the stock.

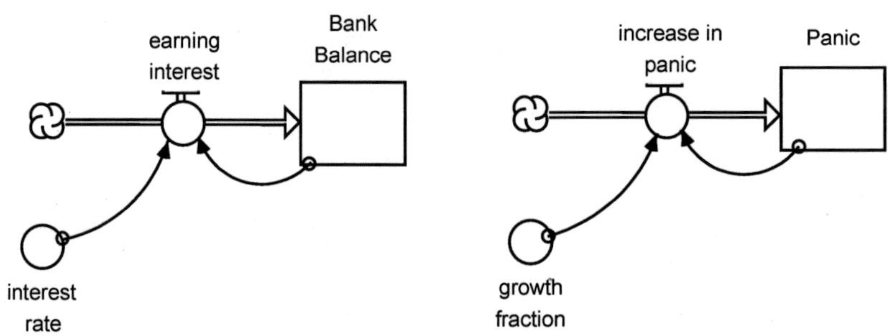

Figure 6-16.
Examples of Compounding Templates.

Chapter 7

Constructing "More Interesting" Paragraphs

Closed-loop & Non-linear Thinking

In Chapter 6, we looked at "simple" feedback loops. In this Chapter, we'll relax the two conditions that define a loop as "simple." We'll allow the parameters associated with the loop to vary, and extend the links that constitute it to more than one "sentence." As you'll see, relaxing these two constraints will enable feedback loops to generate a very rich portfolio of dynamic behavior!

Allowing Parameters to Vary

Before we extend links to create feedback loops involving multiple sentences, let's see what behavioral richness we can engender by allowing parameters to vary within a single-sentence feedback loop structure. Figure 7-1A depicts a simple, reinforcing loop. Left to its own doing, as we saw in Chapter 6, this loop will cause Customer Base to grow *exponentially*, and without limit!

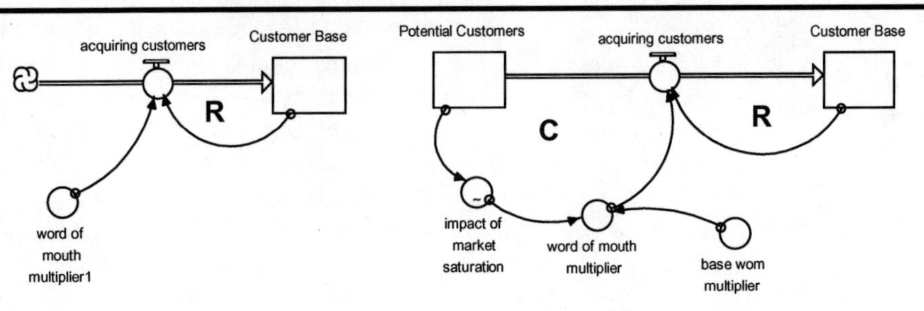

A. A Simple Reinforcing Loop ***B. Adding a Counteracting Loop***

Figure 7-1.
From "Simple" to "Non-simple" Feedback Loops.

Figure 7-1B adds a counteracting loop. The coupling point between the reinforcing and counteracting loops occurs in the variable "word of mouth multiplier." Rather than remaining constant, word of mouth multiplier is "impacted" by a market saturation effect. The equation for word of mouth multiplier is: base wom multiplier * impact of market saturation. The first term is a constant. The second is variable. It depends *in some way* on the stock of Potential Customers. The "in some way" turns out to be interesting, important, and one of the more powerful features in the *ithink* software. But before examining this feature, I want to be sure you "see" the counteracting loop.

The loop works as follows: after Potential Customers falls below some level, the word of mouth multiplier begins decreasing as the stock continues decreasing. This relationship reflects the fact that it is increasingly difficult for a member of the existing Customer Base to find someone left in that stock to "infect" with their enthusiasm. This is true both because there are fewer people remaining in the Potential Customers stock, and because those who do remain are the least disposed (for whatever reason) to become members of this particular Customer Base (or they would have become "infected" earlier). As the impact of market saturation "multiplier" falls, the wom multiplier falls, and hence so does the rate of outflow from the Potential Customers stock—thereby slowing the decline of the stock.

The counteracting loop thus brakes the decline of the Potential Customers stock, and in the process "cools off" the run-away reinforcing loop. What pattern of behavior do you think will result from this interaction between a counteracting and reinforcing loop?

If you were thinking S-shaped growth, you were correct—as Figure 7-2 indicates. When there are plenty of people left in the Potential Customers stock, the impact of market saturation does not yet "kick in." This means that the reinforcing loop is operating unopposed, compounding at a *constant* percentage rate—that rate being equal to the base wom multiplier. We therefore should expect *exponential growth* of the Customer Base. And that is exactly what occurs early in the simulation. If you look at the trajectory traced by Customer Base up to about year 12, it is exponential. After about year 12, or so, Customer Base grows progressively more slowly until, by the end of the simulation, it pretty much ceases growing altogether.

What's going on is that as the magnitude of the Potential Customers stock is drained, the market saturation effect becomes progressively stronger. You might be wondering: How does that innocent-looking little "impact of market saturation" variable pull this off? It's able to pull this off, courtesy of a very important and powerful feature in the *ithink* software. That feature is called a "graphical function."

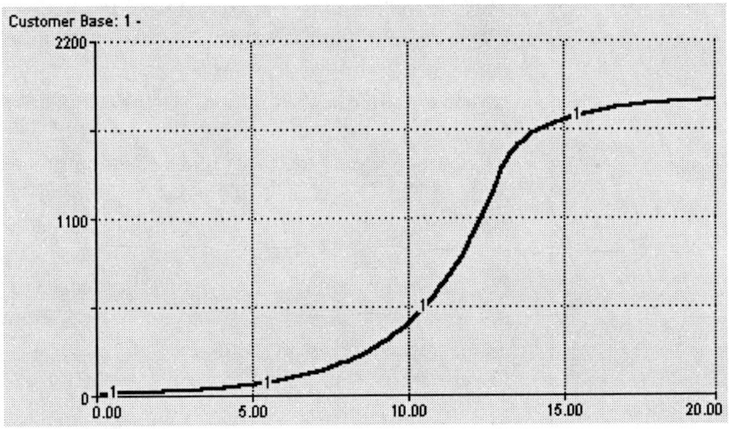

Figure 7-2.
The Behavior of the Coupled Counteracting & Reinforcing Loop System.

The Graphical Function

Take a quick peek back at Figure 7-1B. If you look closely at the converter "impact of market saturation," you will see a sign (albeit a subtle one) of a "loss of innocence!" The little "~" on its face designates it as a "graphical function." Graphical functions express relationships between an input variable and an output variable. They indicate how an output variable changes as the associated input variable varies in magnitude. Graphical functions enable non-mathematically-inclined (as well as mathematically-inclined!) people to express such relationships *without* having to write a mathematical expression. Instead, you draw the relationship by dragging your mouse across an X:Y grid. If you double-click the variable "impact of market saturation," you'd be confronted by something that looks like what you see in Figure 7-3.

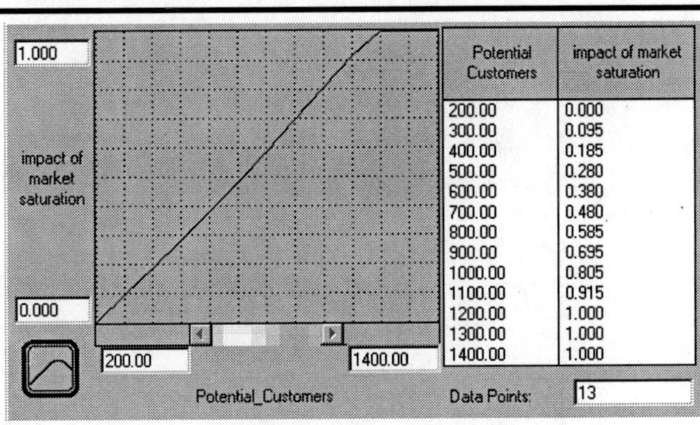

Figure 7-3.
The "impact of market saturation" Graphical Function.

This "something" is a graphical function. It is *not* a graph over time. It's a graph that indicates how an output variable changes as a consequence of movements in an input variable. In this case, the "impact of market saturation" is the output variable. The values it takes on will be determined by the value Potential Customers takes on. As you can see, if the magnitude of Potential Customers remains at or above 1200, the impact of market saturation remains neutral (i.e., the "multiplier" equals 1.0). When Potential Customers dips below 1200, the value taken on by the "multiplier" becomes less than 1.0, and then declines pretty much linearly with the decline in Potential Customers. As it does, it drives the word of mouth multiplier—the parameter determining how strongly the reinforcing loop is compounding—down toward zero, progressively quashing further growth of Customer Base.

In technical terms, what's happening is called a "shift in feedback loop dominance." Remember back to Chapter 6. Whenever a reinforcing and counteracting loop were both in action—one controlling the inflow to, the other the outflow from, a stock—either the stock's magnitude grew exponentially, underwent exponential decay, or remained constant. That's because when compounding and draining fractions are held constant, either the reinforcing loop dominates, or the counteracting loop dominates—or *neither* loop dominates (because they exactly offset each other). And whatever dominance situation is created by the choice of parameter values, *persists*, because the parameter values remain constant!

However, once we allow one or both parameters to vary, loop dominance relationships are no longer fixed! For example, in the illustration at which we've been looking, the *reinforcing* loop is initially dominant. During its reign, Customer Base grows exponentially. Then, as the stock of Potential Customers is drained, the *counteracting* loop progressively grows in strength. And, as it does, it increasingly neutralizes the *reinforcing* loop—shifting the pattern of exponential growth to a "homing in" pattern, characteristic of *counteracting* feedback loop-dominated systems.

Shifts in feedback loop dominance are one of the things that cause systems to generate "surprises." Such shifts are responsible for the "nonlinear responses" (discussed in Chapter 2) in which large pushes sometimes yield barely discernible reactions, whereas small tickles can unleash avalanches! Shifts in feedback loop dominance are caused by variation in the associated parameter values (i.e., the "productivity terms" associated with the loops). In *ithink* models, such variation is most often implemented by using a graphical function. It also is possible to vary such parameters "discretely" by using IF-THEN-ELSE type logic. However, in most cases, doing so is a violation of "10,000 Meter" Thinking. As such, I'll not treat discrete, or threshold, variation here. You will find examples of the use of various Boolean algebraic expressions to discretely shift feedback loop dominance in the Sample Models folder that accompanies the software. The *Help Files* associated with the software also provide detail on how to construct such expressions. But again, for the most part, if you are embracing a Systems Thinking viewpoint, the graphical function will almost always be your weapon of choice for engendering shifts in feedback loop dominance.

Graphical functions are thus very important devices. Formulating them is somewhat an art, but mostly a science. An Appendix to this Chapter relates that science to you. It would be a good idea to spend some time making sure you understand the information in the Appendix—both the mechanical, and the conceptual, aspects!

Extending Links to Create "Multiple Sentence" Feedback Loops

You've now seen how relaxing the assumption of constancy, with respect to the parameters that determine the strength of a feedback loop, can enrich the repertoire of dynamics a system can exhibit. The next bit of relaxation will be with respect to the "extent" of the feedback linkages themselves. All of the feedback loops we examined in Chapter 6 included only one sentence (i.e., one noun/verb assembly). We're now ready to see what can happen when we extend the links constituting a feedback loop to include *more than one* sentence.

Figure 7-4 illustrates a two-sentence feedback loop structure. The loop happens to be *counteracting* in nature. Its purpose is to maintain Inventory at a target level. The "strategy" for doing so is to adjust Labor upward or downward so as to regulate the volume of producing. Here's how the feedback loop works… Initially, the selling volume is constant, and Labor is at a level that causes the producing volume to just exactly equal the selling volume. As a result, Inventory remains constant at its "target" level (the target is "buried" inside the hiring & firing decision diamond). As long as Inventory remains at target levels, the hiring and firing volume will remain at zero. And, as long as the hiring\firing volume remains at zero, Labor will remain constant. The system is in steady-state.

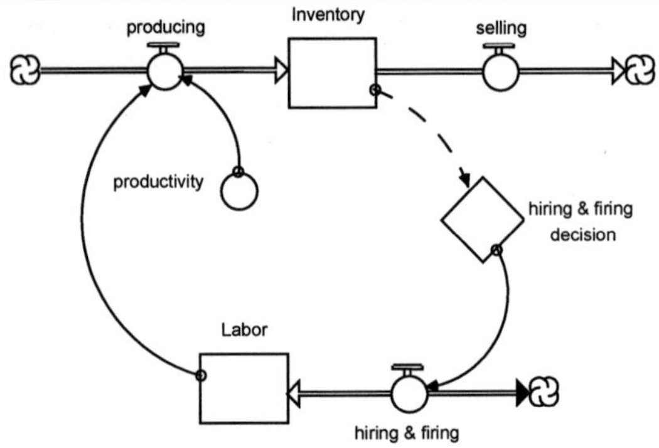

Figure 7-4.
A Simple, Two-sentence, Counteracting Feedback Loop.

But you know how Systems Thinkers *hate* systems that remain at rest. They want to see dynamics! To coax this system into strutting its stuff, we'll step-up the previously-constant selling flow to a higher, constant volume. Mentally simulate what you think will unfold in response to this disturbance.

Did you guess the pattern that you see in Figure 7-5? If so, bravo! Most people don't. I'll offer a brief "anatomical" explanation here. But first, recognize that this simple-looking little structure generates some pretty wild and wooly behavior! Linking sentences via feedback loops really expands the associated behavioral repertoire.

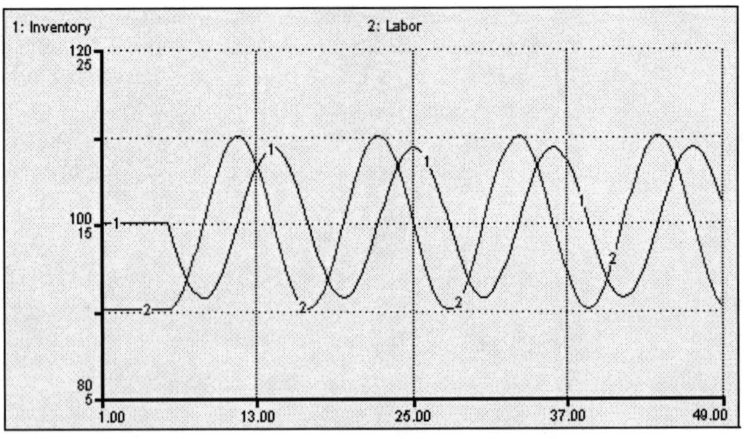

Figure 7-5.
The "Natural Frequency" Response of the Inventory/Labor System.

Here's what's going on …As soon as the step-increase in selling (the *outflow* from Inventory) occurs, Inventory starts falling because the producing flow volume (the *inflow* to Inventory) remains at its previous steady-state value—which is less than the now stepped-up selling volume. When Inventory dips below target levels, hiring "kicks in." The resulting increase in labor drives up the producing volume. However, until the producing volume increases to equal the selling volume, Inventory will continue to fall. Make sure this all makes sense before continuing.

Okay, so what happens to Inventory at the point when hiring has caused an increased stock of Labor to drive up the producing volume so that it now, once again, just equals the selling volume?

If you said, Inventory ceases declining…Bene! However, notice something that's very important to understanding these dynamics. At the point where inventory has ceased declining, it is as far away as it's ever going to be from its target level! Do you see this?

And so, when the producing volume has increased to the point where it is once again equal to the selling volume—a condition for steady-state to be re-achieved—Inventory is as far as it's ever going to be from its steady-state level! We now have a system that is very seriously out of whack! The flows associated with a given stock are in equilibrium at exactly the point where the stock is as far as its ever going to be from equilibrium. This is precisely the condition that must prevail in order for a "sustained oscillation" to occur.

Let's continue a bit more to ensure you understand what's going on. When Inventory is as far below its target level as it's going to be (i.e., the negative discrepancy between the two is at a maximum), the rate of hiring will also be as large as it's going to be. This means that the rate at which the stock of Labor is expanding will be at a maximum, and hence that the producing volume will be *increasing* at its maximum rate, right at the point where that volume is just equal to the selling volume. So, as stock of Labor continues to expand, the producing volume will follow suit, soaring right on by the selling volume. And, as it does, Inventory will begin to re-build (i.e., the inflow to the bathtub will now exceed the outflow), and the rate of hiring will hence slow.

However, as long as Inventory levels remain below target levels, hiring will continue, and hence the producing volume will continue to increase beyond the selling volume. At some point, Inventory levels will have re-built back up to exactly equal target levels—another of the conditions necessary for the system to re-gain its steady-state. At that point, can the system come to rest?

Uh-uh. Because at that point, the producing volume—though it will now cease increasing—will stand as high as it's ever going to be *above* the selling volume. That means there's way too much Labor on board. So, while Inventory has re-achieved its steady-state level, Labor is as far as it's ever going to be above its steady-state level. Do you see the problem? It's called "perfectly out of phase" goal-seeking! And given this feedback structure, it can never get back "in phase."

Bottom line: Although this system is being regulated by a *counteracting* loop, that loop is not capable of returning the system to equilibrium. It will try. It will goal-seek its heart out! But because of the nature of the counteracting structure, this system will continue to oscillate for eternity (or for as long as your laptop battery lasts, if you're on an airplane).

Combining Variable Parameters and Extended Links

Let's now add a *second* counteracting loop to this system. We'll do so by allowing one of the previously constant parameters to become variable.

The particular parameter that we'll make variable is "productivity." Productivity determines the *strength* of the connection between Labor and the producing flow (which is to say, the strength of the counteracting feedback loop). That is, the *larger* the value productivity takes on, the *smaller* the amount of Labor that will be needed in order to elevate the producing volume by a given amount (because each *unit* of labor will contribute a larger increment to the producing volume). Conversely, smaller values for productivity will lessen the strength of the counteracting loop because they would mean that *more* Labor must be brought on to raise the producing volume by any given amount.

Suppose we were to able strengthen the counteracting loop both by boosting productivity whenever the producing volume needed to increase, and by lowering productivity whenever that volume needed to be cut back. Such variation occurs naturally in most work situations. Swollen work backlogs tend to inspire focus, buckling down and getting the job done (i.e., productivity rises). Lean backlogs enable people to drink more coffee and share more water cooler conversation (productivity falls).

To implement such a variation in productivity, we'll rely upon our old friend the graphical function. The resulting new "structure" looks like what you see in Figure 7-6.

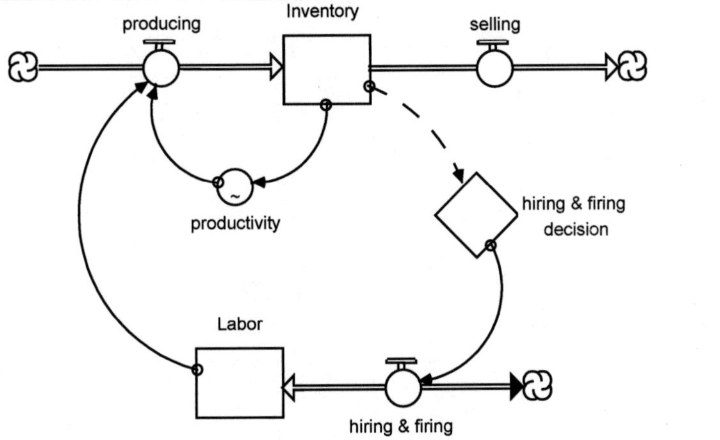

Figure 7-6.
Allowing "productivity" to Vary.

Notice that by linking Inventory to productivity, we've added a second *counteracting* feedback loop. This second loop works in concert with the first one, which is to say, amplifies its strength! It carries some of the burden of causing the volume of the producing flow to increase (and decrease) as Inventory levels rise and fall with respect to target. For example, rather than having to crank up producing *solely* by bringing on additional labor, some of the increase in the producing volume can be delivered via elevated productivity levels.

So, what effect do you think adding this second counteracting loop will have on the system's behavior? Will it heighten or dampen the instability the system was exhibiting? And why?

Such questions confound intuition. One of the significant contributions of the *ithink* software is that it serves as a tool for checking intuition, and for exploring the why. With continued use, your capacity for intuiting dynamics will be strengthened—as will your ability to articulate the associated "how comes." Figure 7-7 shows what happens to the system's behavior when the second counteracting loop is added.

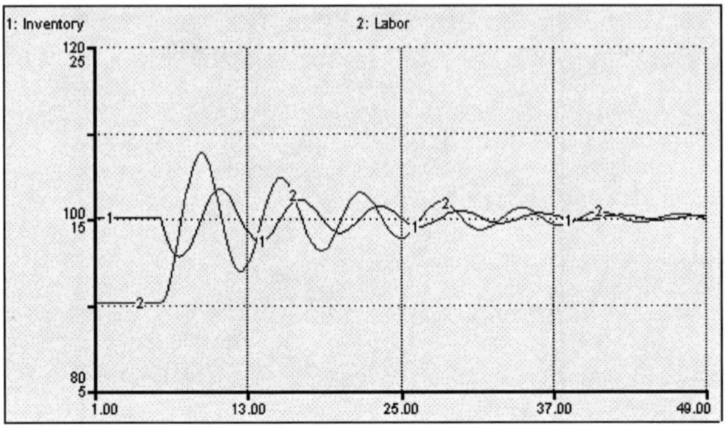

Figure 7-7.
From Sustained to Dampened Oscillation.

As the Figure shows, activating the new loop *dampens* the oscillation. A simple explanation goes as follows…Instead of Labor expanding to its maximum at exactly the point where the producing volume is at a maximum above the selling volume, producing can now reach its maximum point above selling *before* Labor reaches its maximum (because productivity is *also* boosting producing!). This means that not as much Labor needs to be hired on the upswing, and hence not as much needs to be shed on the downswing. That, in turn, means even fewer people need to be hired on the *next* upswing, and thus even fewer still need be shed on the subsequent downswing…and so on. The system is thus able to progressively settle back down into a steady-state (barring further externally-produced disturbances).

Feedback Loops: In Summary

A feedback loop is an ingenious and incredibly powerful "structure." Feedback loops abound in physical, human-made, natural, and social systems. They enable these systems to maintain internal balances, and also to grow. They guide evolutionary adaptation, and preside over catastrophic collapses. Feedback loops *self-generate* all manner of dynamic behavior. Excite one and you will set in motion an ongoing dynamic, not a one-time response. The pattern that dynamic will trace depends on the relative strength of the various feedback loops that make up the system, and how those strengths wax and wane over time. The graphical function in the *ithink* software, by serving as a coupling point between loops, is often the vehicle for enabling such waxing and waning to play out.

You are now well-prepared to begin capturing in your *ithink* models the feedback loops that exist within the systems you are seeking to represent. You will see lots more examples of feedback loops throughout the remainder of this Guide and in the sample models that accompany the software. Capturing the feedback loop structure of a system, in an operational way, is the essence of the difference between building models with tools like spreadsheets versus using the *ithink* software. Viva la différence!

What's Next

In the next two chapters, several examples of generic feedback loop structures are provided. You will find these little "infrastructures" to be very useful as building blocks for populating the models you construct with the *ithink* software.

Appendix:

Formulating Graphical Functions

This Appendix describes two principles to keep in mind when formulating graphical functions, and then goes on to provide a "cookbook" of steps to follow in formulating them.

Principle 1.
The Ceteris Paribus Principle

Graphical functions are used to capture a relationship that you hypothesize to exist between two, and only two, variables whose interaction you are thinking about against a "ceteris paribus" (all other things held constant) backdrop. When you sketch into the graphical function the curve you feel captures the relationship you are seeking to represent, the slope of that curve should (in general) not change direction! If it *does*, think hard about whether you are not implicitly including the impact of one or more other variables in your formulation of the relationship. Let's take an example to clarify the point.

"Schedule pressure" is often brought to bear on workers when a project falls behind schedule. The idea is that such pressure can cause people to increase their focus on the task at hand, and hence increase their productivity—speeding the project forward, and hopefully putting it back on schedule. A description of the relationship between levels of schedule pressure and resulting levels of productivity usually goes something like this...In the absence of schedule pressure, productivity is less than it could be because people will not focus well without feeling some pressure from a deadline. As schedule pressure rises up from zero, productivity increases for a while. But, beyond a certain point, schedule pressure becomes dysfunctional because it weighs too heavily on workers. Implementing the preceding logic into a graphical function would yield something like what you see in Figure 7-8.

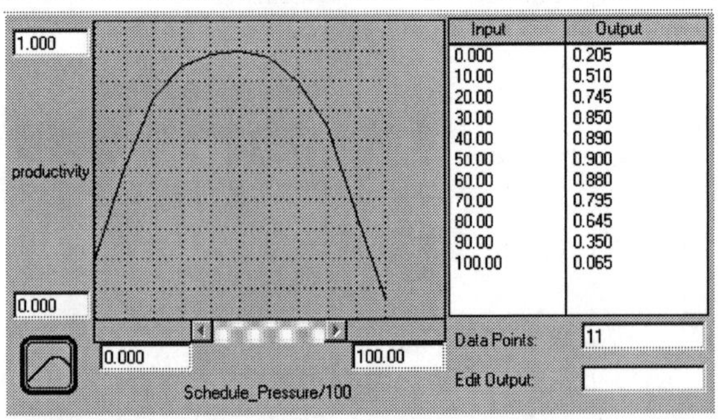

Figure 7-8.
A Schedule Pressure/Productivity Graphical Function.

Clearly this is a curve whose slope *changes direction.* Let's think more carefully about the assumptions that underlie it. How does schedule pressure *directly* impact workers? Not, what actions does schedule pressure cause workers to take, but how does it directly impact them? It is this latter question that you want to ask when formulating a graphical function.

Schedule pressure usually takes the form of a project manager reminding workers of impending deadlines at a higher frequency than normal, and also with a greater sense of urgency. This may, in fact, cause workers to take certain actions as a result. They may, for example, work longer hours, take fewer breaks, focus more on the tasks at hand, and so forth. Once they start doing such things, they don't stop doing them as schedule pressure mounts because of the schedule pressure, itself! They may stop doing them because they are feeling fried, or miss time with their families, or for other reasons—but not because schedule pressure is increasing!

The *direct* impact of schedule pressure on productivity is therefore probably to increase it—though the impact certainly saturates. Schedule pressure can't have a positive impact, and then at some "magic point" all of a sudden reverse the direction of its impact! The perceived change in direction of impact is, in fact, due to unconsciously introducing other things (like burnout, waning motivation, etc.) into the thinking process. The "other things" don't belong in the *same* graphical function! If you do not carefully screen them out, your models can yield misleading conclusions when you simulate them.

For example, in the preceding illustration, what if workers *already* were experiencing some level of burnout from, say, a previous project. Now, assume they are just beginning to fall behind on the current project (i.e., zero schedule pressure has been applied to date). The graphical function relationship described in Figure 6-8 would suggest that you could *increase* worker productivity by applying some schedule pressure. However, clearly that would *not* be the outcome if workers already were feeling frayed at the edges!

Be certain the "thought experiments" you conduct in formulating graphical functions involve two, and only two, variables! Screen out "other influences" on the output variable.

Principle 2.
Think Out of the Historical Box

The second important principle to follow when formulating graphical function relationships is: *Be sure to estimate any relationship over its full potentially realizable operating range, and not just over a range that may have been historically-observed.* Many people feel uneasy about formulating graphical function relationships in general. This is, in part, due to the fact graphical functions often are used to capture "squishy" relationships. But even when the relationships are more tangible—such as, say, the impact of price on demand—people often have issues with venturing outside historically-observed ranges for the relationship. For example, historically, price may only have ranged plus or minus 25% from its current value. And so, this is the extent of the range many people feel comfortable with including in the associated graphical function. "Beyond this range, we have no solid empirical data," is what we often hear.

But think about it…If you want your model to be able to shed any light on what *could* happen if price were dropped to zero, or boosted by 50%, you *must* provide *some* estimate of price elasticity over this range! Oftentimes, real insights emerge when you drive a system to operate outside its historical operating range. If your model's graphical function relationships are not estimated over their full, potentially-realizable operating range, you will forfeit the opportunity to have the model "surprise" you! Model results, in these cases, could be "crazy." But with an ithink model, it's always possible to discover how those results are being brought about, and you can therefore always separate "craziness" from genuine "new insight." I have witnessed the latter on a sufficient number of occasions to feel very strongly about the importance of principle number two.

Cookbook Guidelines for Formulating Graphical Functions

Let's now look at some general guidelines to follow when formulating graphical functions.

The guidelines that follow are arrayed in a progression of steps. Following these steps, in the order presented, will generally enable you to formulate reasonable graphical function relationships, whether you are doing so alone, or working to elicit such relationships from a management team.

Step 1. Apply Ceteris Paribus Principle

Think only of the relationship between the input variable and the output variable, holding all other variables impacting the output variable constant.

Step 2. "Normalize" the Input Variable

Normalizing is accomplished by dividing the input variable by some *appropriate* quantity. Not all input variables require being normalized. For example, percentage variables (like market share) and index-number variables (e.g., variables that are scaled 0-100, like motivation, self-esteem, and burnout) need not be normalized. Other variables that have a compact range also can remain un-normalized.

Normalizing has a couple of important benefits. First, it makes movements in the input variable easier to think about because a normalized range usually ends up being something like 0 to 1, or 0 to 2, rather than some much larger *absolute* range, like 0 to 1000 or 500 to 5000. When a range is 0 to 2, it's much easier to think about changes in the input variable in percentage terms. That is, if the input variable increases from 1.0 to 1.25, that's immediately recognizable as a 25% increase. If an input variable's range is, say, 0 to 10,000, it's difficult to know at a glance how much of a percentage increase a move from, say, 570 to 730 constitutes.

A second benefit of normalizing is that it makes the relationship "scale independent." If you use *absolute* ranges for input variables, you will have to re-calibrate your graphical functions if those absolute ranges change, or if you apply your model to a different organization or group within the same organization (because the absolute ranges would likely be different). But, by normalizing, you convert to *relative* quantities. So, for example, if Cash is your input variable, the question would shift from "If Cash falls to $83 million..." to "If Cash falls to 50% of its initial level.

Choosing an appropriate "normalization" variable often takes a little thought. Sometimes, simply dividing the input variable by its starting value (i.e., its value at the outset of the simulation) works quite well. Other times, dividing through by a variable that has different units-of-measure works better—such as revenues per employee, or sales per region.

Step 3. Establish Ranges for the Input and Output Variables: (apply Principle 2)

Be sure to establish ranges that permit full possible movement of both input and output variables, not just movement that has been historically-observed. Remember that graphical functions do not extrapolate outside their defined ranges. Instead, they retain the first and last output values that you have assigned.

Step 4. Determine the Direction and Nature of the

Remember that if the slope of your graphical function *changes* direction, you are probably including more than one input variable in your thinking. By "nature of the slope," I mean...Does the curve saturate? Is it linear? S-shaped? And so forth. Make explicit a behavioral argument to support your choice of a curve, and include it in the Document cache of the graphical function equation dialog so that others can understand your rationale.

Step 5. Identify Extreme Points and, if Appropriate, a "1,1" Point

Begin with the low-end x point (input value), and establish the associated y point (output value). Then, do the same for the high-end x and y points. In some cases, particularly if you are using "impact of..." variables, you will also be able to establish a so-called "normal point" or "1,1" point. When an "impact of..." variable (usually a "multiplier") takes on a value of 1, it means it is exerting a *neutral* impact. A normalized *input* variable usually takes on a value of 1 in the initial condition, or when the variable is at its "normal" magnitude.

Step 6. Sketch a Smooth Curve Through the Established Points

Whether you have only two extreme points, or those two points plus a "normal point," trace a *smooth* curve through the points. If you have some "magic points" in your curve (some points at which sharp discontinuities occur), look very carefully to be sure you can justify what you've drawn.

Chapter 8

Storylines, Part 1:
Main Chain Infrastructures

With basic parts of speech, sentences, and paragraphs under your belt, you are now ready to begin composing short stories. The next two Chapters will help you in these efforts by providing some classic "storylines." This Chapter presents six examples of what we call, *Main Chain Infrastructures*. Main Chains create a spinal cord for your model. They consist of a series of stocks linked by flows. A good example: a supply chain stretching from manufacturer through distributor and wholesaler to retailer. Chapter 9 presents examples of classic, non-main chain infrastructures.

For each Main Chain, we:

- provide a brief verbal description
- identify issues that can be addressed using it
- suggest ways to customize it for your own applications
- identify the name of the corresponding *ithink* model.

As you become familiar with these main chains, you will begin to appreciate how broadly applicable they are. I strongly encourage you to refer to this section of the Guide as you pursue your modeling efforts.

Human Resources Main Chain

Description

The Human Resources Main Chain provides a highly-aggregated representation of the flow of human resources through an organization. Employees are hired into the organization at the "Junior" level. They then either quit, or move to "Mid-Level." Mid-Levels either quit, or move to "Senior" status. Movement along the chain is governed by level-specific quit fractions and promotion times. All quitting and promoting flows are represented using the "draining" template.

A map of a Human Resources Main Chain Infrastructure appears in Figure 8-1.

Issues to Explore

The model illustrates an important behavioral characteristic of Main Chain infrastructures: *Main chains will seek to distribute material among their stocks in proportion to the relative magnitude of the associated residence times*. The "residence time" (in this illustration) is composed of a combination of the average time before being promoted and the average time before quitting. For example, if, on average, employees remain Juniors for 2 years, Mid-Levels for 4 years, and Seniors for 8 years, the Main Chain will seek to distribute total headcount among the three levels in a 2-4-8 (or, a 1:2:4) ratio. Such a ratio may be quite different than the ratio an organization is seeking to maintain for economic, or span-of-control, reasons. Unless people realize that any such Main Chain has an "implicit goal structure" with respect to distribution of headcount, they can end up "fighting the physics!" The "physics" always win…though you can delay the victory by working very hard against the implicit goal structure!

Suggested Extensions

1. Make promotion times depend on the target distribution of employees among the three classes. That way, for example, if the chain is getting top-heavy, promotion times for Juniors and Mid-Levels would be increased.
2. Tie quit fractions to promotion times—so, for example, as promotion times for Juniors are increased, quit rates for Juniors would also increase.
3. Allow hiring into all three classes.

Model on Disk

"*HR Main Chain*" (in "*Intro to Systems Thinking*" folder).

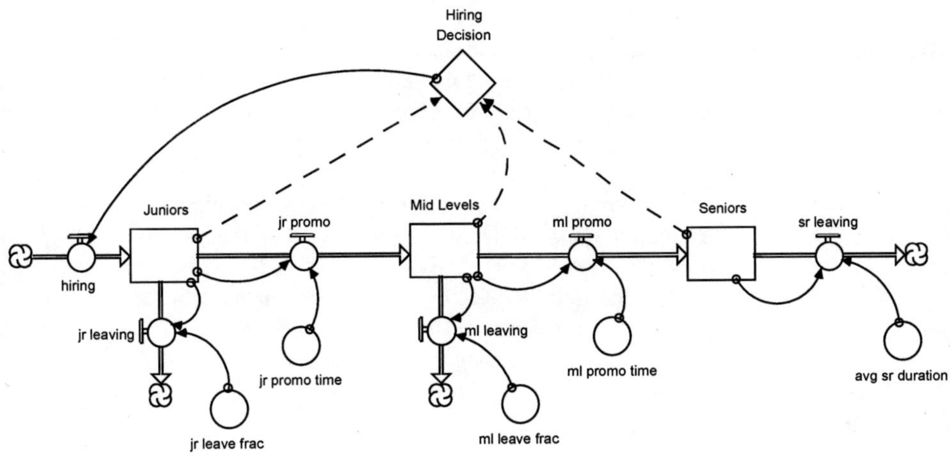

Figure 8-1.
"Human Resources Main Chain Infrastructure."

Customer Main Chain

Description

This chain represents the states through which customers move, from "potential" to "active" users. A map of a Customer Main Chain Infrastructure appears in Figure 8-2. As the map shows, there are many pathways through which customers can exit the system.

The "draining" template, or some slightly modified variant, is used to characterize all but one of the flows. For the *becoming hot, losing potentials*, *purchasing*, and *losing interest* flows, two processes are at work. The first is the time it takes to move through the stage (*time to prospect* and *time to make purchase decision*). The second is the fraction of those passing through the stage who move onward to the next stage (versus out of the system, *frac who get hot* and *frac who buy*).

Issues to Explore

An interesting issue to explore with this model relates to the relative magnitude of the inflows to, and outflows from, the stock of *Active Users*. Many marketing and sales strategies focus on the inflow side—seeking to increase the "hit rate" on sales calls, for example. Often overlooked, but equally important, are activities associated with the *outflows*. Maintaining a healthy base of customers involves *both* attracting new customers and retaining existing customers. Using this infrastructure as a starting point in the examination of a marketing strategy can help to ensure that both sets of activities receive adequate attention.

Suggested Extensions

1. Make the constants in the model (e.g., *time to prospect, time to make purchase decision, frac who buy, frac becoming inactive*) depend upon things like advertising, direct mail, trade show participation, product quality, and responsiveness of customer service.

2. Add new categories of customers. For example, disaggregate the stock of *Active Users* into novice and experienced.

Model on Disk

"*Customer Main Chain*" (in "*Intro to Systems Thinking*" folder).

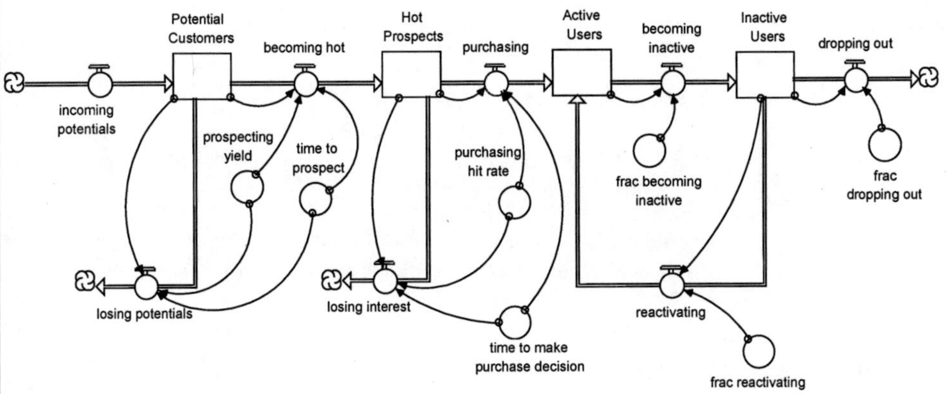

Figure 8-2.
"Customer Main Chain Infrastructure."

Administrative Main Chain

Description

The Main Chain infrastructure depicted in Figure 8-3 represents the sequence of activities constituting an administrative process. Note the presence of a re-work loop, and the use of Conveyors.

Issues to Explore

- Use the infrastructure as a starting point for a process re-engineering application.
- As you customize this structure for your own application, disaggregate the key activities represented by Conveyors.

Suggested Extensions

1. Modify the chain to reflect the key processes in your system.
2. Add support infrastructures (see Chapter 9) to provide visibility into possible resource constraints.
3. Add cycle-time metrics to "keep score" on simulated process improvement policies (see the *ithink Help Files* for details on cycle-time)
4. Set inflow limits and capacities for Conveyors. Add Queues in front of Conveyors to handle "capacity exceeded" conditions (available in the *ithink Analyst* version only).
5. Use variable (rather than fixed) transit times for the Conveyors.
6. Make Conveyor leakage fractions depend on other conditions within the system.

Model on Disk

"*Administrative Main Chain*" (in "*Intro to Systems Thinking*" folder).

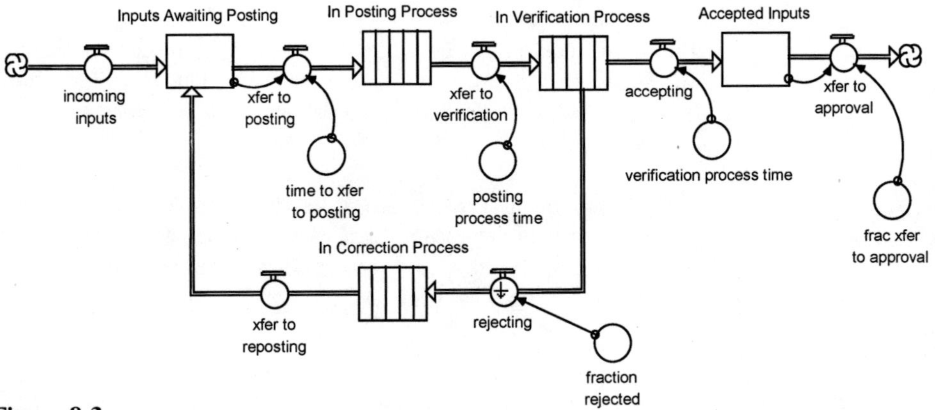

Figure 8-3.
"Administrative Main Chain Infrastructure."

A Manufacturing Main Chain

Description

The Main Chain infrastructure shown in Figure 8-4 represents a simple manufacturing process. A re-work loop is included in the process. Note that four of the stages in the Main Chain are represented using Conveyors.

Issues to Explore

- In many manufacturing processes, backlogs and inventories are excellent barometers of system performance. *Raw Materials* and *Awaiting Inspection* are key performance barometers in this Manufacturing Main Chain. Continual build-up of either stock is a sign that the system is unbalanced.
- As you customize this chain for your specific application, think through the interconnections between the chain and other business processes.
- After identifying these interconnections, represent and simulate them by adding the needed additional structural elements.

Suggested Extensions

1. Generate *raw matls ordering* based on product demand and inventory levels.
2. Add financial score-keeping.
3. Extend the chain to account for additional steps in the manufacturing process.
4. Make the transit times for one or more of the Conveyors variable.
5. Calculate cycle-time and financial metrics.
6. Use a Sub-model to provide drill-down details on the *Work in Process* activity.

Model on Disk

"*Manufacturing Main Chain*" (in "*Intro to Systems Thinking*" folder).

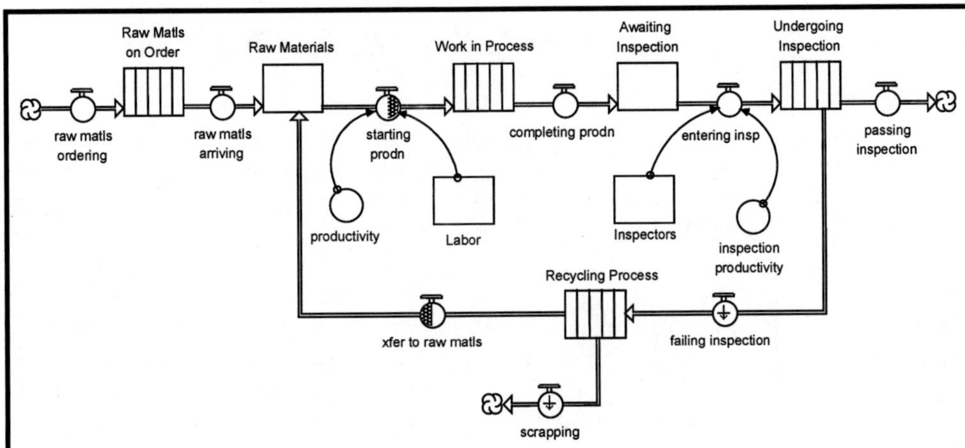

Figure 8-4.
"Manufacturing Main Chain Infrastructure."

Sequential Work Flow Main Chain

Description

This infrastructure provides a generic representation of a sequential work completion process. Tasks are assumed to unfold in serial fashion: work associated with task 2 does not begin until a certain level of task 1 work has been completed. A map of a Work Flow Main Chain Infrastructure appears in Figure 8-5.

Issues to Explore

- This Main Chain can serve as the foundation for a model-based project management "flight simulator." Such a model provides an excellent vehicle for exploring the impact of various managerial and staffing policies on project cost and completion time.
- Extend the chain to include additional tasks.
- Experiment with different resource levels, re-work fractions, task completion targets, and initial amounts of work for each task.

Suggested Extensions

1. Include additional tasks to be completed.
2. Use a *resource allocation support infrastructure* (see Chapter 9) to allocate a single resource among the various tasks.
3. Add a cycle-time structure to calculate task-completion times.

Model on Disk

"*Work Flow Main Chain*" (in "*Intro to Systems Thinking*" folder).

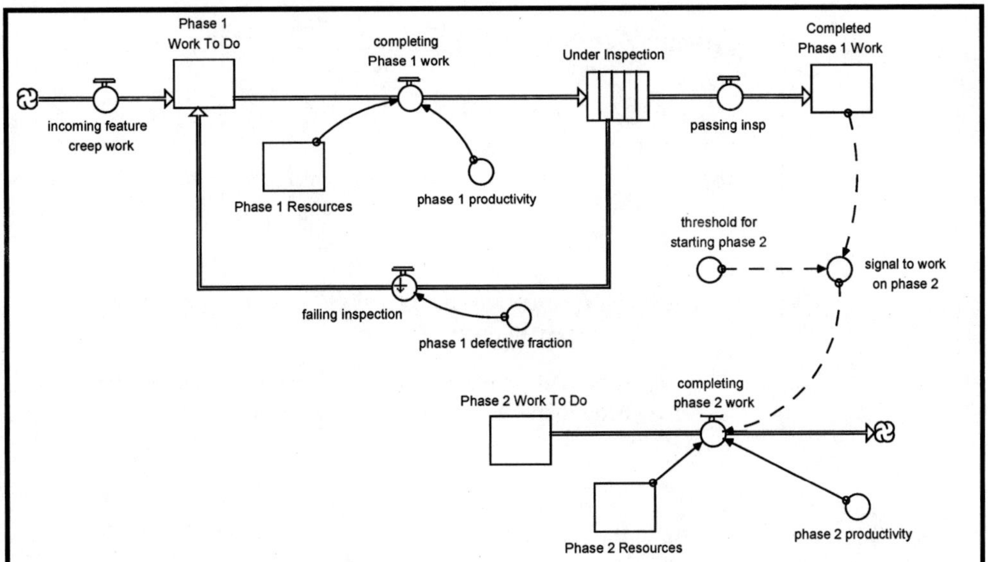

Figure 8-5.
"Sequential Work Flow Main Chain Infrastructure."

Queue/Server Main Chain

Description

This infrastructure uses the Queue and Oven capabilities of the *Analyst* Version to represent a simple queue/server process. A Poisson distribution is used to represent the *arriving* flow. A map of a queue/server Main Chain infrastructure appears in Figure 8-6.

Issues to Explore

- Use this infrastructure when you need to analyze your process from a "discrete" vantage point.
- Explore different arriving rates and service times to learn what relationship between the two best balances arrival volume with service times.

Suggested Extensions

1. Use array capabilities to manage the visual complexity associated with a large number of servers.
2. Feed back service times to the *mean arriving rate*.

Model on Disk

"*Queue Server Main Chain*" (in "*Intro to Systems Thinking*" folder).

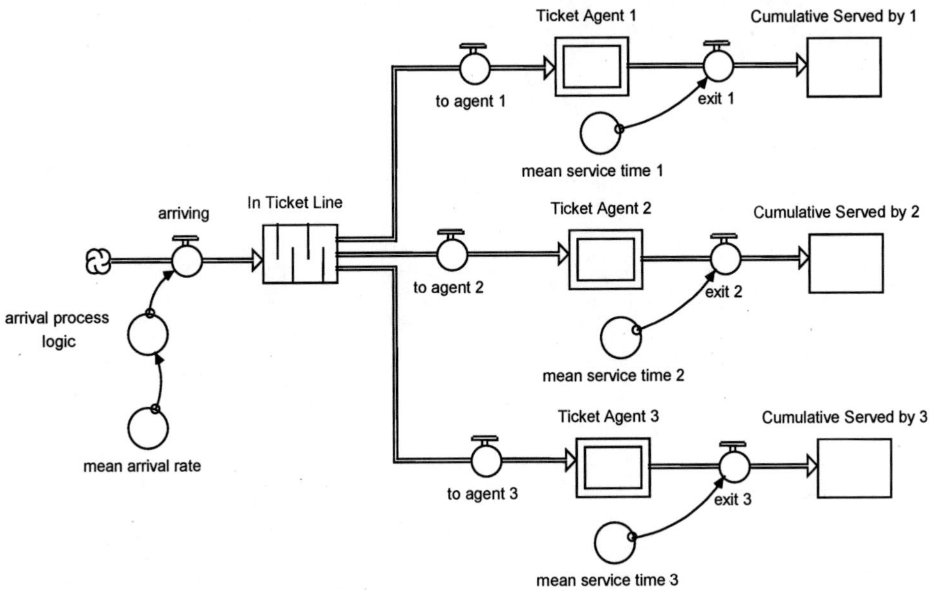

Figure 8-6.
"Queue/Server Main Chain Infrastructure."

Chapter 9

Storylines, Part 2:
Support Infrastructures

This Chapter presents the second category of high-level, "classic" infrastructures that so often appear in *ithink* modeling. We call them, *Support Infrastructures*. We've grouped them into four categories:

1. Resource Infrastructures
2. Production Infrastructures
3. Score-Keeping Infrastructures
4. Miscellaneous Infrastructures

For each infrastructure, we:

- provide a description
- suggest extensions for customizing the infrastructure
- identify the corresponding *ithink* model.

Resource Infrastructures

Human Resources: *Single Tier*

Description

This structure provides the simplest possible representation of an HR system involving hiring and attrition flows. The *hiring* decision includes two components: replacement of attrition and hiring for growth. The *attriting* flow is represented using a "draining" template; an *attrition fraction* is applied to the *Headcount* stock.

A map of a One Tier HR Infrastructure appears in Figure 9-1.

Suggested Extensions

1. Include a *Pool of Candidates* out of which hiring is done. Include a feedback link from the *Pool* to *hiring* (because the hiring process will be constrained when candidates are not available in sufficient quantity).
2. Include feedback from other components of the model (such as financial score-keeping metrics) to *target growth percentage*.
3. Add feedback from variables such as morale to the *attrition fraction.*

Model on Disk

"*One Tier HR Infras*" (in "*Intro to Systems Thinking*" folder).

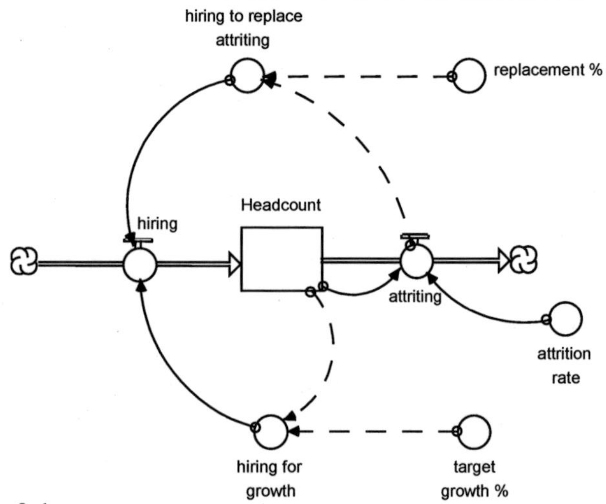

Figure 9-1.
"One Tier HR Infrastructure."

Human Resources: *Two Tier*

Description

This structure builds on the one-tier infrastructure by adding a second employee category. In this example, a Conveyor is used to represent the *Rookies* in the organization. Note the "leakage flow" that is used to depict *rookie attriting.*

A map of a Two Tier Headcount Infrastructure appears in Figure 9-2.

Suggested Extensions

1. Include additional employee tiers.
2. Add a Pool of Candidates out of which hiring is done.
3. Include feedback to *target growth percentage* and/or *attrition fractions*.
4. Convert *Rookies* to a Reservoir; then use "draining" processes to represent *rookie attrition* and *coming up to speed.*

Model on Disk

"*Two Tier Headcount Infra*" (in "*Intro to Systems Thinking*" folder).

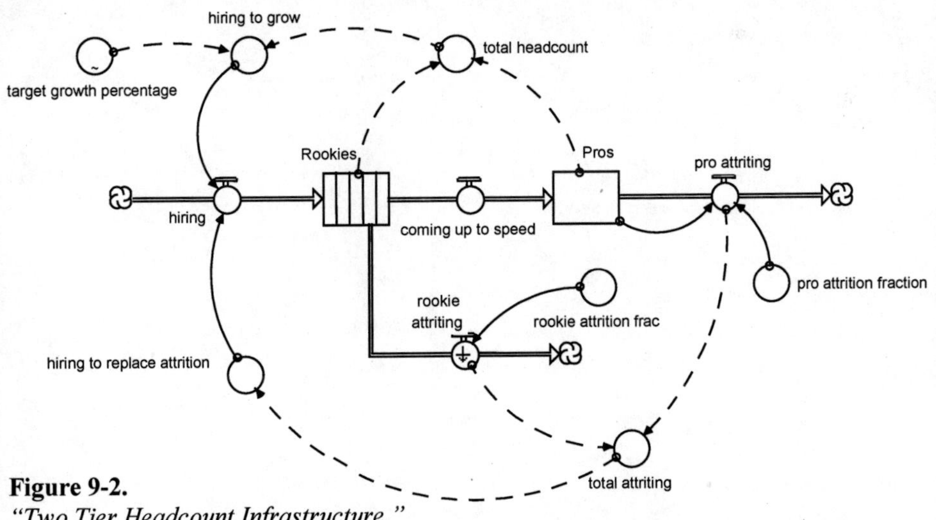

Figure 9-2.
"Two Tier Headcount Infrastructure."

Human Resources: *Attribute Tracking*

Description

Use this infrastructure when you wish to track an attribute associated with a particular stock in your model. The structure calculates a moving average of the attribute. Note that the structure makes extensive use of the co-flow process described in Chapter 5.

A map of the Attribute Tracking Infrastructure appears in Figure 9-3.

Suggested Extensions

1. Tie other conditions in your model to *learning productivity*.
2. Feed back *avg knowledge level* to *hiring* and *attrition*, as well as to the *knowledge per new hire* and *knowledge per exitee*.

Model on Disk

"*Attribute Tracking Infrastructure*" (in "*Intro to Systems Thinking*" folder).

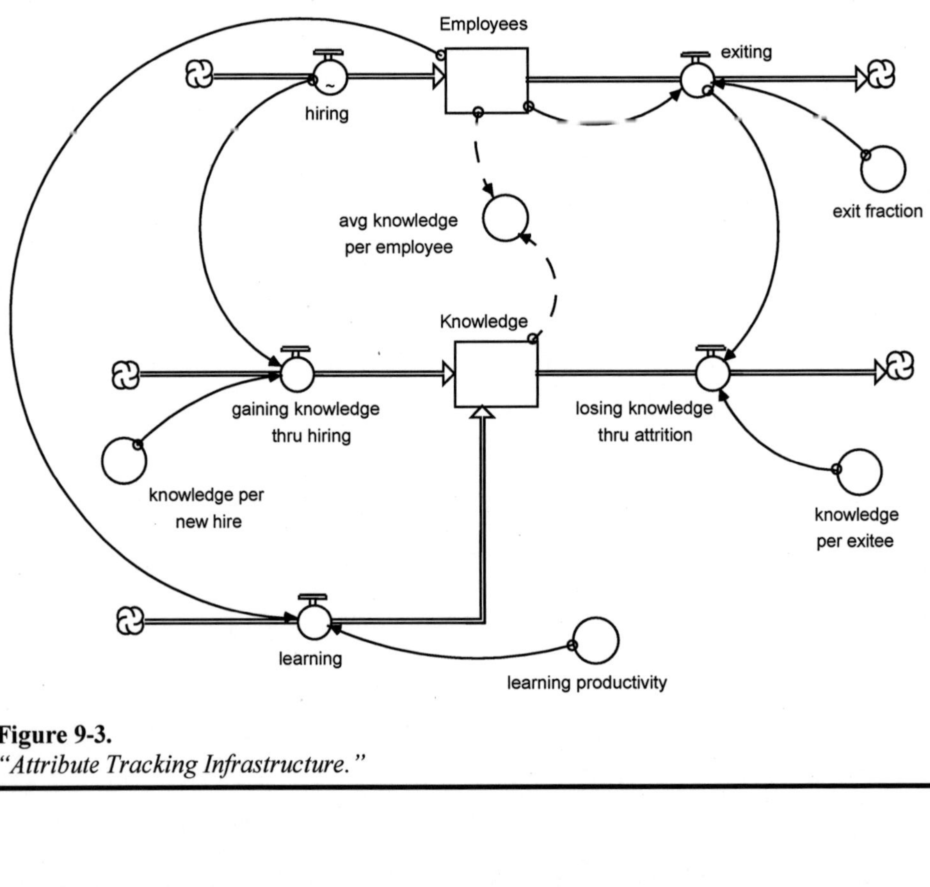

Figure 9-3.
"Attribute Tracking Infrastructure."

Human Resources: *Productivity*

Description

Human resource productivity is a very important variable within almost any model involving employees. This structure includes two key determinants of productivity: morale and skill level. The structure provides a good example of how "soft" variables can be modeled using the *ithink* software. See Chapter 13 for more information on modeling qualitative concepts.

A map of the Human Resources Productivity Infrastructure appears in Figure 9-4.

Suggested Extensions

1. Drive *Morale* with variables within the system.
2. Tie *avg skill level* to a variety of variables in the system.

Model on Disk

"*HR Productivity Infra*" (in "*Intro to Systems Thinking*" folder).

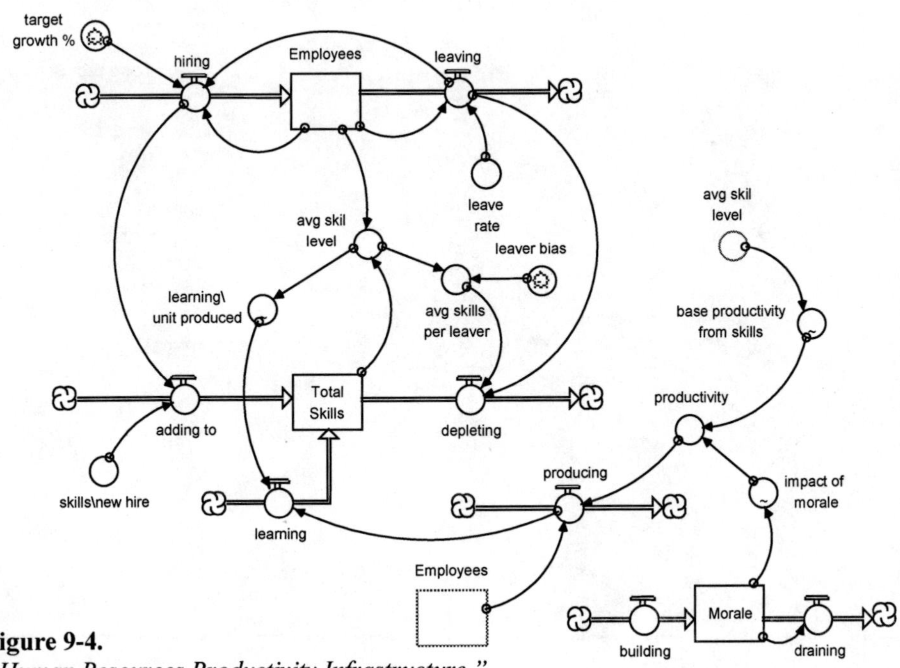

Figure 9-4.
"Human Resources Productivity Infrastructure."

Human Resources: *Burnout*

Description

This structure can be integrated into the productivity structure depicted in Figure 9-4. Burnout serves as the context for the extended example that appears in Chapter 13 (modeling qualitative concepts).

A map of the Human Resources Burnout Infrastructure appears in Figure 9-5.

Suggested Extensions

1. Tie Burnout to Morale and Morale to Burnout.
2. Link *productivity* to a *producing* flow that depletes a *Work Backlog* stock as it builds a *Completed Work* stock. Use *Work Backlog* to determine the number of *hours worked per day.*

Model on Disk

"*Burnout Infra*" (in "*Intro to Systems Thinking*" folder).

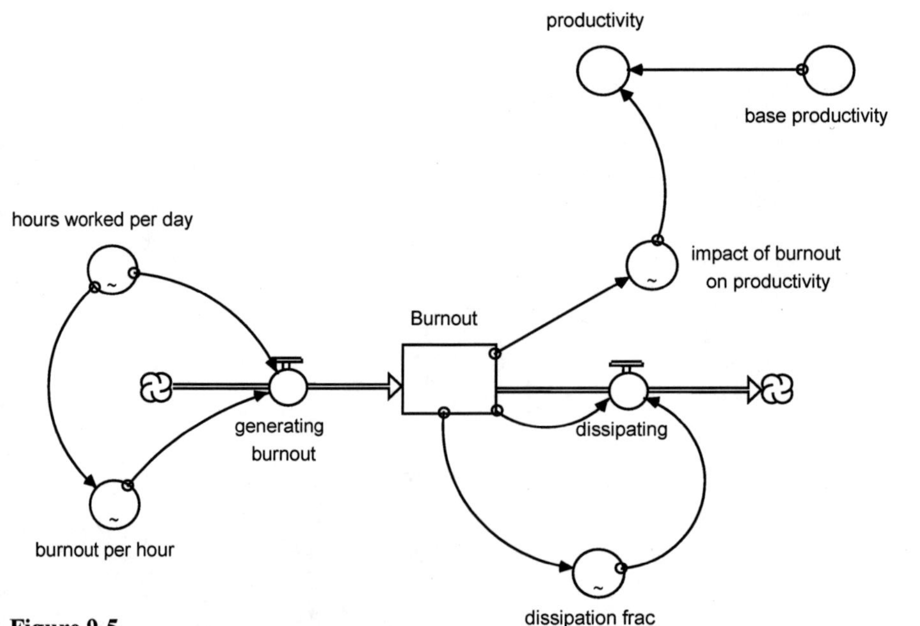

Figure 9-5.
"Human Resources Burnout Infrastructure."

Human Resources: *Resource Allocation*

Description

This infrastructure is useful when you wish to allocate a single resource pool among multiple tasks. The allocation algorithm is based on the notion of "squeaky wheel gets the grease." That is, resources are allocated in proportion to how much work resides in each backlog. More work, more resources. *productivity* serves as a weighting factor in the allocation. To see why, consider the following example. Suppose Backlog 1 has twice as many tasks in it as Backlog 2. This suggests that it would get twice the resources allocated to it. But, say the productivity in completing Backlog 1's tasks is *double* that of completing Backlog 2's tasks. In this case, the algorithm would allocate an *equal* amount of resources to each backlog.

A map of the Human Resources Resource Allocation structure appears in Figure 9-6.

Suggested Extensions

1. Include additional tasks.
2. Allow productivities to vary.
3. Incorporate additional biases, or weighting factors, into the allocation algorithm.

Model on Disk

"*Resource Allocation Infrastructure*" (in "*Intro to Systems Thinking*" folder).

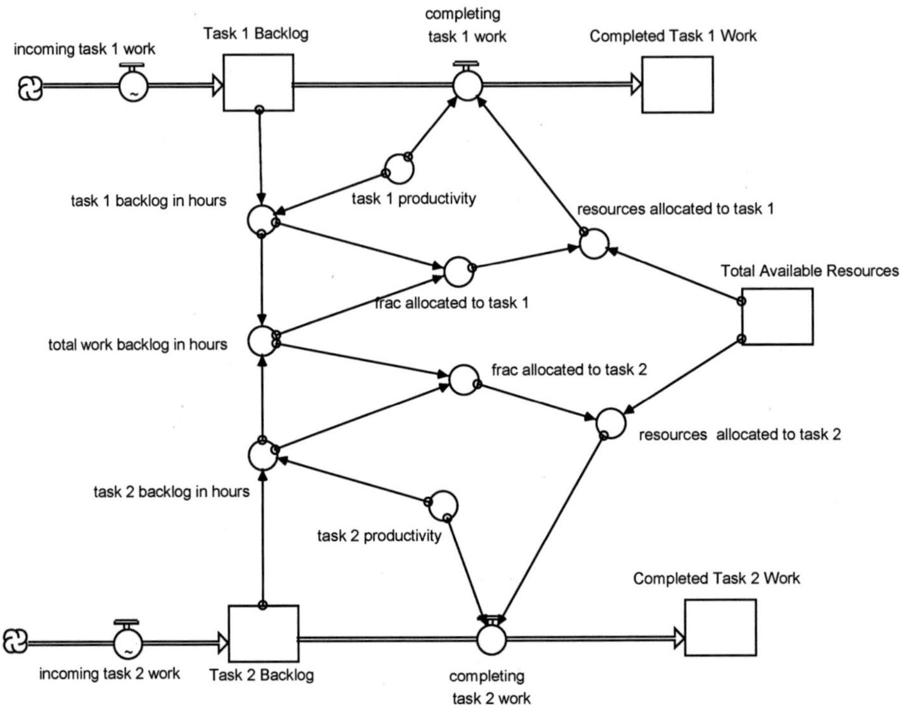

Figure 9-6.
"Resource Allocation Infrastructure."

Physical Capital

Description

This structure uses a conveyor and a reservoir to keep track of the aging and (straight-line) depreciation associated with physical assets. The structure can be very handy if you're issue is asset management.

A map of the Physical Capital Infrastructure appears in Figure 9-7.

Suggested Extensions

1. Add other sources of investment.
2. Disaggregate the structure to address assets with different economic lifetimes.

Model on Disk

"*Physical Capital Infrastructure*" (in "*Intro to Systems Thinking*" folder).

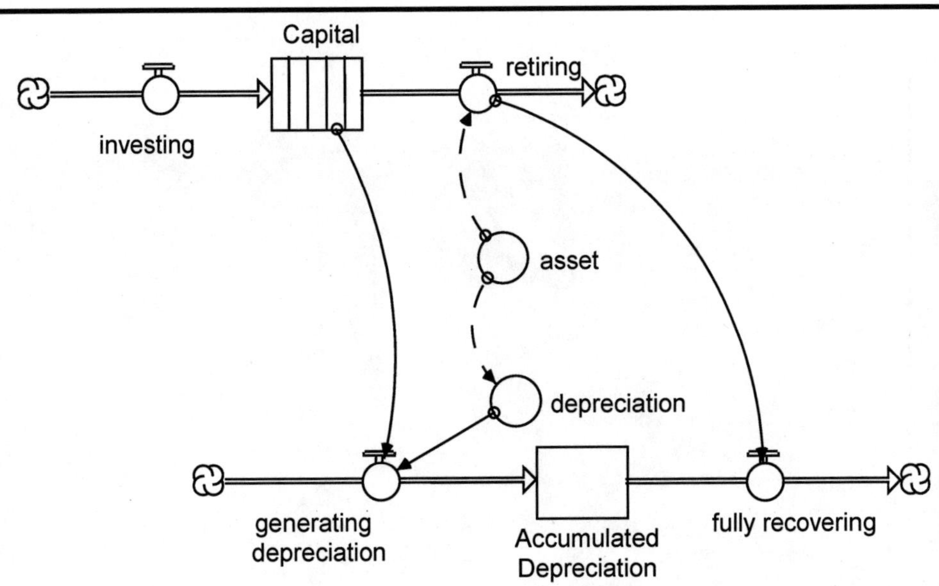

Figure 9-7.
"Physical Capital Infrastructure."

Financial Resources

Description

This infrastructure provides a basis for cash flow analysis. Note the conversion of an absolute quantity, *Cash*, into a relative measure, *liquidity*. It is often easier to work with *relative* measures because you can think in terms of numbers that are fractions and multiples of 1.0, rather than large absolute numbers.

A map of the Financial Resources Infrastructure appears in Figure 9-8.

Suggested Extensions

1. Include additional categories of expense.
2. Determine category-specific impacts on liquidity.

Model on Disk

"*Financial Resources Infrastructure*" (in "*Intro to Systems Thinking*" folder).

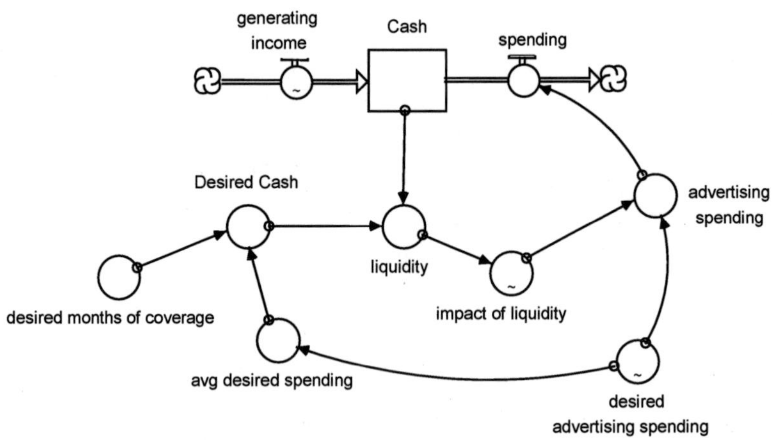

Figure 9-8.
"Financial Resources Infrastructure."

Political Capital

Description

Use this infrastructure as a template for capturing perceptions or memories. Notice that the stock *Recent Transgressions* has a draining flow attached to it. This flow represents the "fading away" of the memory of past transgressions that occurs with time.

A map of the Political Capital Infrastructure appears in Figure 9-9.

Suggested Extensions

1. Make *chips per resource per time* and/or *chips spent per transgression* depend upon the stock of *Recent Transgressions*.
2. Make *chips per resource per time* depend upon the stock of *Political Chips*.
3. Make *time to forgive* depend on *Recent Transgressions*; the bigger the latter, the longer the former.

Model on Disk

"*Political Capital Infrastructure*" (in "*Intro to Systems Thinking*" folder).

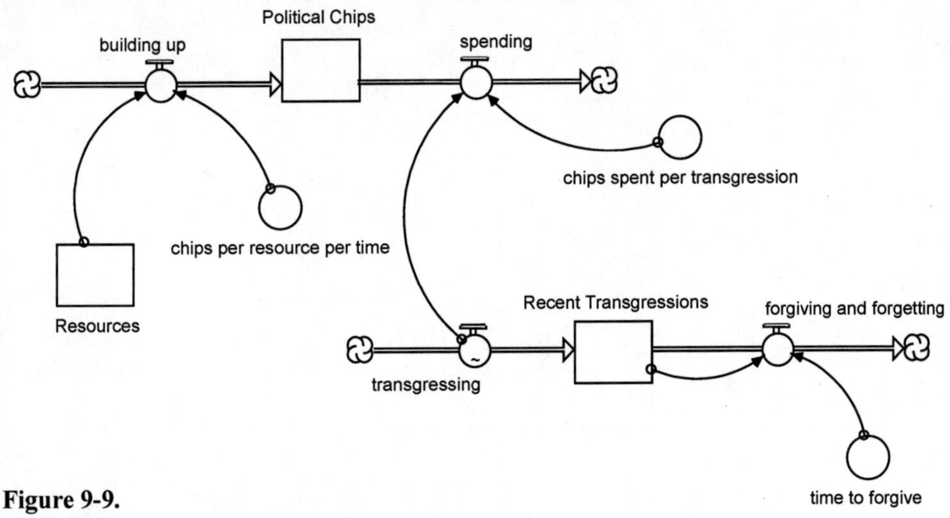

Figure 9-9.
"Political Capital Infrastructure."

Production Infrastructures

Product Production

Description

This infrastructure depicts several key aspects of a basic producing process. There are several "nuggets" captured in this infrastructure. These include overtime logic, a variable target inventory structure, and activity-based learning, to name a few.

A map of the Product Production Infrastructure appears in Figure 9-10.

Suggested Extensions

1. Include other determinants of productivity.
2. Wire *overtime hours* to an accumulation of Burnout (which affects *productivity* and *attrition fraction*).
3. Tie *experience per u of prodn* to *average experience.*

Model on Disk

"*Product Production Infrastructure*" (in "*Intro to Systems Thinking*" folder).

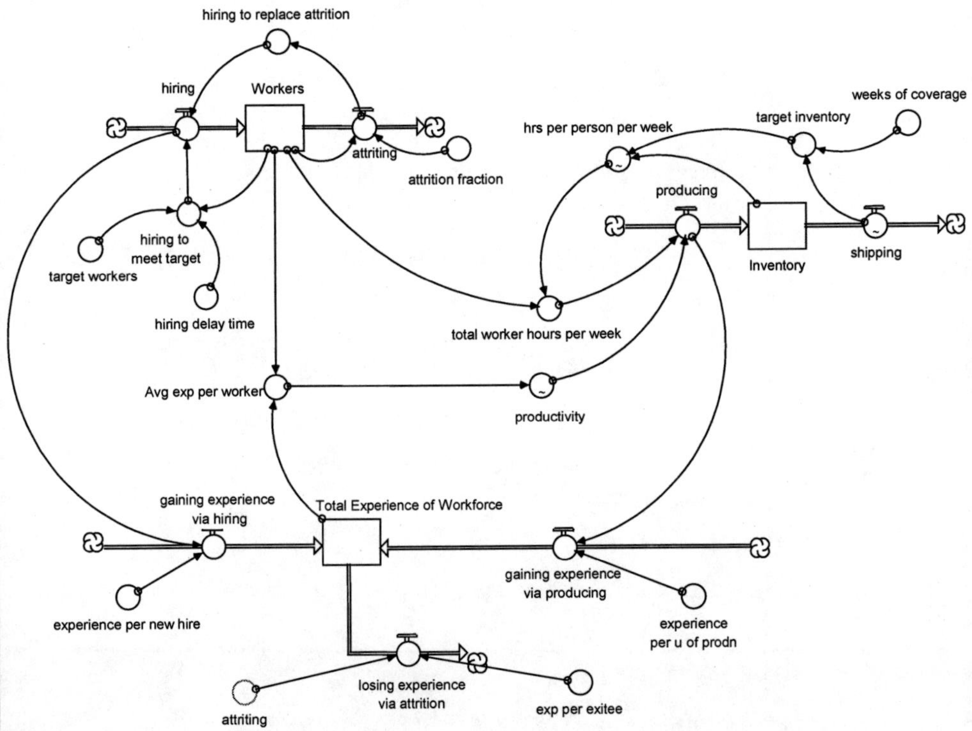

Figure 9-10.
"Product Production Infrastructure."

Service Production

Description

Like the product production infrastructure, the service production infrastructure integrates several smaller structures into an operational depiction. For example, note the two tiers of service workers with tier-specific productivities. The principal "score-keeping" variable in this structure is *service lead-time*, which feeds back to impact demand.

A map of the Service Production Infrastructure appears in Figure 9-11.

Suggested Extensions

1. Add an outflow that causes *generating service demand* to be cancelled (as, for example, *service lead time* grows).
2. Add flows to represent the buildup and loss of *Clients*.
3. (*Analyst Version*) Use cycle-time functionality to calculate *service lead time.*

Model on Disk

"*Service Production Infra*" (in "*Intro to Systems Thinking*" folder).

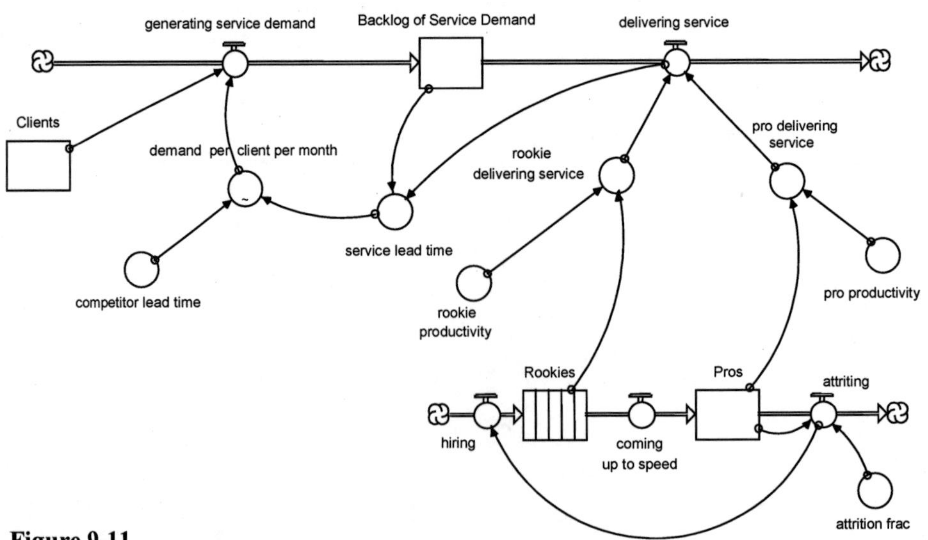

Figure 9-11.
"Service Production Infrastructure."

Score-keeping Infrastructures

Financial: *Cash Flow & Profit*

Description

Use this infrastructure as the nucleus of a financial score-keeping sector. Conveyors are used to represent the delays inherent in the receipt of *Receivables* and disbursement of *Payables*. Note that *writing off* is defined as the "flow-thru" outflow from the *Receivables* Conveyor, not as you might intuitively think, by the leakage flow. This is because write-offs represent customer obligations that have "traveled the entire length" of the Receivables Conveyor without "leaking in." The receipt of receivables (i.e., *inflowing cash)* is represented by the leakage flow.

A map of the Cash Flow Infrastructure appears in Figure 9-12.

Suggested Extension

Calculate liquidity (see Financial Resources infrastructure presented earlier in this chapter) and feed it back to spending.

Model on Disk

"*Cash Flow Infrastructure*" (in "*Intro to Systems Thinking*" folder).

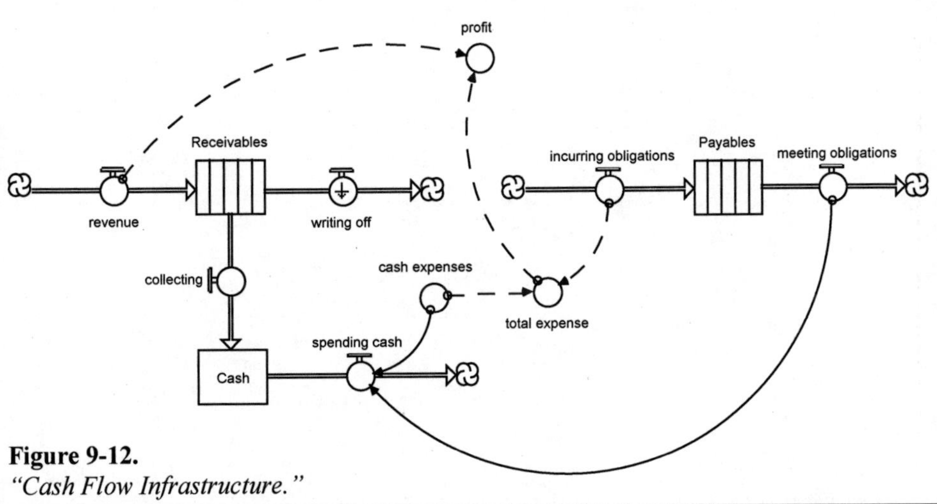

Figure 9-12.
"Cash Flow Infrastructure."

Financial: *Debt*

Description

This infrastructure represents the essential mechanics of debt incurrence and repayment. The structure allows for the variation of interest rates over time through the inclusion of both a *prevailing interest rate* and an *avg interest rate* (associated with existing debt). Note the similarities between this structure and the human resources attribute-tracking infrastructure presented earlier in this Chapter.

A map of the Debt Infrastructure appears in Figure 9-13.

Suggested Extensions

1. Feed back *Cash, Debt,* or other barometers of financial well-being, to determine credit-worthiness.
2. Include Long-Term Debt, which is taken on to underwrite physical capital acquisitions.
3. Use *Conveyors* to track *Debt* and associated "Total" interest rate, so as to yield a more accurate calculation of *debt service.*

Model on Disk

"*Debt Infrastructure*" (in "*Intro to Systems Thinking*" folder).

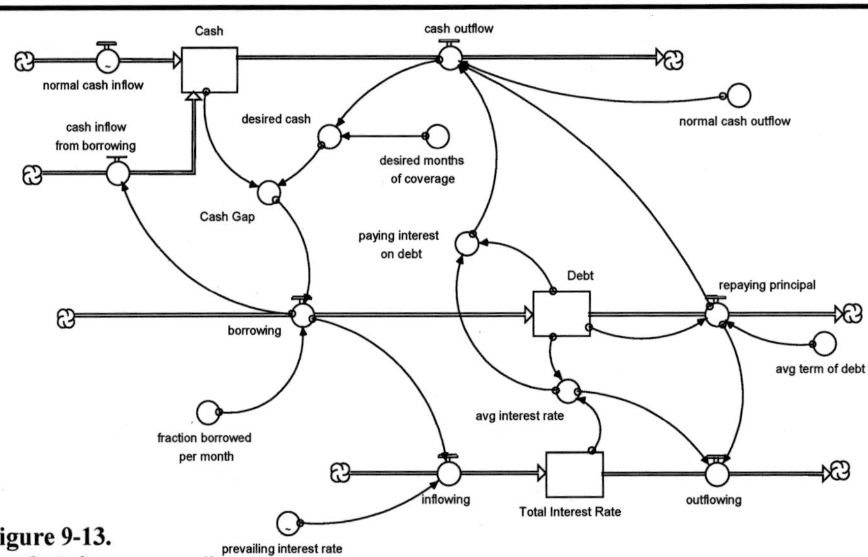

Figure 9-13.
"Debt Infrastructure."

Market Share & Relative Attractiveness

Description

Use this structure to generate market share. Market share is defined as a firm's revenues as a percent of total market revenue. The assumption is that sales are driven by the attractiveness of a firm's product relative to the competition's offerings.

A map of the Market Share Infrastructure appears in Figure 9-14.

Suggested Extensions

1. Add flows to price to enable it to vary dynamically.
2. Add firms to the market.
3. Include additional components of relative attractiveness (i.e., product performance, quality, lead-time, service quality, reputation, etc.).

Model on Disk

"*Market Share Infrastructure*" (in "*Intro to Systems Thinking*" folder).

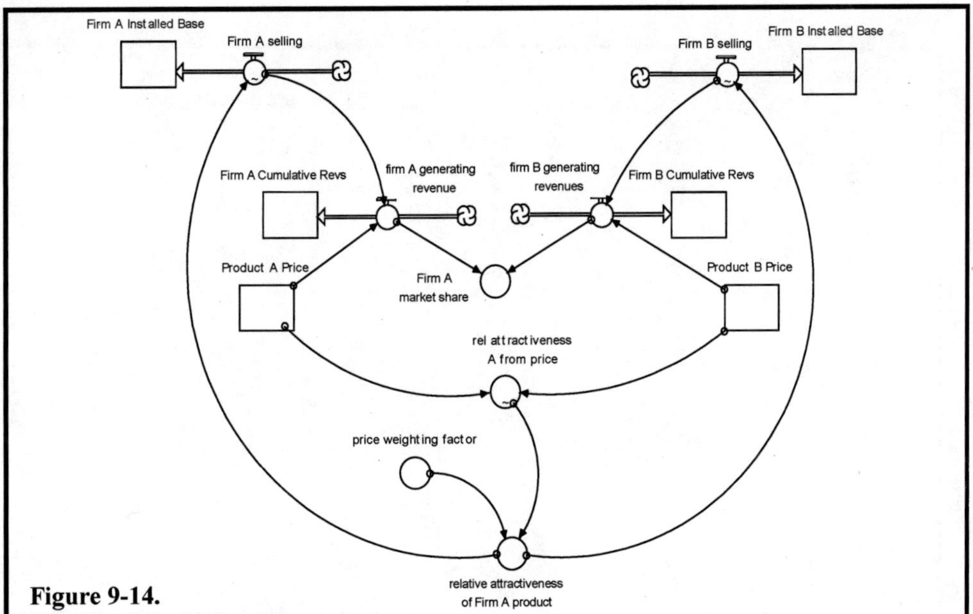

Figure 9-14.
"Market Share Infrastructure."

Perceived Quality

Description

This simple infrastructure can be used to generate some surprisingly sophisticated patterns of behavior. The structure is a stock-adjustment template (described in Chapter 5). However, the adjustment time parameter, *delay in adjusting perceptions*, rather than being a constant, is a graphical function. The graphical function depicts an asymmetry in adjusting perceptions. When *actual* quality is *less* than the current perceived value, the adjustment is rapid ("bad news travels fast"). When actual quality is *greater* than perceived, the adjustment time is much longer, reflecting the "once burned, twice shy" phenomenon many customers exhibit in their perceptions of a product's quality.

A map of the Perceived Quality Infrastructure appears in Figure 9-15.

Suggested Extension

Tie *Perceived Quality* to a bias in perceiving the current indicator of quality.

Model on Disk

"*Perceived Quality Infra*" (in "*Intro to Systems Thinking*" folder).

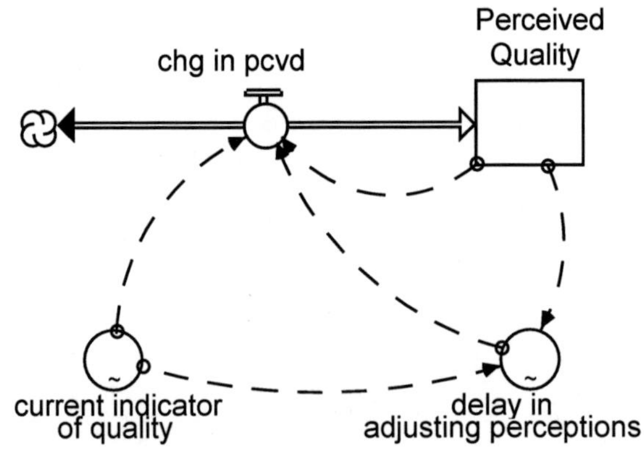

Figure 9-15.
"*Perceived Quality Infrastructure.*"

Miscellaneous Infrastructures

Pricing

Description

This structure does a nice job of handling situations in which a markup (expressed as a % over cost, and which can vary) is applied to a unit cost, in order to generate a price. Here, the *Markup Percentage* changes as a result of your price relative to the competition's.

A map of the Pricing Infrastructure appears in Figure 9-16.

Suggested Extensions

1. Include relationships that drive cost; e.g., experience curves, technology advance, etc.
2. Include inputs, other than competitor price, that cause the markup percentage to change.

Model on Disk

"*Pricing Infrastructure*" (in "*Intro to Systems Thinking*" folder).

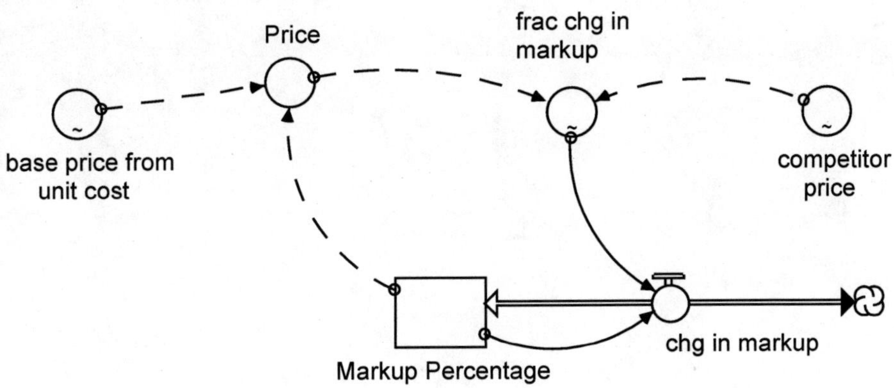

Figure 9-16.
"*Pricing Infrastructure.*"

Ordering

Description

Use this infrastructure when representing an ordering process that restocks an inventory, where there is a delay in the associated delivery process.

A map of the Ordering Infrastructure appears in Figure 9-17.

Suggested Extension

Make "coverage terms" dynamic—experiment with a just-in-time inventory system.

Model on Disk

"*Ordering Infrastructure*" (in "*Intro to Systems Thinking*" folder).

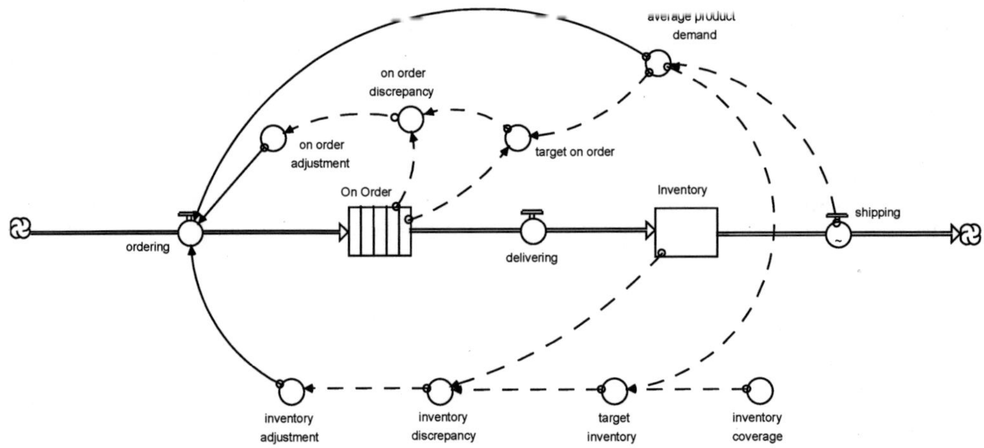

Figure 9-17.
"*Ordering Infrastructure.*"

Shipping

Description

This infrastructure provides a simplified representation of a shipping process. It can be quite useful when shipping is a necessary activity in, but not the primary focus of, your model. Note that the units-of-measure of the stock *Shipping Capacity* are units per time (just like the *shipping* flow!).

A map of the Shipping Infrastructure appears in Figure 9-18.

Suggested Extensions

1. Allow for retirement of *Shipping Capacity*.
2. Tie *adding to capacity* to conditions within the model.

Model on Disk

"*Shipping Infrastructure*" (in "*Intro to Systems Thinking*" folder).

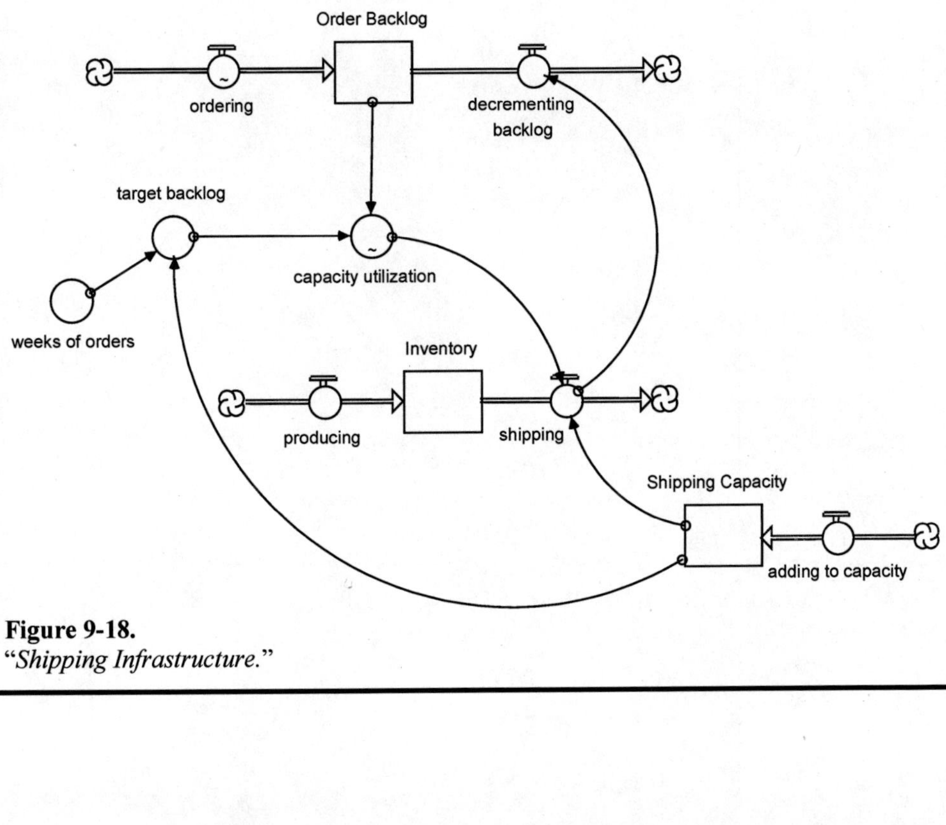

Figure 9-18.
"*Shipping Infrastructure.*"

Part 3

"Writing" Short Stories

Mastering the *Thinking Skills*, *Language*, and *Concepts* of Systems Thinking is essential in order to "write" a good short story (or novel, for that matter). But it's not enough to master each of these separately. Good "writing" is an *emergent* capability. It emerges when all three come together synergistically. It's like basketball. You can learn the skills, you can understand the strategy, you can rehearse the defenses, but good basketball emerges only when it all comes together under game situations.

The way to get better at "writing," and basketball, is to practice. First you have to know what constitutes "good form," so that your practicing pays off. Chapter 10 provides an overview of a "best practice" writing process. Read it and you'll have a picture of what it is you'll need to get better at.

Once you've got a "big picture" laid out on a piece of paper for the intellect to grasp, it's time to get the viscera involved. The way to do that is to watch a classic execution. That's what Chapter 11 is about. It "walks you through" an actual application. Thinking skills, language, concepts, client issues, and software mechanics, are all wrapped up together—as they are in any real application. However, I have tried to shine light on the various pieces, making key points about "good practice" all along the way.

Chapter 12 then provides an annotated "cookbook," offering guidelines for each step in the modeling process. This Chapter should serve as a valuable reference as you build your writing skills through application.

Finally, Chapter 13 offers some guidelines, and encouragement, for modeling "soft" variables. These variables often represent high-leverage points in a system, and usually also stimulate the most interesting discussions. Shying away from them because they are "squishy," will never win you a Pulitzer.

Chapter 10

An Overview of the "Writing" Process

Writing, like model-building, is highly a creative process. Nevertheless, there is a set of "steps" that define a systematic process. In this Chapter, you'll get a quick run-through of those steps. The purpose is to provide a framework for the illustrative application you'll walk through in Chapter 11. Detailed guidelines to help you with your real-world execution of each step then appear in Chapter 12.

First, I'll provide an overview of the steps in diagram form. Then, I'll provide a brief description of each.

The Steps

Figure 10-1 diagrams the steps in the model-construction/learning processes.

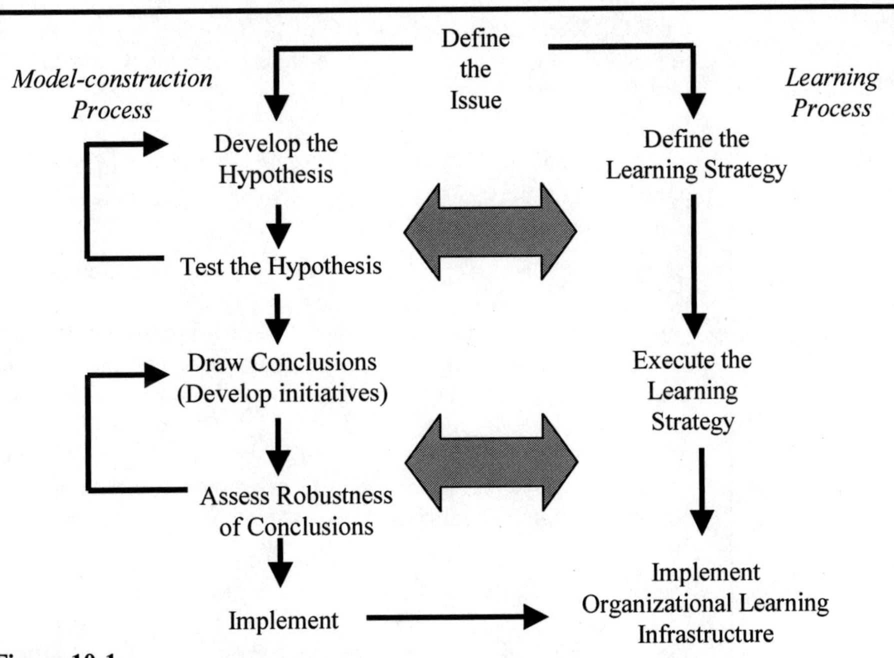

Figure 10-1.
The "Steps" in the Model-construction/Learning Processes.

The sequence of steps appears more linear than it is when actually executed. In reality, you will do a lot of iterating down, then back up *and across*, through both sets of steps. Note the parallel stream of *model-construction*—the left fork—and *learning process,* the right fork. Note also the large two-headed arrows that link the two streams. The intent of these arrows is to reinforce a very important point: *the streams may run in parallel, but there must be a lot of interplay between them!* Stated more crudely, *models constructed in "back rooms," with little regard for how others are going to learn from them (other than, "I'll share my conclusions with people"), go nowhere!*

It is my very strong conviction that as soon as an issue is cast, an associated learning strategy should be developed and then executed in parallel with model development. That strategy should continue to be in effect *after* "implementation" (the final step in the modeling stream). Recall that Chapter 1 argued that one of the reasons we have difficulty honing our mental models is that the feedback we need from what happens *after* we implement our initiatives, never finds its way back into the mental models that originally underwrote those initiatives. In large measure, that's because mental models usually are not made explicit and preserved. As a result, there's no way to update them with the feedback that comes from actual outcomes.

Until this loop back to the mental model is closed, it will be essentially impossible for us to get much smarter about how to make our initiatives more effective!

The Steps

I'll discuss model-construction steps first, and then treat the associated parallel learning process. This is being done for clarity of presentation purposes, not because that's the way the overall process actually should be executed.

Define the Issue

Everything pirouettes off purpose. And, way too often model-building efforts embark with no clear statement of purpose to guide them. Until you can state clearly and succinctly (in words, first) the purpose of the model-building endeavor in which you are about to engage, do not double-click the *ithink* software! In addition to a verbal statement, it's also a good idea (for a variety of reasons discussed in Chapter 12) to develop one or more graphs of patterns of behavior over time for variables that define either the past performance that you wish to change, the future performance you would like to bring about, or a combination of the two.

Generally speaking, there are two categories of purpose for *ithink*-based modeling efforts. The first is to create an "operating tool." The second is to create a "learning tool." In principle, there is no reason why a single model can't serve both functions. In practice, however, this is very rarely the case.

Operating tools are "answer generators," decision-support vehicles. The associated *ithink* models tend to be large, and to place a premium on having numerically-precise parameter values. By contrast, the distinguishing characteristic of learning tools is that they are small. Yes, size really *does* matter if what you are trying to do is "re-program" the mental models that people carry around in their heads. And small is *always* beautiful in this arena!

Let me be clear about what a learning tool does, because the name may suggest that it is "academic" in nature. Nothing could be further from the truth! Learning tools change mental models, shift entrenched viewpoints, and inspire insights that create new visions, strategies, and processes. They are able to do these things because they can be directly compared to prevailing mental models. In order to be so compared, it's essential that these models be clear, simple and visual.

There is no way people can imprint on their brains the "plumbing" that constitutes the typical operating tool. The diagrams are too large, and contain too many connections, too much algebra, and too many decimal places, to hold in one's head. By contrast, the stock/flow topology of an *ithink*-based learning tool *is* capable of being burned into a visual cortex. People actually can conjure up the picture of the *ithink* diagram in their mind's eye. And when they do, they can use it to facilitate mental simulations. For most learning tool models, precise numbers are not as important as having internally consistent numbers. The insights that arise from such models are not dependent on the absolute values of model parameters, but rather on getting the nature of the interrelationships right—running the wires correctly, nailing the delays, capturing the non-linearities.

Over the 20 years or so that I've been constructing models with and for clients, I've developed a distinct preference for learning, over operating, tools. Not that the latter are unimportant. It's just that, in my experience, people too often head for the trees before they have enough of a sense for the forest. As a result, much of the effort that's put into honing the fine points of a strategy, process design, operating policy, or Balanced Scorecard, is "barking up the wrong tree!" My approach is always to press for an understanding of the forest *before* examining root hairs. Often, the result is that such examinations end up either being deferred, or canceled—saving valuable time, attention, and money.

Develop the Hypothesis

Once a clear picture of the issue being addressed is developed, the next step is to articulate a hypothesis that people feel can account for the phenomenon of interest. Obviously, here, knowledge of structure-behavior pairings can be very helpful. For example, if the issue is an exponential run-up in costs, it'd be wise to search for reinforcing loops. If instability is the concern, you'd be on the lookout for counteracting loops operating "out of phase" (as you saw in Chapter 6). And, so forth.

However, sometimes the historical patterns don't suggest a particular feedback loop structure, or there *is* no historical pattern because you're implementing something brand new. In these cases, you are thrown back on your knowledge of main chain infrastructures and other dynamic organizing principles, such as you saw in Chapters 8 and 9. You put down a simple stock/flow assembly and just "play" to see what you can learn. The model then evolves from there.

Test the Hypothesis

By hook or by crook, you get "something" down in a simple *ithink* diagram, and then you *simulate* it. Next, you scrutinize the resulting dynamics to see if they "make sense," or suggest anything interesting to explore further. In the "classic" cases, you replicate the pattern of historically-observed behavior that was established in the "defining the issue" step. Doing so means you have an "entertainable hypothesis." It does not mean your model is "valid." It just means that you have an explanation that "holds water," and is thus interesting to expose to others around the organization to determine *how much* "water" people think it holds. You should continue refining your hypothesis through numerous rounds of testing (both simulation-based *and* conversation-based!) until you (and others) are satisfied that it adequately explains the challenge, or issue, you're facing.

Draw Conclusions

Once you've got a solid model/hypothesis to work with, the next step in the process is to use that model to draw some conclusions about how to best address the issue at hand. You'll be looking for high-leverage points, and trying to anticipate unintended consequences. Computer simulation will be very helpful in tracking the ramifications of each intended action/initiative in both space and time.

Assess Robustness

Be it a strategy you're designing, a process you're reengineering, a revision you're making in an operating policy, or the development of an acquisition plan, you'll want to "what-if" the heck out of it. The idea is to understand just how "robust" the conclusions you've drawn really are. Under what scenarios (variations in *external* conditions) do they prevail, and under which do they crumble? In addition, you'll want to determine how sensitive the efficacy of your initiatives is to variation in the values of *internal* parameters. Understanding the range of external and internal conditions under which your initiatives remain "the best course of action," enables you to be proactive about adapting to "outside the box" circumstances should these arise.

Implement

The last "modeling" step is "implementing." This isn't so much something you do with the model itself, as it is something you do *better* because of having constructed and exercised a model. What's important to note is the link between "implement," and "implement organizational learning infrastructure." It is this link that enables us to hone our mental models over time.

We're now ready to hop over to the parallel track in which a learning strategy is defined and executed.

Define the Learning Strategy

Any such strategy begins with the question of "who builds the model?" Is it a situation in which an "expert" Systems Thinker (or two) constructs the model, or do non-experts—usually a group larger than two—grope along through a process, often facilitated by an expert? Both processes can work, although the former runs the afore-described risk of turning into a "back room disconnect" type exercise. Whichever approach to model construction is taken, it is vitally important that a process for sharing the model conceptualization, and associated intermediate products (both maps and computer-simulatable models) be established at the outset.

No matter how effective the "along the way" learning strategy that you put in place turns out to be, there always will be some number of people—either people new to the organization, or people who simply could not participate in the original model-building effort—who did not make the journey. As such, it's important to develop a process that will enable these people to become enrolled in what should become an "ongoing discussion," or ongoing process of "thinking together." Such processes can benefit from development and deployment of strategy labs, "flight simulators," multi-player simulations, and other *ithink*-based software products, as well as from processes like Strategic Forums™ that also rely on simulation models as engines for learning.

Execute the Learning Strategy

The single most important determinant of successful execution of any learning strategy is the degree of commitment to it that is evidenced by people at senior levels within the organization. Lip service doesn't work. Senior managers must really want to have the organization, or at least some set of people within it, learn. Absent this commitment, *no* learning strategy will get very far execution-wise. Having exacted such a commitment, it's possible to proceed with designing a portfolio of software artifacts and processes capable of bringing the entire organization to a deeper level of shared understanding about a broad range of issues facing the organization.

Implement Organizational Learning Infrastructure

One piece, an important one, of executing the learning strategy is development of an *ithink*-based "organizational learning infrastructure." A full organizational learning infrastructure would have more than just an *ithink*-based component, but here we'll focus only on that component. Central to the *ithink*-based infrastructure is a server-based inventory of maps and models that would be maintained and operated much like a reference library. At any time, anyone with access to the repository (which presumably would be any employee of the organization) could download a particular model, review the associated assumptions, run simulations to test initiatives or conduct what-ifs, and also to *propose modifications*. A formal process would be established for reviewing all proposed modifications before any updates to the "golden master" were implemented.

Over time, through this "ongoing review process," the degree of alignment in underlying mental models across the organization would increase. More people would literally "be on the same page," thereby facilitating execution of any initiative being implemented by the organization. In addition, the *quality* of the models in the repository would be systematically ratcheted upward over time as feedback from reality weighed in and was used to re-tool model assumptions. And, as the quality of the *ithink* models improved, so too would the quality of the associated mental models. Real organizational learning would come to pass.

What's Next

You now have an overview of the process for using Systems Thinking and the *ithink* software to improve the effectiveness of the performance-improvement initiatives that you develop. In the next chapter, I'll walk you through the process by looking at a couple of actual (though disguised) applications while illustrating some of the key principles of "good practice." Then, in Chapter 12, I'll offer a cookbook of guidelines and principles for executing each step in the process.

Chapter 11

Illustrating the "Writing" Process

As noted in Chapter 10, models constructed with the *ithink* software tend to fall into two major categories: Learning tools and Operating tools. In this chapter, I'll strike a compromise. I'll walk you through the "writing" of a Learning tool in some detail. The example is a real, albeit disguised, client application. At the end of the example, the learning tool will undergo an evolution into an Operating tool. And so, you'll get some sense for how both tools emerge from the "writing" process. I'll use the "steps" in the process outlined in the previous chapter to frame the discussion. These steps are reproduced in Figure 11-1 for convenience.

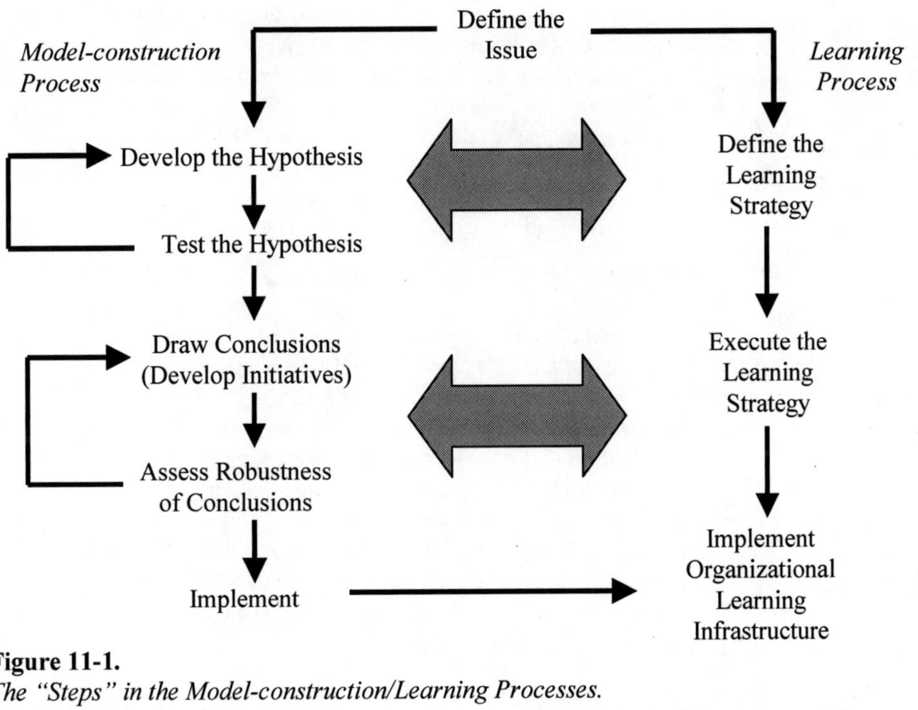

Figure 11-1.
The "Steps" in the Model-construction/Learning Processes.

"Writing" a Short Story

The particular short story I'll recount here has the distinction of being one of the shortest ever written. The description of how it was written is much longer than the story itself! Yet it is also one of the most impactful in terms of clarifying an important issue, generating insight, and inspiring productive action.

The Backdrop

The client associated with this illustration is a technology firm that was founded by an engineer, and renowned for its engineering culture. The firm took pride in shipping the "hottest box" in the business! Revenues and profits had steadily climbed every year the firm had been in business. However, over the last couple of years an issue had been simmering within the organization. That issue now was beginning to boil, and the CEO decided to engage the senior management team in taking a hard look at it. The issue's key protagonist was the VP of the customer service organization. This gentleman, let's call him Jake, was *not* an engineer—and he was quite okay with that. He dressed sharply, used (what engineers felt was) hip language, was gregarious, and had a reputation for being "loud" (cube-rattling laughs, boisterous hallway conversations, etc). In physical appearance and operating style, Jake stood in sharp contrast to the image of the firm's archetypal engineer.

Jake also stood accused of being an "empire builder." When called on the accusation, engineers were quick to marshal data to support the view. Over the last several years, headcount and budget for the "field" organization (particularly, customer service) had grown far more rapidly than the associated numbers for the engineering ranks—though engineering headcount and budget were both also expanding at a pretty healthy clip. In addition, the share of the firm's revenues coming from customer service was expanding relative to that being generated from the sale of hardware.

Engineers felt the company's image as a technology leader was being threatened by Jake's very visible non-engineering persona. The engineering community also was troubled by the fact that an increasing share of the total operating budget was being allocated to the customer service organization. The growing allocation was widely perceived to be the result of behind-the-scenes "political maneuvering" by Jake. The feeling was that this maneuvering, as the revenue picture reflected, was turning the company into a service delivery organization and away from the core mission upon which the firm was founded. Many fingers pointed at Jake. Jake, and his growing army, worked at ignoring the criticism. Their position: *Look at the bottom line*! The CEO was sympathetic to both positions, and needed some way to get some resolution before armed conflict erupted!

Defining the Issue & Learning Strategy

Had I been an OD consultant, I would have probably defined the issue as Jake-centric, and then proceeded to look at what might be done to produce a better match for him with the dominant engineering culture. In fact, later on, after we had completed our work, an OD consultant was retained, and did produce some good results following this kind of an approach. However, had I been an OD consultant, the CEO would not have brought me in at that time. Instead, knowing something about "this systems stuff," he wanted to see if maybe it could "get beyond personalities" to see if any "physics" were involved. I was young, naïve, and game.

It was clear from the outset that members of the senior management team had little time or interest in building the Systems Thinking skills needed to investigate the issue on their own. So, this was a case in which an outside expert was going to "build the model." Nevertheless, I was determined that the team emerge from the investigation having not just improved their understanding of the particular issue at hand, but also acquired some general Systems Thinking skills.

I began by interviewing *each* member of the senior management team. It is vitally important that each member be interviewed if there is to be an "event" associated with the investigation. Leave anyone out, and that person is almost certain to be "an issue" during the event! Such interviews are useful for "taking the pulse" of the team. They also shed light on interpersonal dynamics, and help you to gain a broad picture of the organization.

From the interviews, I produced two to three graphs of key variables over time to see which, if any, caught the team's attention as being a good "summary" of the issue. Team members pretty quickly converged on the pattern depicted (camouflaged) in Figure 11-2.

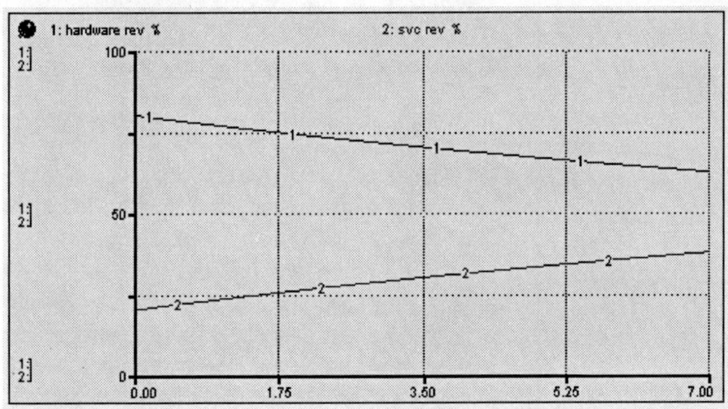

Figure 11-2.
The Relative Expansion of Service Revenues.

Revenue was a closely-watched barometer within the organization as a whole. The team felt that the relative ascendance of service revenue was symbolic of the decline in the relative importance of the engineering organization.

Once this picture was "in front" of the team, the issue was both focused and made operational. Everyone could look at a simple dynamic pattern of behavior and say, "Yes, that's it!" For me, the picture defined a crystal clear purpose for the modeling work. As is often the case, that purpose was best articulated through a question: *Is there a plausible hypothesis, other than empire-building, that can account for the relative ascendance of service revenues?*

Develop the Hypothesis

As the interview process quickly revealed, the firm's business was very complex. There were many diverse product lines, serving numerous market segments, across widespread geographies. The abundance of "gee whiz" technology further added to the complexity. There was this chip, and that bus, and the brand new thingamajig coming out next quarter. Talk about root hairs!

My deep-rooted "10,000 Meter Thinking" gut told me the relative ascendance phenomenon was not the result of root hair-level relationships. But even if it hadn't, good Systems Thinking practice (and good science, Occam's Razor) would have dictated that I not begin thinking at that level. So, I pushed *way* back from the root hairs, back beyond the trees, to a point way atop the forest. I asked myself the following question: *If I were building the simplest possible model of this firm's business, what's the first stock I'd put on the screen?* This is much like the question posed in Chapter 2 about the first variable you'd include in an operational model of milk production. It's an approach I use all the time for "muddling my way" toward a hypothesis. It's kind of a "Let's just get something simple onto the screen and see what it'll do when we simulate it," approach. It almost always turns up something interesting. In this case, it did more than that. It quickly cracked things wide open...for me. I then had to worry about how I was going to "bring everyone else along." But first things first...

In the privacy of my own home, I slapped down a stock called "Installed Base." The stock represented the aggregate number of "boxes" the company had out there in customer hands. Taking a top-down approach, I made no effort to disaggregate "boxes" into the firm's numerous product lines, to disaggregate customers into the wide variety of market segments the company served, or to disaggregate the location of those customers by geography. Was this model looking and feeling like the real company? Absolutely not! Was it a good starting point for investigating the issue? Absolutely yes! One of the advantages of being able to do at least some of this work "off line" is that you are afforded the luxury of starting simple—you don't have to beg, plead, grovel for, then finally, insist on, it to the client.

Once the Installed Base stock was firmly in place, I asked the next (obvious) question: *What flows are associated with this stock?* There were basically two. The first was an inflow; call it sales (I would have preferred "selling," but the client would have thought this strange). The second was an outflow; call it "retirements." I decided to see if I could get away with ignoring the outflow for the time being. I justified doing so because: (1) the issue was cast in revenue terms, and the outflow didn't generate revenue, (2) the outflow rate was quite small relative to the sales/inflow rate, and (3) over the time horizon of interest, the next five years, there would not be a very substantial number of retirements relative to the large volume of sales that were projected to occur. Basically, I was being relentless in my pursuit of the simplest possible model that could account for the phenomenon of interest. You should be similarly relentless!

And so, my first-pass map, looked like what you see in Figure 11-3. Pretty unimpressive, huh? This provides another good example of the old adage: Don't judge a book by its cover! Unimpressive looking? Yes. Unimpressive? No way! Let's see why.

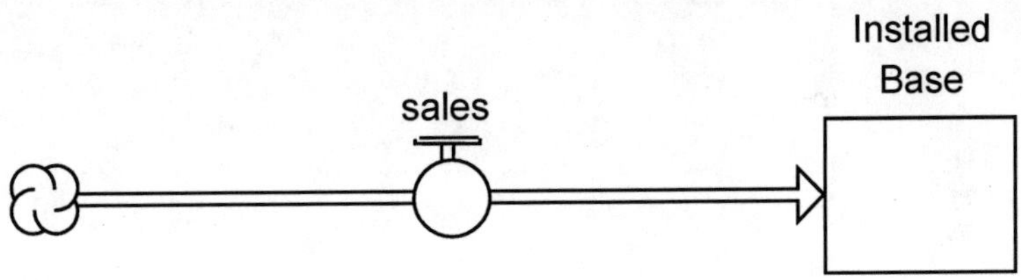

Figure 11-3.
A First-pass Map.

Test & Revise the Hypothesis

Once you get a preliminary map, before elaborating it, "test" it! Remember, you are looking for the *simplest possible* hypothesis that can account for the phenomenon. And you just might have it staring *you* right in the face. So, find out! You do that by *simulating* the model. My colleague, Steve Peterson, has coined a very useful expression. He says, very wisely, "*Never stray too far from a simulatable model.*" Burn the expression into your memory and keep it top-of-mind whenever you're building models. It will save you endless amounts of time, and tons of frustration. Simulate. Then, if need be, revise/extend, and then simulate again, and so forth. Very short cycles of hypothesize, test...hypothesize, test...is definitely the way to go.

So, I wanted to simulate the little fella I had in front of me. Would I—on a Saturday afternoon, with no access to the client's corporate databases—allow my desires to be stymied by the absence of "real numbers?" Most assuredly not! And I hope you won't allow yourself to be so stymied, either. In fact, even if you *do* have ready access to reams of infinitely-precise numerical data through SAP, Oracle, or the ERP system of your choice, I would urge you not to avail yourself of the opportunity—at least not at this point in the process. Before looking for any real numerical data, you should literally just "throw some numbers into the model." Then, look at the resulting *patterns of behavior over time*, not the resulting numerical values! As long as you are choosing the numbers you're throwing in, choose nice, simple numbers—not big, strange ones. And, if reasonable, choose them in such as way as to put the model into a steady-state initial condition.

In this case, a steady-state initialization was trivial to achieve. Because steady-state means that all stocks in the system remain unchanging, the only way to achieve that with this model is to set the one inflow to zero. You want to initialize your model in steady-state for the first rounds of testing because it enables you to begin "reading" the story of your model's dynamics from the beginning. That is, the model is sitting there in perfect balance, you "hit it" with something bare minimal to disturb it, and the story begins unfolding. Initializing your model in an out-of-balance condition is equivalent to fast-forwarding the story to some point in the story-line, and then freezing it there. When you initiate a simulation, you are "unfreezing" the story at that point. You have no idea how it got to that point, and the action already is fast and furious (as the system seeks to restore its balance, or grows/collapses with abandon). Steady-state is good for initial tests of hypotheses!

To implement a steady-state testing strategy, you also need what are referred to in the trade as "idealized test inputs." These are the "somethings" you use to "knock" the system out of its steady-state resting place. The two favorite weapons of choice are the STEP and PULSE functions (both available as *ithink* Builtins). The idea here is to just barely "ping" the system to "call forth" its natural frequency response, and to do so without "driving" it (i.e., imposing dynamics from an external source).

I decided to use the STEP function as my test-input. Because sales were initially zero (as dictated by steady-state considerations), I stepped them up from 0 to 10 at time 3. When I did, I got the result depicted in Figure 11-4. The response, though easily anticipated, upon reflection proved very interesting. It suggests something important about the relationship between the sales rate and the associated pattern of behavior traced by Installed Base. If the flow of sales remains constant, the Installed Base will grow linearly. This means that if the firm continued to sell its "boxes" at a constant rate (i.e., no growth in the hardware part of the business), the basis for its customer service business would nevertheless *increase* at a constant rate.

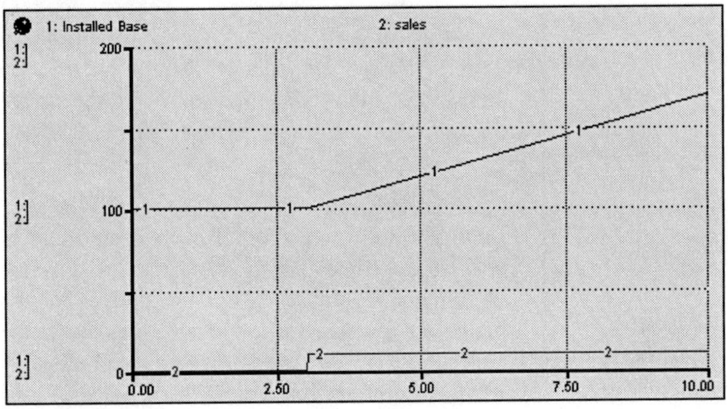

Figure 11-4.
Response to a Step-increase in Sales.

Hmmm...this made me wonder what might happen if the firm's hardware sales business was growing instead of just remaining constant. So, did I leap up, run out and comb through annual reports to collect accurate sales data for the preceding ten years and use it to drive the model? Not exactly. Instead, I used another "idealized" test input. This time it was the RAMP function (another *ithink* Builtin). Figure 11-5, shows the results...

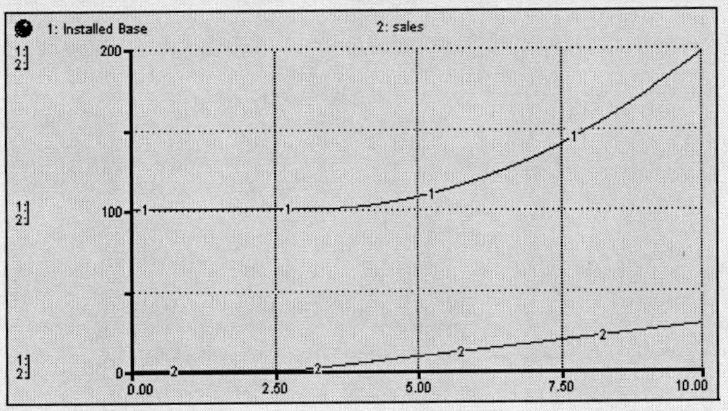

Figure 11-5.
Response to a Ramp Input.

The plot *thickened*! If the firm's sales were to grow linearly, its Installed base would grow something more than linearly (the mathematical term for the resulting curve is "quadratic"). To make a short story even shorter, no matter what pattern the sales inflow took on (be it constant, or any kind of growth), the resulting Installed Base pattern *always* trumped it! This makes intuitive sense because the stock is *accumulating* the values of the inflow (i.e., it contains the current value, plus all previous values), while the inflow contains only its *current* value.

And so, this dirt simple little model was saying something actually quite profound (and yes, also quite obvious—*once it had been made so*!). It appeared that the fundamental "physics" of this business was dictating an evolution (albeit an "inadvertent" one!) of the activity, and hence the revenue split, within the business. If you sold "boxes," and also serviced them, the latter activity was destined to ascend over time relative to the former activity because "box sales revenue" depends on the flow while "box service revenue" depends on the stock. No assumption of "empire building" needed. An evolution was inexorably "in the physics!"

The plot got a little thicker when I added revenue to the picture. Doing so yielded the model you see in Figure 11-6…

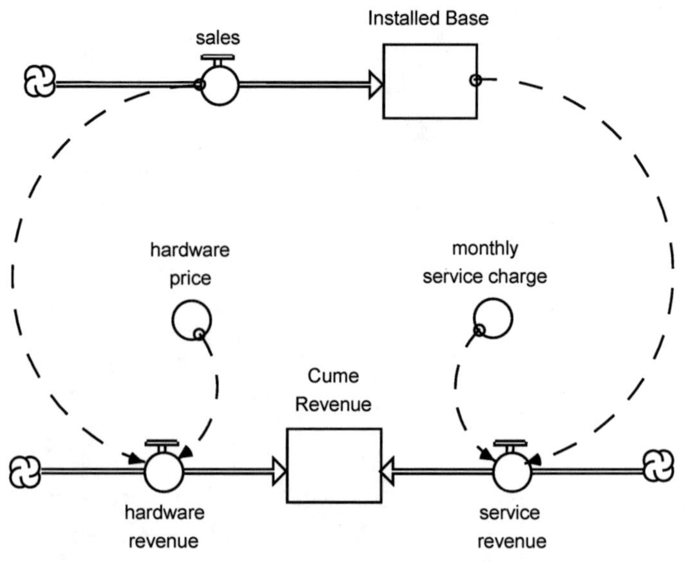

Figure 11-6.
Adding Revenue.

The first thing I did with this new model was to "sanity-check" the mental simulation results derived from computer-simulating the sales/Installed Base model. That is, if the two prices were neutralized (i.e., set to 1.0), would service revenue (as a percent of total revenue) ascend relative to hardware revenue? The result of this computer simulation is depicted in Figure 11-7. As you can see, the mental simulation results held. But the amount of ascendance was a lot more than had actually been observed to occur. That's OK, I thought, because the values of the numbers in the model were nowhere close to the firm's real numbers. I was happy, at this point, that the qualitative pattern of behavior I was seeking was in evidence.

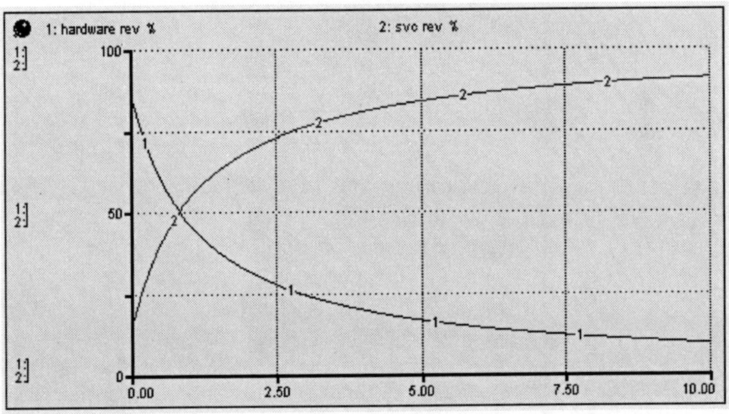

Figure 11-7.
Sanity-checking the Base Model.

The next step in testing the hypothesis was to "throw in" some numbers for the two prices. Doing so is a good illustration of what is meant by looking for "internally consistent" numbers, rather than "absolutely precise" ones. Clearly the price of a "box" must be considerably greater than what someone would pay on a monthly basis for a service contract. How much greater? Twice as much? Ten times as much? Probably closer to the latter than the former. And so, I "threw in" a number for hardware price that was 10 times greater than the number for service charge. Figure 11-8 shows the results...

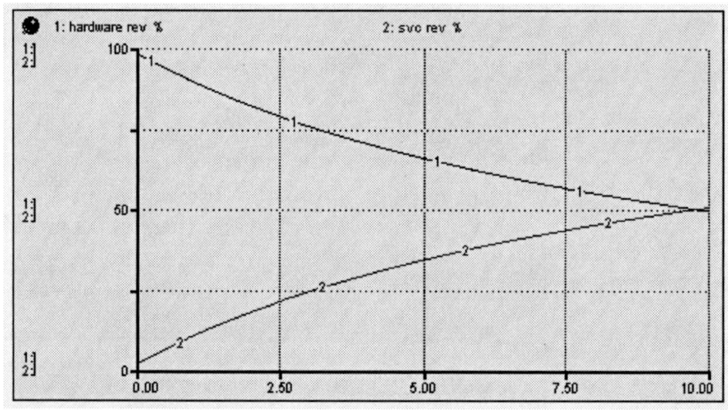

Figure 11-8.
Putting Prices in a Relatively Accurate Perspective.

The picture was now beginning to look a little more like the real pattern, and still without much effort to "tune the numbers." But in thinking about prices, it occurred to me that they probably wouldn't remain in a constant proportion over time relative to each other. Instead, I expected hardware price to grow more slowly than the monthly service charge—which is the same thing as saying that hardware price would *decline* relative to the service charge. My reasoning was that hardware price is driven by technology, where the name of the game is always faster, smaller, cheaper—more for the same or less price. By contrast, service charge was based largely on the cost of delivering service, and the major component of that cost was labor—the cost of which tends to continuously escalate over time.

And so, again undaunted by the lack of any precise numbers, I threw in some patterns of escalation for the two prices. I allowed the service charge to escalate more rapidly than the hardware price. The results appear in Figure 11-9. Three things to note…First, again, no major surprises. Second, I really needed to do some tuning because the model was generating too much relative expansion. And third, it sure looked like an interesting story was developing! The nutshell version: *The basic physics of the business dictated a relative expansion of service activity, and the physics governing the relative price of the two products (hardware and service) served to accelerate that expansion.* Engineers would understand this story. They might not *like* it, but they would understand it.

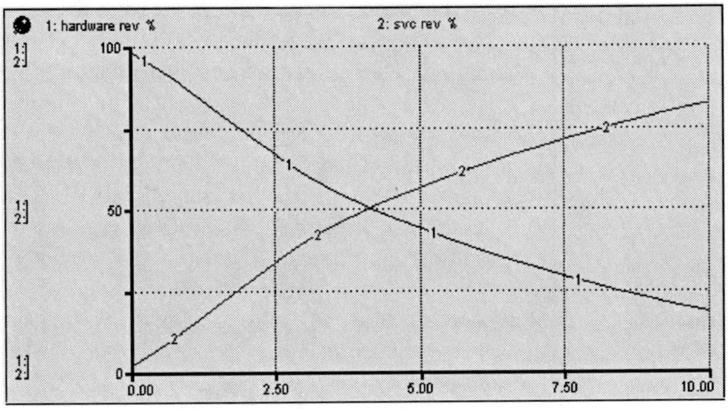

Figure 11-9.
Accelerating the Relative Expansion.

I faced several challenges at this point in the process…

First, I really did finally need to do some tuning of numbers. It's fine to play with relative, internally-consistent numbers "off line." But when the stage lights come on, the lack of numerically-precise numbers can distract a client from the real story-line. However, notice something important in this regard. Waiting until this point in the progression to worry about precise numerical values winnows data collection down to the barest minimum. I knew precisely what numbers I needed. And, with my data collection agenda so precisely defined, I didn't set off on a lengthy expedition to collect reams of data (most of which would not be germane to the story-line). Furthermore, I hadn't delayed the start of serious thinking—or worse, ruled that thinking "not possible"—because the numbers either didn't exist in the form required, or weren't deemed accurate enough!

Second, I had learned a good deal. I knew an "event" was scheduled. I had to come up with an effective process for enabling members of the senior management team to discover the storyline for themselves, and then to determine whether it made any sense.

Third, I had yet to give any consideration to the always-important question: "Okay, great, so even if the storyline does make sense, what can we do about it?"

The first challenge was the easiest to address. I really only needed a few numbers, and they were pretty easy to come by. The major issue was aggregating sales and pricing numbers. I was never going to generate an exact tracking of the history with this model. It simply was too aggregated. My strategy was to take this issue head on. I told team members that the model they were about to see was the *simplest possible* representation that could shed light on what was possibly going on. I added that we could spend a lot of time making the model track history more precisely by disaggregating it, but I felt that was a very poor use of everyone's time. I told them they either bought the story, or didn't buy the story, and that the "validity" of the story didn't depend on the precise tracking of history. Rather it depended on whether the "structure" of the model (i.e., the relationships contained within it) made sense to them. If they bought the structure, they bought the story. They "bought" this argument (and ultimately the associated story, as well). Doing so was tantamount to recognizing that what they had in their hands was a "learning tool," *not* an "operating tool."

The second and third challenges, I'll discuss as illustrations of two of the key steps in the process.

Executing the Learning Strategy

How do you "bring people along" a particular learning path that you have already traversed? The first thing you must do is recognize that this is in fact the nature of the challenge. Too often the challenge is perceived to be: *Tell the client what you have learned.* This is not the place to debate the merits of a "discovery oriented" versus a "transmit oriented" approach to learning. I'll simply report on my experience. I have had overwhelmingly more success with a discovery-oriented approach. As such, I'll describe such an approach to sharing the learning.

In this case, the approach began by arranging for computers to be in the room at the "event." I then designed a progression of simple computer simulation-based exercises to be executed in teams of two to three people. The progression followed the path that I had traced in my experiments. The first exercise was based on a single stock and single inflow. It allowed team members to experiment with various patterns for the inflow (i.e., sales), beginning with the simplest possible pattern and moving on from there. The second exercise added the revenue scorekeeping. And, so on. Each exercise was "de-briefed" by a whole-group discussion. This enabled everyone to recount their version of the story that was unfolding. At various points during the event, questions about the simplicity of the model were raised and discussed. In this case, no "show stoppers" emerged—which is to say, team members felt that although the model wasn't numerically accurate, there wasn't anything about its structure that rendered unacceptable the conclusions it was surfacing.

After a morning of working their way through a progression of simulation-based experiments, and lots of associated lively discussion, the group was satisfied that they had reached a shared understanding of what was driving the "relative expansion" phenomenon. Following a lunch break, the team returned to address the, "So, what are we going to do about it?" question.

Drawing Conclusions & Assessing Robustness

In this case, the conclusions that emerged were greeted with a general sense of fatalism. The relative ascendance of service revenue was generally perceived to be an inexorable result of "physics," rather than something brought about by the firm's operating policies, or business processes. But was this really the case? One VP didn't think so.

A half-hour into the afternoon session, this VP averred that if we really wanted to stay a technology company, we could "third party" our service operation. Not a radical suggestion in today's rampant out-sourcing environment, but at the time, the suggestion was radical. Other suggestions were less radical in nature, but there was a lot of discussion about what they should do. Significantly, not one of the suggestions focused on Jake!

In this case, the learning tool developed to support building understanding of the causes of the phenomenon of interest, was not detailed enough to support a very extensive investigation of alternative measures for addressing the team's concerns. The team needed something that was more of an operating tool at this point. In particular, the model needed expense logic that would allow the profitability implications of various alternative courses of action to be examined. As a result, the remainder of the session was used only to surface possible alternative courses of action. Then, following the meeting, the model was expanded to enable it to support the analysis of alternatives, to include assessing their robustness.

In my experience, this is the best way for the need for constructing an operating model to arise. A learning tool is used to clarify the issue, enhance understanding, and stimulate creative thinking about alternatives. Once the "playing field" is identified, resources can be usefully allocated to readying that field for simulating "game situations." But first, it's important to know whether you're playing soccer or basketball! Learning tools satisfy this (too often overlooked) need.

In the interests of illustrating "good practice"—though the brief analysis I'm about to discuss didn't actually take place in reality—before exiting the "Draw Conclusions/Assess Robustness" phase, you really should take a hard look at your model's boundary. Every model has both an *extensive* and an *intensive* boundary. The former refers to how broadly you have cast the net in terms of what you've included in the model. The latter refers to the depth with which you've represented what you've included in the model. Reality is both infinitely broad—everything really is connected to everything else—

and infinitely deep—you can just keep peeling back the layers, and there's *always* another level. The challenge in writing a good short story, creating an impactful movie, and in constructing a good model, is to make good decisions with respect to how broad and how deep.

In this illustration, clearly we did not go very deep! One stock was used to depict the accumulation of lots of different models of hardware. A single, overall average price of that hardware was employed. The model clearly was a very highly-aggregated representation. Although very high-level, the representation was pretty broad, in the sense that it spanned the entire organization—from hardware to customer service, including finance. This is the profile of most good Systems Thinking models: broad, but not very deep (disaggregation-wise).

To challenge the boundaries, you should ask questions like: If I disaggregated hardware into categories of models, would that change my conclusions? What if I included marketing? And so forth. Here, I will illustrate only one such challenge, a challenge to the *extensive* model boundary. Recall that I made a decision early on not to include an outflow from the stock Installed Base. A good test of the extensive model boundary of the model would be to include this flow (it represents people "turning over" their current "boxes") and then see under what conditions it made a difference to the conclusions. In concept, the flow could make a difference because if its volume was significant, perhaps the Installed Base would not be growing relative to the sales flow, and as a result, hardware sales revenue might grow faster than service revenues. Adding the flow to the model yields a picture that looks like Figure 11-10.

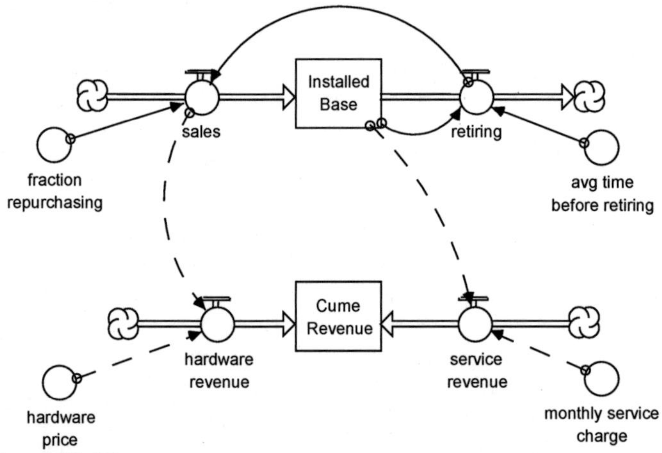

Figure 11-10.
Challenging the Extensive Model Boundary.

As the Figure indicates, adding the flow brings with it some additional relationships. In particular, a fraction of those who retire their existing hardware repurchase new hardware from the firm. If the repurchase fraction is large, any outflow volume would in effect be neutralized because what went out the back door would come back in the front! In fact, this is exactly what the firm had experienced over its lifetime—a very high repurchase rate. And so, the decision to ignore the outflow from the Installed Base turned out to be a good one. It simplified the analysis, yet didn't significantly impact the conclusions. If the firm's repurchase rate were to, for whatever reason, plummet, the pace of the relative expansion dynamic would certainly change and the conclusions would then have to be re-examined.

Implementation & Development of Organizational Learning Infrastructure

Implementation, in this case, moved forward on two tracks. The senior management team wanted to roll out the learning tool, and associated exercises, to their organizations. Given that the "learning event" was short and well-defined, it proved relatively easy to reproduce. In addition, at my urging, the progression of models was preserved for "organizational learning" purposes. True organizational learning can be said to occur (with respect to an issue) only if the associated understanding and insight is somehow disembodied and then maintained, *independently* of the human resources that inhabit the organization at any particular point in time. The progression of "relative expansion" models, and associated exercises, met these criteria. They became the first model-based contribution to the firm's organizational learning infrastructure.

The second implementation track had to do with decisions concerning what, if any, actions to take as a result of the new level of understanding. Development, and subsequent exercising, of an operating tool was used to facilitate movement along this track.

"Writing" a Novel

The same process used to develop Learning tools is applicable in developing Operating tools. In practice, the process takes longer to execute because the associated models are larger—not so much in breadth, primarily in depth. In particular, the same need exists to define an explicit learning strategy up-front. The danger of "leaving a client in the dust" (no matter who is doing the model-building) is very much greater for Operating tools. Again, that's primarily due to the size of these models. Hence, if an Operating tool is to be embraced (i.e., used!), a lot of thought must be given to both "learning along the way," and "learning through use."

Learning along the way

One "learning along the way" strategy that has proven highly effective is to construct the model in a progression of *top-down* spirals. The first spiral would yield a model not much larger than the Learning tool. Two questions should be asked at that point (and at the end of *each* turn on the spiral). The first is: "Is the model good enough, can we stop now?" If the answer is "yes," there's no need to ask the second question, which is: "What is it likely we will gain by going another turn around the spiral?" If the answer to the second question is: "The model will be more realistic (or something close)," STOP! That's not a good enough reason to keep going. It's *always* possible to make a model more realistic. In the process, the model becomes more and more clogged with detail that obscures understanding and extinguishes insight. Make sure there is a solid rationale for going around another turn, and don't make the turns very wide! Remember: "Never stray too far from a simulatable model!"

Another aspect of an effective "learning along the way" strategy entails the use of "sectors" (see *Help Files* for detail on sectors). There might be a human resource sector, a finance sector, a manufacturing sector, a customer sector, etc. As each sector is "brought into being," circulate straw man maps that allow members of the organization who are not directly involved in the modeling activity to provide reactions. Then, convert the sector maps to computer-simulatable models and set it up so that people can easily simulate each sector in isolation first, then in pair-wise combinations, and so forth. Be sure to follow the "initialize in steady-state, disturb with idealized test-inputs" approach for each sector. Doing so will greatly increase the likelihood that people will be able to understand what's causing the overall model to generate the behavior it's generating.

Learning in Use

In my experience, two important things are essential to any effective "learning in use" strategy. "Effective," here, means "beyond those who constructed the model." The mere existence of either thing does not guarantee success. However, the absence of either virtually assures a lack of success. The two are: effective "storytelling," and an effective "Flight Simulator." The two are not independent, and in most successful applications, complement each other very well. Let's examine each in turn.

Storytelling

No one but the person/people actively engaged in writing a "novel," and highly-experienced Systems Thinking practitioners, can easily "make meaning" out of the stock/flow diagram. Even if *great* care is used in laying out the plumbing—avoiding crossed wires, using sectors, thinking carefully about overall map topology—large maps are inherently difficult to "read." Written novels have a first page and a last, and they're broken into chapters. Where do you begin reading a large map? Upper-left corner? Middle? Wherever your eye happens to land first? Imagine trying to read a large novel whose pages were torn out, page numbers erased, and then taped, not in numerical order, up onto a wall. That's pretty much the situation people face when trying to "make meaning" out of a large stock/flow map.

What "storytelling" enables you to do is to literally "tell the story" of a model's structure (*Help Files* provide detail on Storytelling). In storytelling, a model's structure is unfurled (one small chunk at a time) at a speed that is controlled by the "reader." You choose what will be unfurled, and in which order. You also decide whether to associate a textual, graphic, sound, or movie-based annotation with each chunk that's unfurled. For very large models, sometimes highly-aggregated, reduced-form representations of the "real" model structure are used in storytelling sequences. However you "get the job done," it is essential to provide some sort of a reader-paced unfurling of model logic if people are to gain any real understanding of why a novel's plot unfolds as it does.

But really effective storytelling sequences do more than just unfurl structure. They associate a simulation with each major piece that's unfurled. For example, once a critical main chain is unfurled, or the sub-plot associated with a particularly important feedback loop is revealed, it's important to building a reader's understanding that a pattern of dynamic behavior be associated with that unfurling. The full story is told only when a reader can associate "structure" with "behavior." Pausing at various milestones within an overall unfurling to enable the user to conduct a simulation of "just that piece" (in isolation) is what really drives understanding deep into the viscera.

Storytelling is an essential component of any "in use" learning strategy. It is primarily used either up-front to enable "readers" to develop some sense of a "big picture," or it's used at the "back-end" as a means of enabling people to make sense out of a "Flight Simulator" experience they've just completed.

Flight Simulators

The bottom line on operating tools is that people who were not involved in constructing the underlying models can generate understanding and insight from using them. Generating understanding and insight is not the same thing as "having fun," although enabling an end-user to have fun *can* be part of an effective "learning in use" strategy.

In order for a "reader" to generate understanding and insight from a large model, it's essential that the model be outfitted with a Dashboard. Models so-outfitted are called "Flight Simulators." Good dashboards consist of one or more screens (with a strong preference for, one) that provide input and output devices, as well as access to information that will be useful during the simulation experience. An example of a simple Dashboard appears in Figure 11-11.

Input devices, such as knobs, sliders, and graphical input devices should first enable "pilots" to specify what kind of aircraft they're going to be flying (by modifying initial conditions and underlying behavioral relationships), and under what conditions (by modifying scenario parameters). Then, once "takeoff" occurs, these devices enable pilots to enter the decisions that will determine how well the flight goes—do they "crash and burn," or successfully navigate the turbulence they'll face. Such flight simulators do not always create a "game" situation. I have constructed numerous so-called Strategy Labs, which offer flight simulator dashboards but none of the other trappings of a "game" environment.

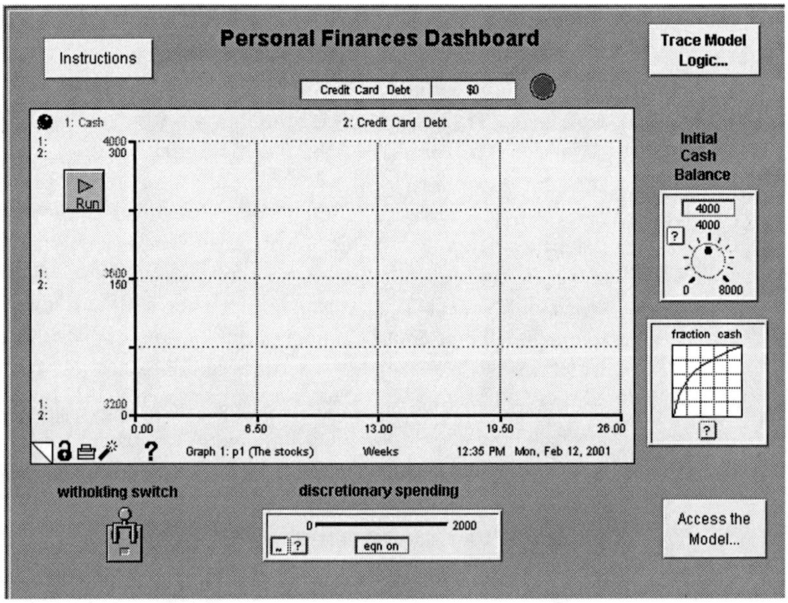

Figure 11-11.
A Simple Dashboard.

Output devices consist of graphs, tables, numeric displays and warning flashers, all of which inform pilots of the status of their flight. Are we running out of fuel? Are we flying at our target altitude? Are we encountering turbulence? And so forth. It is by interpreting the information provided by output devices that pilots arrive at their next set of decisions.

Access to non-Dashboard information frequently takes the form of buttons that navigate to a glossary of model variables, background information on numeric values and data sources, intelligence on the competitive environment, and so forth.

Good dashboards make it easy for people to understand how to implement what they want to implement, and also provide some sense for how various decision levers are "hooked up" to things in the underlying business environment. What dashboards, alone, cannot do is to help pilots to understand the *systemic consequences* of their decisions! They may know that if they pull that lever, this is the direct consequence. For example, hire ten people…get ten new employees. Cut the training budget by 20%…reduce operating expenses by this-and-such. But if *direct* consequences were all people needed to understand, complex models and flight simulator interfaces wouldn't add much value. It's the *unintended* and *unforeseen* consequences of decisions and actions that people need help with. And it is here that too often flight simulators come up way short!

Many flight simulators provide a compelling "game" experience, but no way to understand why you get the results you're getting! What's missing is what we call "JITJWN" coaching. The acronym stands for: Just-In-Time, Just-What's-Needed. What it means is providing a pilot—at a critical in-flight juncture—with just enough coaching to both surface some implicit assumption that's driving their decision-making at that point, and also to help them right the airplane! The only way to ensure that this coaching "arrives" JIT, is to program it to be triggered by the model! A good way to ensure such coaching is triggered at the appropriate moment is to tie it to Dashboard decision levers. For example, right after a pilot decides to lay off workers, boost prices, or slash a training budget, a good JITJWN coaching sequence would: pause the simulation, make explicit what the pilot's mental model underlying the decision must have been, and then offer a slightly enhanced set of assumptions (closing a feedback loop, including an unforeseen impact, etc.). Ideally, the enhancements that are offered lead pilots to reconsider their decision—which, in turn, helps to right the airplane (if it's not too late on the current flight).

Over the course of several flights, good JITJWN coaching will not only alter the specifics of the particular mental model underlying the decision-making for that flying situation, it will begin to outfit the pilot with a better set of general "meta assumptions" (remember back to Chapters 1 and 2!). And this is what real learning is all about.

A good JITJWN coaching architecture is both time-consuming and difficult to construct! It takes an ability to empathize with end-users, so that coaching messages are couched using visual metaphors and language that connect with peoples' imagination. It also requires a careful inventorying of possible "in-flight" situations a pilot might encounter—so you're certain you've got coaching to cover all of the important ones. Finally, it takes a lot of thought with respect to the sequencing of coaching messages. Good coaching architectures ensure that end-users are not so inundated with "help" that the fun of the flying experience is obliterated. Coaching sequences should be distributed across a series of simulations, allowing pilots the time to assimilate changes to their mental models, and to then get some flying experience using the modified mental models before again being "confronted" with alternative assumptions.

Designing an effective "in use" learning strategy is indeed a challenging endeavor. But the alternative is unacceptable: a largely useless large model, an unread novel.

In Conclusion & What's Next

In this Chapter, I've walked you through the steps in the "writing" process. As I hope you've seen, good practice does not consist of "writing" in isolation and then publishing your work for others to read. The writing process itself must be "social." The purpose of this process must be "learning together." Otherwise, your short stories and novels will fall on deaf ears.

The Chapter also strongly supports my explicit bias toward Learning tools *before* Operating tools. If you find yourself leaping right into constructing an Operating tool, I urge you to push back your perspective and also to push back on those who may be driving you deep into the weeds. In the absence of a clear view of the forest, Operating tools tend to get very ugly very quickly. I have seen too many people disappear into the swamp, their models never to be seen again outside the confines of their laptops.

If and when you *do* get around to constructing operating tools, do not ignore the "along the way" and "in use" learning processes. If you do, you are certain to experience disappointing results in terms of widespread use and acceptance of the tool.

In the next Chapter, I'll present a cookbook of guidelines that should help you in executing each step in the modeling/learning processes. Remember that mastery of the Systems Thinking skills that stand behind the execution of the process steps is essential to realizing full impact.

Chapter 12

Guidelines for the "Writing" Process

Both writing and constructing a model, are *creative* processes. Creative work, by definition, is not something you produce by simply adhering to a prescribed set of guidelines associated with a well-defined set of steps. This said, after teaching Systems Thinking, and using it with clients for more than twenty years, I can say with great confidence that there is a set of steps—and a set of guidelines/principles of good practice associated with those steps—that "work." By "work," I mean that if someone follows them, the likelihood they'll produce a model that underwrites understanding, inspires insight, and guides effective action, increases significantly. It makes sense to read the material in this Chapter carefully, and to keep it near as a reference when you are engaged in modeling activity.

The Chapter begins with four quotes from four sages. The quotes establish an excellent context for any modeling effort. Next, I'll provide a diagram that depicts the general challenge you'll face in seeking to construct a model. This picture will help you to keep in focus what you are always trying to achieve when building a model. Following this, I'll use the "steps" in the modeling process (the framework presented in Chapter 10, and reiterated in Chapter 11) to organize the presentation of guidelines and principles of good practice.

Words of Wisdom

Some pretty smart people have pronounced on the nature of good modeling practice. Figure 12-1 presents the words of four such sages.

"All models are wrong. Some models are useful."

Deming

"Seek simplicity...then, distrust it."

Whitehead

"The best explanation is as simple as possible...but no simpler."

Einstein

"Perfection is attained not when there is nothing left to add, but when there is nothing left to take away."

St. Exupèry

Figure 12-1.
Quotes to Ponder.

Deming and Whitehead make the point that all models are "wrong" because all models are simplifications of reality. If the simplifying has been done well, the model becomes *useful* for a particular purpose—but never for all purposes! No model is *true*. If you find yourself trying to prove the one you've built is, throw some cold water in your face…or better yet, on your model!

Einstein and St. Exupèry sound the KISS theme (Keep It Simple, Stupid), albeit invoking more elegant prose to do so. The simplicity theme is an *extremely* important one! Attempting to "model the system" is the most common cause of "crash-and-burn" in modeling efforts. People end up with gargantuan models that they either never succeed in rendering simulatable, or if they do succeed, have absolutely no idea why the model is producing the behavior it's producing. Do not set out—or be seduced, cajoled, or berated into—"modeling the system." If you find yourself (or your client) looking at the real system and saying, "Hmm…that's not in the model, yet." Stop! Rather than being guided by an issue-based purpose, the purpose will have become to include in the model virtually everything that's in the real system. Resolve now never to make this mistake and you will save yourself (and your client) the wrenching agony of defeat—and believe me, it really does hurt to be defeated in this way!

The Fundamental Challenge You Face in Building a Model

When you decide to construct a model, you've been motivated to do so by some real-world issue, challenge, or problem. When you look at the environment within which the issue has arisen, what you usually find is a multi-dimensional collage of sights and sounds and personality and politics and soap opera and slapsticks. In short, it's a jumble! And, somehow, you have to get from this exquisitely rich admixture to a somewhat abstract (albeit operational) diagram that is composed of (hopefully) only a few boxes, pipes, wires, and maybe a couple of circles buried in a rogue Decision Process Diamond.

The fundamental challenge in building a model is then to capture the essence of the issue, system, or process you're looking at, without allowing the abundance of interesting, but extraneous, detail to cloud the picture. The diagram shown in Figure 12-2 should help to operationalize the challenge. It's intense. Savor it for a few minutes...

The axes in the Figure represent the two dimensions by which we can characterize any model's adequacy as a representation of reality: *breadth* and *depth.*

The horizontal axis represents breadth. How expansive a picture is the model trying to take in? Is it laser-focused on a small, tightly bounded slice of reality that's been carefully excised for study? Or, does it seek to capture an extensive landscape of connections to other pieces of reality? How much tunnel or peripheral vision does the model reflect?

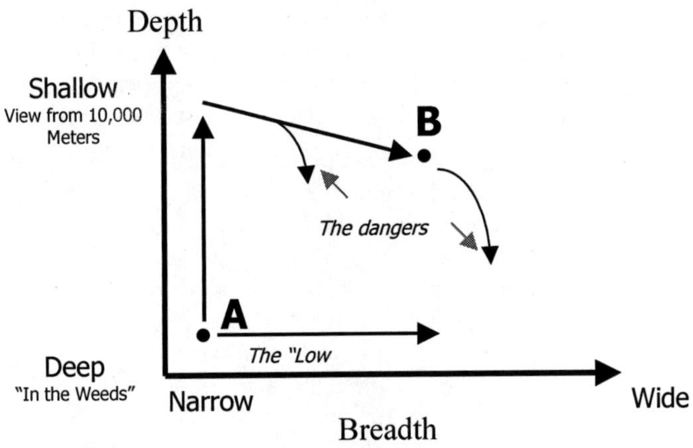

Figure 12-2.
Positioning the Modeling Challenge in Breadth & Depth.

The vertical axis represents the depth captured by the model. It ranges from shallow to deep—from the view from 10,000 Meters, to the blow-up of the root hairs. How aggregated is the picture being painted by the model? Is our concern addressing the generic issue of instability in inventory levels, or are we delving into the details of part number BL4378P in thirty-four different inventory locations?

Thus far, we've described depth and breadth in *structural* terms. It's also useful to offer a *behavioral* interpretation for these two dimensions. Behaviorally, a deep, narrow perspective corresponds to a focus on a specific event, or set of events. A shallow, broad perspective sees longer-term patterns. So, are we talking about inventory cycles as a general phenomenon unfolding over the last couple of years, or the details of last quarter's stock-out? Are you interested in the structural relationships responsible for higher than desired quit rates, or are you concerned with why Susan Jones departed yesterday? Do we focus on the premature demise of a particular start-up firm, or the higher than average death rates for start-ups in general?

Given this structural and behavioral interpretation of the two-dimensional depth/breadth space, we now can pose the fundamental challenge you will face in constructing models. Point A (in Figure 12-2) represents where most mental models "live." They tend to be pretty highly detailed and pretty narrowly focused. We know *our* piece of the rock—the part that affects us—quite well! And, we are also very concerned with specific events, because each major one has an important impact on our lives. Point B is in the region where "systems" models reside—both a shallower (more aggregated, less detailed) and broader (more peripheral connections, more patterns) position in the space. The challenge is then: *How does one get from point A to point B, avoiding the slippery slope danger along the way, and then remain there (i.e., keep from sliding down into the weeds)?*

The answer that we've discovered works best for getting from A to B brings to mind Camus' *Myth of Sisyphus.* In the essay, Camus metaphorically depicts the human condition as one in which we must struggle hard and long to roll a huge rock up a very steep mountain path, only to see it quickly tumble down the other side. And, even with the knowledge of what will happen upon attaining the summit, Camus feels you must work with conviction at rolling the rock once more. For Camus, life's meaning lay in putting forth the disciplined effort—he called it, "lutter vers les sommets" (fighting for the summits)—*not* in any of the resulting achievements.

In getting from A to B, like Sisyphus, you will face a serious uphill struggle. That struggle, as Figure 12-2 suggests, will begin right at the outset of the modeling effort. You will need to begin by wrenching your perspective (and likely your client's, if you have one), up out of the weeds—i.e., the detail of the operating environment in which they are enmeshed. You'll need to embrace the 10,000 Meter Thinking. As was true for Sisyphus, you will need to exercise a lot of discipline throughout the journey in order to keep from sliding off the slope. And, also like Sisyphus, much of the learning will occur along the way (not after you arrive). But there are also some important differences between Sisyphus' challenge and the one you'll face in seeking to travel from A to B.

First, Camus' protagonist was at least assured of being on a path toward a summit. You are afforded no such assurance. In fact, many people are encouraged to choose a *horizontal* path leading rightward from point A. We refer to this path as "the low road." People traveling it are "modeling the system!" One sure way *not* to get to B, is not to set out for B in the first place! I've already described the agony of defeat that *with certainty* awaits those who seek to "model the system." It isn't pretty. Stay off the low road!

The second difference between the pathway traveled by Camus' hero, and the one you should be seeking to tread, is that most of your journey is on a slight *downhill*! Following an initial very steep vertical ascent, the rest of the trip consists of expanding the breadth of your view, while being careful about admitting extraneous detail (don't lose your footing!). Remember that it's always possible to add more detail, for cosmetic and face validity purposes, *after* you've understood what you need to understand. The first order of business is building the understanding.

The third difference between Sisyphus' journey and your own is that it is not preordained that your "rock" will roll back down again! That can happen. But it doesn't *have to* happen. One of the most common causes of it happening is "clients." After seeing an initial, simple version of the model, interest is piqued. Clients point out that while "interesting," the model would be "even better" if it just included a few more things. The next version is, again, "Good…but." So, a new "punch list" of "must adds" is developed. After awhile, as the model continues to gain visibility, stakeholders from across the organization come to feel they, too, must put *their* imprimatur on it. When this happens, you are in free-fall toward the weeds.

One of the best ways to avoid being nudged into free-fall is to make sure your client is lashed together with you on the slope. That is, involve them in the boundary-setting decision-making process. Make their involvement an explicit part of your learning strategy. Encourage your client to struggle with you to understand why a model is doing what it is doing, and engage them in trying to develop clear, intuitive explanations that others can understand.

With this prelude to the process in place, we're now ready to look at some Guidelines for the modeling/learning process…

Modeling Process Guidelines

The diagram depicting the steps in the modeling process is reproduced as Figure 12-3. For each step, I have provided some Guidelines and "Best Practice" principles to help you in the execution of the step. Guidelines for the modeling steps precede those for the Learning steps—this is strictly for clarity of presentation and not intended to suggest a priority, or that in practice the two would be executed this way.

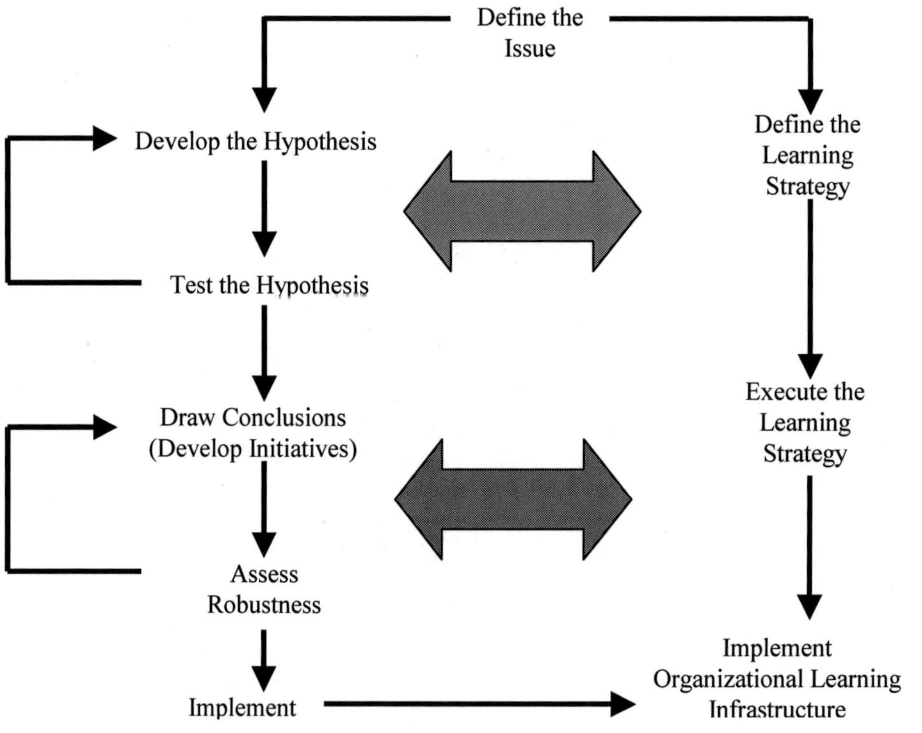

Figure 12-3.
The "Steps" in the Model-construction/Learning Processes.

Step 1. Define the Issue

In step one of the process, you are seeking to develop a sharp issue-focus to guide the effort. Most modeling efforts that spin out of control do so because not enough time was taken up front to nail down an operational statement of purpose. Spend the time!

Guideline 1: Write a Clear, Explicit Purpose for the Effort.

- Write your purpose statement on paper. Then, always keep it within sight.
- Couch the purpose statement in terms of gaining an understanding of the relationships responsible for generating a specific problem/ issue for purposes of addressing that issue. For example: "This model is intended to shed light on the causes of inventory instability, for purposes of reducing that instability."
- Never set out to, or be drawn into, "modeling the system."
- Be sure to involve the entire stakeholder community in developing the statement of purpose.

Guideline 2: Develop a Reference Behavior Pattern.

A *reference behavior pattern* (RBP) is a graph over time of one or more variables that best depict the pattern of behavior you're trying to understand/change.

- In cases where there is "history," your RBP should show an "As Is." Your RBP may also include a "To Be" segment—in cases where there is no history (such as in the design of a new strategy or a new organization) this may be all it includes. In developing the "To Be" segment, pay particular attention to how long it is projected to take for performance to achieve "To Be" levels.
- Choose an "interesting" RBP, one that visually depicts "a puzzle" that *cries out* for an explanation.
- Where possible, create the RBP by using *relative* measures. Divide the RBP variable by some benchmark quantity, to screen out issues of absolute growth (this process is called "normalizing").
- Pay attention to the time span over which the RBP is unfolding. Only include things in your model that unfold with a rhythm that's relevant to this time span. For example, if the RBP unfolds over five years, you could include things that play out in quarters or months, but not weeks or hours!

Three illustrations of Reference Behavior patterns appear in figure 12-4.

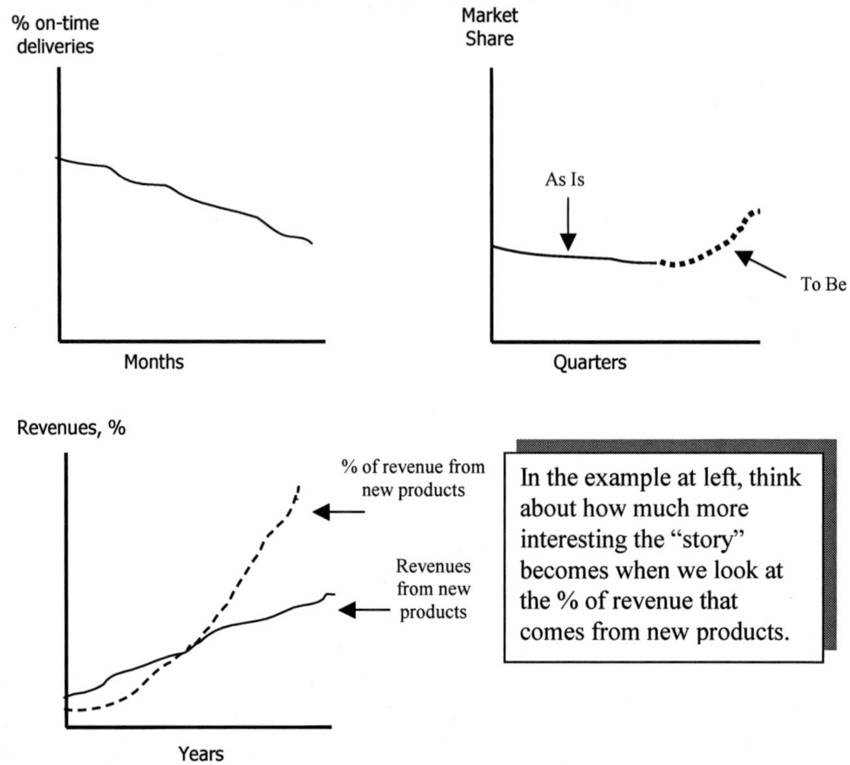

Figure 12-4.
Illustrative Reference Behavior Patterns.

In the example at left, think about how much more interesting the "story" becomes when we look at the % of revenue that comes from new products.

Step 2. Develop the Hypothesis

In this step, you will conceive of, and render, a hypothesis that you believe is capable of explaining the RBP you defined in Step 1.

Guideline 1: Seek a Dynamic Organizing Principle.

A "dynamic organizing principle" is an infrastructure-based, or feedback loop-based, framework which resides at the core of your model. Think of it as providing an underlying theme for your "story."

Some examples: ***Infrastructure-based***

- Time allocation (Chapter 9)
- Percolation in a Main Chain (Chapter 8)
- Attribute tracking (Chapter 9)

Some examples: ***Feedback loop-based***

- Overshoot and collapse (from depletion of a resource base)
- S-shaped growth (shift in dominance) (Chapter 6)
- The two-stock pure oscillator structure (Chapter 7)
- When you're hot you're hot, when you're not you're not!
- Shifting the burden to the intervener
- Eroding goal structures

Main Chain

Guideline 2: Try One of These Approaches: Main Chain, Key Actor, Most-important Accumulation.

A Main Chain is a sequence of stocks connected by conserved (i.e., material) flows. Main Chain infrastructures are described in Chapter 8. A Main Chain provides a physical "backbone" off of which the remainder of your model can pirouette. An illustration of a Main Chain appears in Figure 12-5.

- Ask: *What's flowing through the system?* Note the associated "stages." There should be an accumulation associated with each. If the accumulations/flows from a conserved-flow sequence, you've got a Main Chain.
- Keep your Main Chains as aggregated as possible.

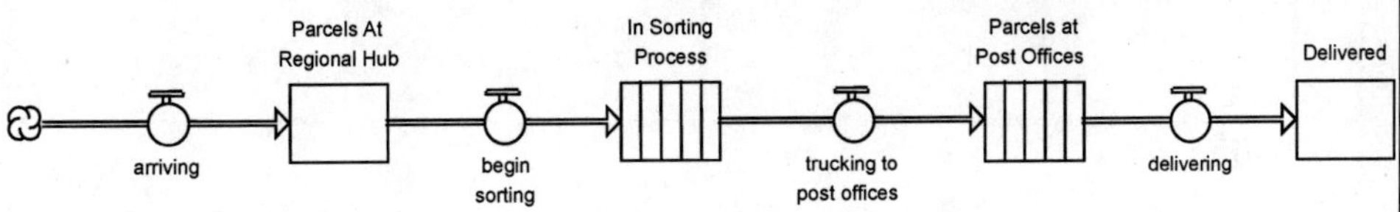

Figure 12-5.
An Illustrative Main Chain.

"Key Actor" Approach

Often, by thinking about the "actors" associated with your model, you can identify a nucleus of essential stocks and flows associated with each.

- Identify the smallest set of Key Actors that you hypothesize to be involved in generating the RBP. Actors often are not individual human beings.

- For each actor, identify the conditions the actor monitors to determine how things "are" within their piece of the system. Conditions may be material (e.g., money) or non-material (e.g., trust). They will most likely be represented as *stocks*.
- Next, identify the actions taken by each actor in response to changes in conditions. The actions will be represented by *flows*.
- Finally, identify the resources that support taking actions. Resources may be material or non-material. Resources will be *stocks* (or converters).
- It's useful to use a "Key Actor Matrix" (illustrated in Figure 12-6) to collect the information on conditions, actions, and resources.

Actor:	**Conditions Monitored**	**Actions Taken**	**Resources Consumed**
Finance Department	• Cash on Hand • Actual vs. Projected Spending Ratio • Remaining Budget Dollars	• Evaluate Spending Request	• Cash • Analyst Person-hours

Figure 12-6.
An Illustrative "Key Actor" Matrix.

The Most-important Accumulation

Identify the accumulation (a stock) you consider to be closest to the "heart" of the issue you are seeking to address. Then, add an inflow and an outflow. You're on your way!

Guideline 3: Use The Generic Flow Templates to Characterize the Flows.

Once you've got some stocks and flows laid out, the next step in developing the hypothesis is to *characterize the flows*. Seek to capture the nature of each flow as it works in reality. Strive to achieve an operational specification by using one of the generic flow templates described in the Appendix to Chapter 6.

- Look at each flow in isolation. Ask: "*What is the nature of activity that generates the flow? How does this activity work in the real system?" Don't* ask: "What are all the factors that *influence* this flow?" Doing so leads to a Laundry List!

- If the activity...

Is a self-reinforcing growth process, use the *Compounding Template.*

Involves passive decay, draining or aging, use the *Draining Template.*

Is produced by a resource, other than the stock to which the flow is attached, use the *External Resource Template.*

Runs in parallel with some other flow, or if the flow tracks an attribute associated with a stock, use the *Co-flow Template.*

Adjusts the stock to some target value, use the *Stock-adjustment Template.*

- Use only one generic template per flow. If another template is needed, create a separate flow. Add only the structure required by the generic flow processes you choose. You can embellish the structure later.

Guideline 4: Close Loops Without Adding More Elements to the Model.

After you have characterized the flows in your map, the next step in rendering your hypothesis is to close loops. It's important to do so without including additional stocks, flows, or converters.

- Look to see if any of the parameters associated with the generic flow templates that are currently constant, should in fact really depend on some other variable *currently on the screen* (many will be, but you're only interested in making them variables if doing so is part of your hypothesis!). Close the resulting feedback loop as illustrated in Figure 12-7.

In the Figure, two loops are closed, turning co-flow and stock-adjustment flow templates with constant parameters, into templates whose parameters are variable. The first loop links the *Knowledge* stock to time being allocated to learning activities. The idea here is that, for example, the desire for more knowledge could lead someone to spend more time engaged in *learning activities*. The second loop links *Knowledge* to *learning productivity*. The notion is that the more someone knows, the more "hooks" they have for learning even more.

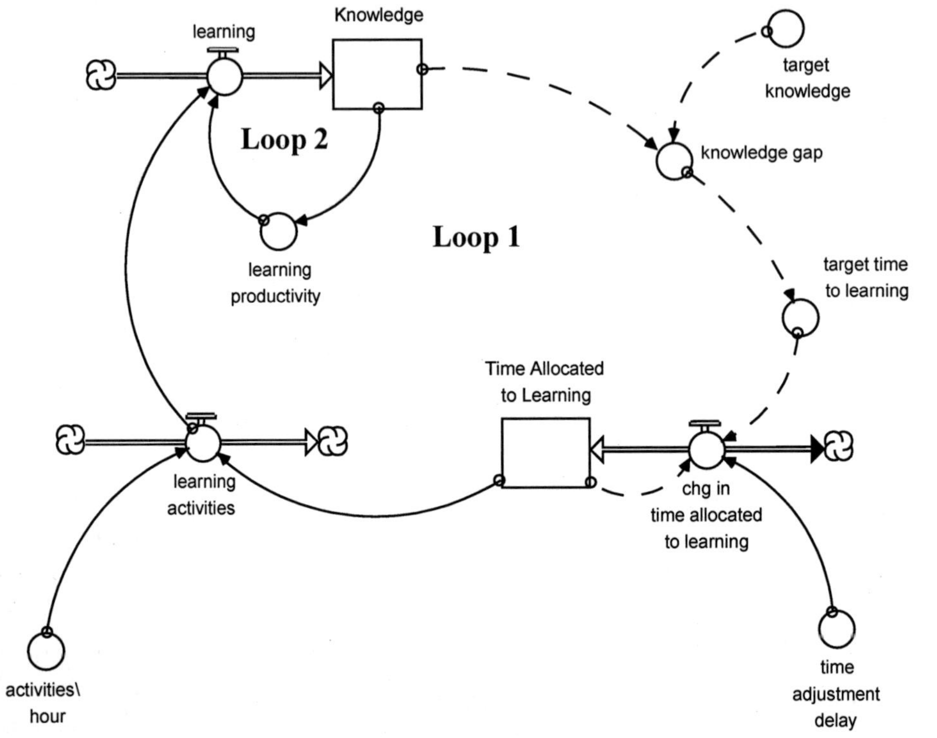

Figure 12-7.
Closing Loops.

Guideline 5: Convert Your Map to a Computer-simulatable Model by Including Equations.

Once you have fleshed out the map, select a chunk (a sector is a good chunk) and make it simulatable—i.e., specify the associated algebra and include numbers.

- Click in the generic flow template equations first.
- Check the dimensional balance of each equation. The units-of-measure of the right-hand side of each equation should be the same as those for the left-hand side. Flows should have the same units-of-measure as the stocks to which they are attached, but with the addition of "per time."
- Avoid "dead buffalos" (a name derived from their appearance on the diagram; see Figure 12-8). Strings of factors that are "correlated," or "influence," are not the same thing as an operational statement of causality. Avoid "Critical Success Factors" Thinking.

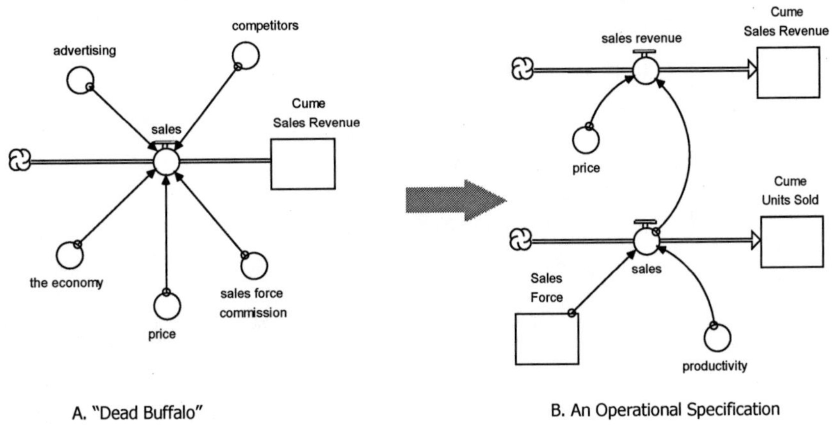

Figure 12-8.
A "Dead Buffalo" vs. an Operational Specification.

Guideline 6: Convert Your Map to a Computer-simulatable Model by Including Numbers.

On first-pass, choose numerical values that initialize your model in steady-state. In steady-state, the net of all inflows and outflows across each stock is zero. See the Appendix to this Chapter for details on initializing models in steady-state.

- On first-pass, favor numbers that are simple and make sense relative to each other, over numbers that reflect actual values taken from the real system. Simple, internally consistent numbers will help you to put the model into steady-state. On second-pass, you can include real-world data, if doing so is shown to be important.
- Favor small numbers (e.g., 0, 1, 10, 100, 1000, etc.) over large ones (e.g., 2.7182818, 97.2222, 1 quadrillion, etc.). By choosing small, numbers, you'll find it much easier to understand what's going on in your model.
- Avoid equations in which more than 2-3 "effect" or "impact of..." multipliers are strung together. Even if each has a value of only slightly less than 1, the resulting overall impact of several such "effects" can be surprisingly large (e.g., 0.9 * 0.9 * 0.9 * 0.9 = 0.66).
- Follow the procedure outlined in the Appendix to Chapter 7 for developing your graphical functions.

Step 3. Test the Hypothesis

Simulating your hypotheses on a computer is designed to increase your confidence that the model you've rendered is useful for the purposes it is intended to serve. These tests also are designed to make you aware of the limitations to the model's utility. Thus, you should emerge from this step both confident in what your model can do, and knowledgeable about its limits.

In order to ensure that you learn as much as you can from each test, before each simulation, sketch out your best guess as to the associated outcome, and articulate your rationale. Then, after the simulation is complete, work to resolve any discrepancies in either actual versus predicted behavior, or in your rationale. If test results so dictate, don't hesitate to cycle back through Steps 1 and 2 of the modeling process.

Guideline 1: Find "Mechanical" Bugs.

- Make a run.
- Investigate any "?" (i.e., undefined entities) that keep your model from simulating.
- If it simulates, choose Range Specs from the Run Menu.
- Look for anomalous values (?, ∞, and negative values that should be positive values).
- Put "offending" variables and associated inputs (or inflows and outflows) into a Table. Set the Table's print interval to DT. Set the Table to report Beginning Balances.
- Run for a few DTs. Run your eye over the values in the Table to determine which variable is causing the problem.
- Repeat the previous two steps until you have identified and repaired all mechanical mistakes.

Guideline 2: Ensure Model is in Steady-state.

- Make a run. Enter the stocks into a Table.
- Set print interval to DT. Set Table to report Beginning Balances.
- Run for one DT. See if any stock changes in value.
- Put the offending stock(s), and its inflows and outflows, into a Table. Fix the problem. Repeat until model is in steady-state.

Guideline 3: Test the "Robustness" of the Model.

- Robustness tests identify formulations that do not hold up "under extreme conditions."
- Incorporate Step and Pulse functions as test-inputs into one or two carefully selected flow equations. The idea is to "shock" the selected stock, knocking it (and the model) out of steady-state.
- Graph the response of key variables. In particular, graph the response of the stock whose flow is being subjected to the shock.
- Use the tracing feature (the "T" on the Graph page that appears after selecting a variable name on the top of the graph page), in conjunction with the "hover to display mini-graph" feature, to help you understand why you are getting the results you are getting.
- Determine whether the model is exhibiting absurd or implausible behavior: stocks going negative when they shouldn't; stocks growing without limit; system returning to the "wrong" steady-

state; response time too short, too long, etc. *Be sure you understand why.* Often you will have omitted a feedback loop; or if it's there, it's too weak/strong.

- If the system exhibits a "high frequency" oscillation in response to any test (i.e., stocks and/or flows jump up and down wildly each DT), check your DT. Halve its value, per the guidelines presented in the *DT: What, Why & Wherefore* section in the *ithink Help Files* within the software. If the oscillation persists, halve it a few more times.
- If the system exhibits a smooth, but ever-expanding, oscillation pattern, be sure that you're using one of the Runge-Kutta simulation methods. See *Simulation Algorithms* in the *ithink Help Files* within the software for details.
- Check model results against the RBP.
- First-pass, look for qualitative similarity. Don't waste a lot of time trying to "track history" exactly unless your purpose (or your boss!) requires it. Be sure you understand, and can explain, the results you are generating.
- Use the tracing feature (the "T" on the Graph page that appears after selecting a variable name on top of the graph page), in conjunction with the "hover to display mini-graph" feature, to help you understand why you are getting the results you're getting.
- If required to "track history," substitute in real-world numbers for constants, initial values and graphical functions. If necessary, also add time series graphical functions to drive the model with historical data.

Steps 4 & 5. Draw Conclusions and Assess Robustness

The next set of tests is aimed at discovering ways to alter (often, to *improve*) the performance of the system. Frequently, behavior patterns being generated by a model are "insensitive" to even reasonably large changes in many parameters. Even though numerical magnitudes change, the pattern of behavior persists. *Sensitive* parameters are those that, when altered, can result in a change in the pattern(s) of behavior being exhibited by a model. Such parameters often are referred to as "leverage points"—a change in their value results in a shift in behavior mode. "High-leverage points" are parameters whose values, when altered only a small amount, result in a shift in behavior pattern. Leverage arises from the fact that the change in parameter value(s) has unleashed the power of a reinforcing, or counteracting, feedback loop that heretofore had been "locked up."

Once some effective initiatives have been identified, it is important to determine how "robust" they are. Do they continue to be effective when the *behavioral assumptions* included in the model, and the assumptions about the *external environment*, are varied? Assessing the former is known as "sensitivity analysis." Assessing the latter is known as "scenario analysis." Both are important in guarding against the "silver bullet syndrome" (i.e., a policy/strategy that works under virtually *all* conditions and all assumptions—*very* few of these exist!).

Guideline 1: Search for "High Leverage" Points.

- Scan the model structure to identify constants and graphical functions that reflect real policy options (i.e., are under the control of decision-makers within the system).
- It often is useful to look for graphical functions that regulate the strength of feedback loops. In particular, look to unleash reinforcing spirals that exist within the non-physical variables within the system (as these variables sometimes offer, as yet un-eaten, "free lunches").
- For each, one at a time, use the Incremental option in Sensitivity Analysis, or the GID (Graphical Input Device, for graphical functions) to assess the amount of leverage the parameter offers.

Guideline 2: Assess Robustness to Parameter Values

- Identify the important "behavioral assumptions" in your model. These are values associated with parameters that are "internal to the system," and hence over which decision-makers within the system can presumably exert some control. For each, conduct a sensitivity analysis with the "high leverage" parameter(s) set at its *altered* value(s). Do the leverage points continue to remain leverage points? Under what conditions do they lose "their magic?" Assess the likelihood of those "magic eradicating" conditions coming about.
- Identify the important "scenario parameters" in your model. These parameters are "external" to the system, and hence decision-makers within the system have little (to no) control over them. For each, conduct a sensitivity analysis with the "high leverage" parameter(s) set at its *altered* value(s). Do the leverage points continue to remain leverage points? Under what conditions do they lose "their magic?" Assess the likelihood of those "magic eradicating" conditions coming about.
- As a result of your analyses, identify the intervention points that are most robust to changes in both internal behavioral and external scenario parameters.
- Identify your model's key *extensive* and *intensive* boundary points (see Figure 12-9).

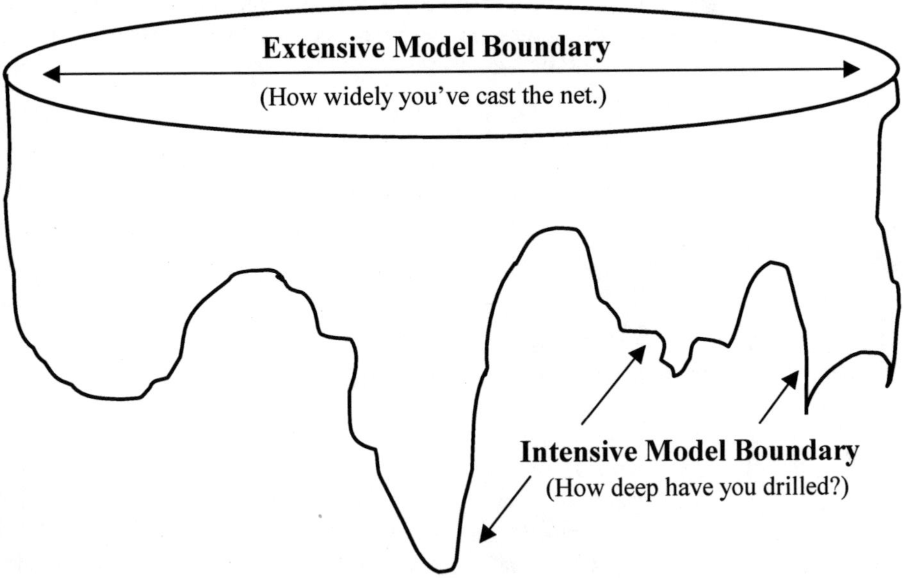

Figure 12-9.
The Concept of an Extensive and Intensive Model Boundary.

Guideline 3: Assess Robustness to Model Boundary Decisions.

- *Extensive* model boundary tests help you evaluate the adequacy of the *breadth* of your model. The clouds on the ends of flows are an explicit indication of breadth. Clouds represent "infinite sources" or "sinks." A cloud says that the stuff flowing into a stock comes "out of thin air" (i.e., doesn't deplete any other stock), and that the stuff flowing out of a stock in your model vanishes into same (i.e., doesn't fill up another stock). Clouds associated with physical flows imply that the stocks being omitted, as well as any associated flows and feedback linkages, are "outside" the scope of your model. The existence of clouds helps to keep you aware you are making these assumptions.
- *Challenge* the clouds in your model! Ask…If I replaced this cloud with a stock, what additional feedback relationships would be introduced into the model? Do I think introducing those relationships might cause me to change my conclusions? If the answer is "yes, to maybe," eliminate the cloud, add the relationships, and simulate!
- *Intensive* model boundary tests help you to evaluate the depth, or degree of disaggregation, of your model. Have you included "too much" or "too little" detail in depicting the elements, activities and

interrelationships in the model? You'll be "challenging" converter, graphical function, stock and flow, representations.

Scan the model for *converters* that are being used as stock substitutes. Consider each such converter in light of your purpose, asking:

- What flows are being left out of the model by choosing to treat the stock-type concept as a converter?
- If I included these flows, how might the system's dynamics be altered?

If the answers to these questions appear interesting, make the required stock/flow for converter substitutions, include any feedback relationships that suggest themselves, and then simulate.

Identify each *stock* that is being used to aggregate a category of accumulations (e.g., doctors, instead of the "umpteen" medical specialties). In light of your purpose, ask if the disaggregation of the aggregate stock is likely to alter your conclusions? If the answer seems worth pursuing, pursue it. Examine each *conveyor* that you've included in your model. Think about the processes it is aggregating. Would explicitly representing the detail of these processes be likely to cause you to change your conclusions? If so, disaggregate! Simulate.

Examine each *flow* in your model. Determine whether the associated activity is represented in enough detail to do justice to the actual process. If not, consider disaggregating the flow to capture a truer picture of the reality. Do you think doing so might alter your recommendations? If so, disaggregate. Simulate.

Examine each graphical function. Think about whether the "on average" assumption embedded in the dependent variable is really justified. For example, in a graphical function representing the "price elasticity of demand" for a good, should the function really be broken down into separate price elasticities for each of several market segments?

Guidelines for the Learning Process

Learning Process

If only the person/people who construct a model learn from it, a huge potential for understanding and insight will go un-harvested. It is vitally important to define an overall learning strategy for your effort. Any such strategy should include an "along the way," and an "after completion" component.

Guideline 1: Define an "Along the Way" Learning Strategy.

- Seek to involve all key stakeholders in the process of constructing the model. This does not mean that everyone in the group has to be involved in writing equations or collecting numerical data. It means that members should weigh in on conceptualization of the model, react to initial strawman maps, and are engaged in simulations of first-round models.
- An "along the way" learning strategy for those *not* directly involved in model construction also must be defined. Do you want to make "maps," outfitted with annotated storytelling sequences, available for perusal and download via the organization's intranet? Do you want intermediate versions of computer-simulatable models made available, perhaps outfitted with Flight Simulator interfaces, so people from around the organization can learn by "playing?"

Guideline 2: Define an "After Completion" Learning Strategy.

- After completion, the model ideally should become part of an on-line *Organizational Learning Infrastructure*. Anyone within the organization should be able to "check the model out" of the Library, review it, and make enhancement suggestions. Enhancements should be implemented via a formal editing process in which some official party controls access to the "Golden Master."
- Any models housed within the infrastructure should have: (1) annotated storytelling sequences to help people "make meaning" out of model structure/behavior, (2) a high-level interface that provides context and documentation, and (3) some sort of user interface that facilitates making changes to parameters and simulating.
- You may choose to convert some models into Flight Simulators or full-blown Learning Environments. *Flight Simulators* provide Dashboards and usually simulate in "pause and resume" mode. Often they include "in character" feedback messages and some means of "keeping score." *Learning Environments* are Flight Simulators that have been outfitted with JITJWN (just-in-time, just-what's-needed) coaching sequences.

Flight Simulator Guidelines

Populate the front-end context portion of Flight Simulators and Learning Environments with icons of the culture (movies featuring the CEO are very effective!) to create as many touch-points with organizational reality as possible. Doing so facilitates suspension of disbelief, drawing end-users into the "magic kingdom." Provide end-users with a clear statement of their mission and a clear picture of "who they are" (what role they are playing) in the drama that is about to unfold. Make the statement of mission operational by explaining the direct impact that each decision lever will have on the system (the indirect impacts—ramification patterns—are what end-users will discover through their efforts to manage the system).

Keep Dashboards simple! Limit the number of decision levers to around five to seven. Limit the number of variables being monitored on the main panel to three to four. If it is necessary to include additional levers, group them and navigate from a central panel to each group (or use a single List Input Device with multiple pages). Additional variables to be monitored should be included on graphs and tables located on a separate screen. Consider whether separating decision levers from output devices makes sense. Be sure to include a "record of decisions" (graphs, tables, or both!) so that learners can re-visit the decisions they have made during the flight.

Do not include more than 20 decision periods (10-15 is optimal). Use Run/Restore rather than Run for your Run buttons so as to prevent learners from accidentally running past the end of a simulation and inadvertently wiping out their record of decisions and their performance achievements. Consider including a Sketchable graph to enable learners to "put a stake in the ground" with respect to the performance results they hope to achieve.

In developing coaching sequences, begin by determining all possible patterns of behavior that learners might produce. For each pattern, think through a "trail of breadcrumbs" that would lead a learner to ask good questions about why they are getting the outcome that is developing. Front-end load with in-character feedback messages, then transition to coaching messages with successive simulations. If learners go too long without feeling they are making progress in building understanding, they will become frustrated. If learners "get it" too quickly, they will de-value the learning experience. Make each coaching vignette short and sweet; *don't lecture*! Pose good questions; present evocative visual metaphors. Remember that learners are in "action mode" and not eager to spend lots of time reflecting!

Learners greatly appreciate pats on the back! Do not underestimate the importance of providing them (both small and large victories should be acknowledged).

Consider including an "Extend Your Understanding" section in which learners can modify behavioral and scenario assumptions so as to "make the model their own" and dispel any notion of "silver bullets."

Summary

The major benefit of working systematically through the modeling/learning process is that, as a result, you will be able to communicate more clearly, more succinctly, and with greater confidence, both about what's causing the issue you've examined and what you might do to effectively address it. You'll also be able to make your learning available to others in an *active* format. People will be able to discover insights and build understanding for themselves. In so doing, they'll be building shared understanding and alignment across the organization.

Appendix:
Initializing Your Models in Steady-State

Achieving a steady-state initialization often is a straightforward process. It's always a useful process to engage in, for two primary reasons. First, steady-state ensures that the parameters in your model are internally consistent. Second, once the model is in steady-state, you'll be able conduct controlled experiments in which you observe the "pure" response of the system to your robustness and policy tests.

In steady-state, the sum of the inflows for each stock is equal to the sum of the outflows for each stock. Therefore, the magnitude of all stocks will be constant.

Guidelines

- Determine how much latitude you have for specifying the value of each flow. Can you *directly* set a value for the flow, or otherwise cause it to be whatever you'd like?
- Once you've determined the amount of latitude you have, use the data which are "most solid" to infer values for those parameters whose values are "least solid." Give yourself plenty of license in determining "less solid" parameter values. Because few real systems are in steady-state, you'll often need to modify numbers taken from an actual system in order to achieve a steady-state. After completing steady-state-based tests, you can substitute "real" values back in. Whenever possible, use algebraic initialization to establish initial values for stocks. We'll illustrate this process using the model pictured in Figure 12-10.

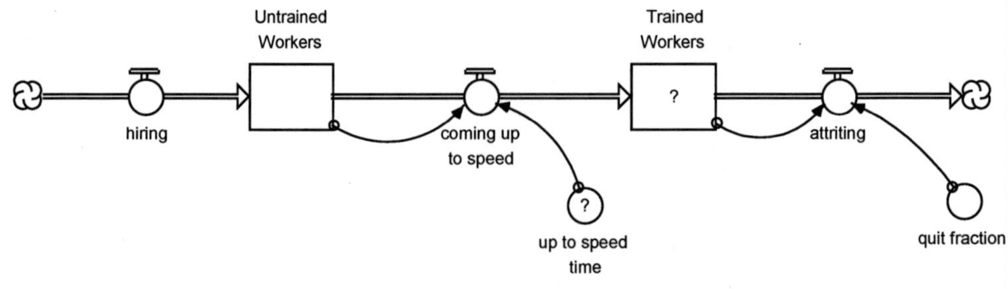

Figure 12-10.
Illustrating Algebraic Initialization.

You may find it useful to work along with this illustration. The model is contained in your Models folder as "Initialization." In this simple model, we know the following with some confidence:

- *Untrained Workers* = 100
- *coming up to speed* = *Untrained workers / up to speed time*
- *attriting* = *Trained Workers * quit fraction*
- *quit fraction* = 0.25
- *hiring* = 50

We'll use what we know with confidence, to solve for the two values we're less certain of (an initial value for *Trained Workers* and a value for *up to speed time*). The solution process will also cause the model to be initialized in a steady-state condition. We'll begin by finding an initial value for *Trained Workers*. In steady-state...

- *attriting* = *coming up to speed*

Substituting the associated algebra for the two flows, we have...

- *Trained Workers * quit fraction* = *Untrained Workers / up to speed time*

Solving for *Trained Workers*, we get...

- *Trained Workers* = *(Untrained Workers / up to speed time)/quit fraction*

[We can now click-in this equation using variables in the Allowable Inputs list of the *Trained Workers* dialog box. The software will then solve the equation at the outset of the simulation in order to arrive at an initial value for *Trained Workers*. Note that, because of the way we solved for this value, it will cause the *attriting* flow to equal the *coming up to speed* flow!]

To wrap up the process, we'll find a steady-state value for *up to speed time*. For steady-state:

- *hiring* = *coming up to speed*

Substituting the algebra...

- *hiring* = *Untrained Workers / up to speed time*

Substituting in numbers...

- 50 = 100 / *up to speed time*

Solving for *up to speed time*...

- *up to speed time* = 100/50 = 2

Following this sort of process is a nice way to use numerical values about which you are reasonably confident to "force out" values for which you have little to no information. At the same time, it yields a steady-state initialization for your model. Two birds with one stone!

Chapter 13

Adding Texture to Your Compositions

Modeling "Soft" Variables

Things like self-esteem, commitment, and trust usually aren't mentioned in the same breath as computers. Such variables are "squishy" and amorphous, while computers are scientific, numerical, and precise. But, you know what? How things go with these amorphous, squishy variables is absolutely vital to the effective functioning of not all, but many, systems in which humans play a role! Leaving such variables out of a model in which you know they belong is tantamount to assuming they are irrelevant to the associated dynamics. Be honest. Can you think of *any* system that includes human beings in which trust, self-confidence, commitment and self-esteem, and (to name only a few) are *completely* irrelevant?

The real issue here is one of model purpose. Many models have as their implicit, if not explicit, purpose, precise numerical point-prediction. "Model, model, on the wall, tell me what interest rates, earnings, sales (pick your poison) will be in the Fall." Three decimal point precision will do, thank you. The fact is, there will never be a precise measure of frustration, confidence, love, or anger. Indeed, measuring such variables is "sticky" even in concept. That's because of the long-recognized "Hawthorne effect;" i.e., the act of measuring, itself, causes a change in what's being measured—physicists know this effect as the "Heisenberg uncertainty principle." So, if a model's purpose is numerically-precise prediction, the kingdom of the "squishy" is almost certain to be decreed off-limits.

Given all this, let's step back and look dispassionately at the situation. Here are the options… You can proceed with a model whose purpose is numerically-precise prediction, but which intentionally leaves out variables you are *absolutely certain* exert some (perhaps, a major) impact on how the system performs. Or, you can sacrifice a certain measure of numerical precision, but not necessarily analytical rigor, in order to include "soft" variables that you know play a critical role in generating the system's dynamics.

Here's some more information that should be useful in helping you to evaluate the two options. Numerically-precise prediction is in fact unattainable, because there are *always* variables that impact outcomes, but that are outside the control of decision-makers within the system (and, hence, unpredictable). Further, pursuing prediction as a purpose belies a reactive, victim-oriented posture—as opposed to, for example, seeking to understand how to design for resiliency/robustness in the face of forces you cannot control! For these purposes, numerical precision is seldom as important as capturing the qualitative essence of the associated relationships. Translation: *squishy variables are welcome!*

In summary, it is not always necessary to include "soft" variables in your models. But when you know these variables are important, you shouldn't intentionally ignore them! This Chapter will show you how to bring "soft" variables to full, first-class citizen status within your models.

Distinguishing Between Quantification and Measurement

One of the reasons people shy away from soft variables is that they fail to recognize an important distinction. That distinction is between *quantification* with *measurement.*

Measurement means: "determining the magnitude of." Often, the result of the determination is expressed numerically. For physical quantities, we have many pre-defined units-of-measure. For example, we have miles, meters, pounds, kilos, quarts and cubic centimeters. It's possible to measure the number of units in a finished goods inventory quite precisely. It's also possible to measure a child's height and weight, the distance to grandma's house, or the diameter of a circus tent, with a good deal of numerical precision.

By contrast, quantification means: "assigning a numerical index to." You can quantify *anything*! There is a certain inherent arbitrariness to the process. For example, if someone asked me to quantify my level of fatigue, the first question I'd ask is…"On a scale from what to what?" When the response came back "0 to 100," or "1 to 10," I could then take a shot at quantifying my level of fatigue. You could, too! And, we could do the same for our level of confidence, lust, envy, commitment, and all the other juicy non-physical variables that spice up our lives!

And so, it's easy to quantify anything. The real trick is to do so in a way that enables you to maintain the rigor-of-thinking associated with the physical (i.e., *measurable*) variables in the model. In fact, there's no "trick" involved…just careful thought, as you're about to see.

Quantifying Soft Variables

I'll use an example of quantifying a squishy variable to illustrate an approach that works. I'll then conclude the chapter by distilling and summarizing the associated process and principles.

The example involves "burnout." Burnout covers a continuum of psychological states. There's the mild fraying around the edges that occurs after burning the midnight oil for a few consecutive nights. There's the "medium broil." You spend a month or two flat out. Your exercise program evaporates. Your diet disintegrates into fast-food and chocolate. Each time you awaken, you swear you'd spent your slumber serving as a well-trafficked off-ramp on the interstate. Finally, there's "deep fried." This vintage usually requires clinical treatment and a long lay off to overcome.

The first step in representing burnout within a model, as with representing *any* such non-physical quantity, has absolutely *nothing* to do with numbers! This is important. The first step is to ask yourself the classic Systems Thinking question: "How does it work?"

Think about it for a second before continuing. How *does* the process of becoming burned out really work?

The diagram presented in Figure 13-1 provides one answer. It suggests that the "building burnout" process is *co-flow* in nature. Building up burnout is coincident with the process of allocating hours to working—and, correspondingly, not enough hours to activities that allow any burnout that has accumulated to dissipate. As the diagram indicates, for each hour worked, a certain amount of burnout per hour is added to the stock of burnout. As the level of burnout builds, it progressively depresses productivity. As productivity falls, other things equal, the work backlog swells even further. This causes workers to "throw" even more hours at the problem—causing burnout to build at an even more rapid clip. A vicious cycle if ever there was one!

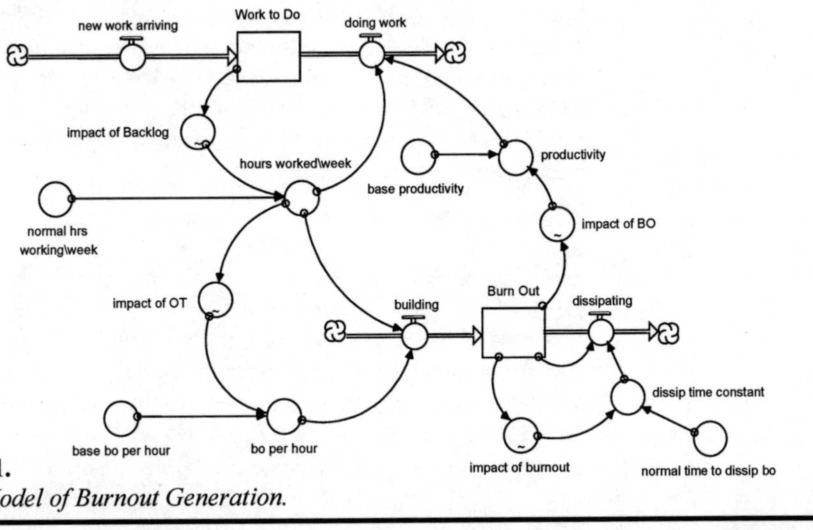

Figure 13-1.
A Simple Model of Burnout Generation.

Much can be harvested from this simple model. First, as already noted, the model illustrates how to capture the way burnout actually builds up—i.e., the formulation is "operational," as opposed to a "factors" statement (these six things "cause" burnout).

Second, burnout is quantified using a 0 to 100 index. A value of 0 means not a trace of burnout; a value of 100 means as deep-fried as it's possible to be. The purpose of the model is not to predict the precise instant at which burnout levels will hit 67.49. The purpose will be something more along the lines of determining which policies will enable burnout to remain at levels that do not significantly depress productivity. Those levels are closer to 20 than they are to 60.

Third, burnout is *operationally-related* to physical variables in the system. For example, it impacts *productivity*, which in turn determines the rate at which work is completed. It also is driven by *hours worked per week*. Operationally weaving burnout-related variables into the fabric of the physical variables within the system makes it possible to empirically calibrate the associated relationships. Let's look at how this process works in a bit more detail.

Look at the variable "bo per hour." It is determined as the product of a base amount of burnout per hour and an impact that comes from how many overtime hours per week workers are putting in. So, how would you go about quantifying either of these two variables? Here's how...

Start with "base bo per hour." Let's just make it, say, 10. You want 1? Okay, 1 it is. Assume, for now, that the "impact of OT" is neutral (i.e., equal to 1.0, because workers are working a normal amount of hours—no overtime). Next, consider the equation for "building" burnout (i.e., the inflow). It is: "hours worked per week" times "bo per hour." If we assume that workers normally work 40 hours per week, this would mean that the inflow to the burnout rate, in a *normal* week, would be equal to 40 per week (because we assumed "bo per hour" to equal to 1)! If 100 is, by definition, the maximum level that Burnout can ever achieve, building 40 units of burnout per week under *normal* circumstances makes no sense at all.

Bottom line: a value of 1.0 for "bo per hour" will not work! A value of 10, which was the first value suggested, would have caused 400 units of burnout to build in a normal week...not just absurd, *impossible*! We are probably looking at values in the vicinity of 0.1 for "base bo per hour"—meaning that a *normal* work week might build 4 units of burnout. Could the number be 0.2 (meaning 8 units of burnout would be built in a normal 40-hour work week)? Probably. Arriving at an agreed-upon value would make for an interesting discussion. But it probably would be difficult for anyone to argue for numbers too much bigger than 0.2.

What we are doing in this process is using the combination of an arbitrary, but consistent, numerical scale (0 - 100 for Burnout) and a physical variable—about which we have solid numerical data (i.e., the number of hours worked in a normal work week)—to "force out" values for a couple of squishy parameters for which we have *no* numerical data! The other squishy parameter value we can "force out" of this particular calculation process is the "impact of OT." Because it multiplies "base bo per hour" to yield "bo per hour," and also because we already have determined that values of "bo per hour" probably lie in the 0.1 to 0.2 range, we can home in on reasonable values for the "impact" variable. The process you'd employ would go something like this...

When you work an 80-hour week, how much burnout do you think you'd generate? Suppose your answer was, say, 40 units. Let's also say you had elected to set "base bo per hour" to a value of 0.1. To generate an inflow of 40 units of burnout, the "impact" multiplier, at 80 hours per week, would have to take on a value of five (because 5 times 0.1 = 0.5; and 0.5 times 80 hours per week = 40). Values too much greater than five for the multiplier would generate too much burnout inflow per week—given that the maximum allowable value for burnout is, by definition, 100. Do you see how the process works?

Let's work through one other example in the burnout model. The "impact of BO," a multiplier that determines the level of productivity, can be empirically calibrated in the previously demonstrated manner. Begin with the "doing work" flow. The numerical magnitude of this flow should be easily obtainable from company data. The flow represents how many units of work (say, tasks, widgets, transactions, etc.) are completed in a week. It is calculated as the product of "hours worked per week" and "productivity." If you know that, say, 80 units of work (whatever those "units" might be) are completed (per person) in a normal 40-hour work-week, then "base productivity" must be 2.0. Base productivity is "impacted" by the level of burnout. To develop the graphical function relationship, impact of BO, you'd proceed like this...

If the level of burnout stood at zero, the "impact" on productivity would be neutral (or 1.0). As the level of burnout increases, the impact on productivity will become increasingly depressive. At the extreme, very high levels of burnout will drive productivity to zero (but no lower). So, the multiplier will range from 0 to 1.0. Discussion would create the rest of the points in the graphical relationship—and then, you'd conduct sensitivity analysis (see *Help Files*) to see whether the various shapes of the curves passing through the (0,1) and (100,0) points made much of a difference to the conclusions that are drawn.

As in the previous calculation, we've relied on common sense, "hard data" where it's available, and arbitrary (yet consistent) index-number scaling for "soft" variables. The combination allows us to "force out" internally-consistent parameter values. The process works! Try it.

Some Guidelines for Quantifying Soft Variables

Leaving "soft" variables out of your model, when you know they are playing an important role in generating a system's dynamics, is the only hypothesis that you can reject with certainty! You'll have little difficulty incorporating such variables into your models if you adopt the following four-step approach:

1. Use a consistent range for all "soft" variables in the model. I recommend 0 to 100. 0 means "complete absence." 100 means 100% (i.e., as much as it's possible to have).
2. If the variable is being represented as a stock, think *operationally* about how the inflow and outflow activities really work. Use one of the *generic flow templates* (Chapter 6) to represent these activities if possible.
3. Use "hard" data to "force out" numerical values for "soft" variables.
4. Conduct sensitivity analysis to see how important the specific values you've chosen are to the conclusions you've drawn. In this context, a parameter is sensitive if it changes the nature of the conclusions/recommendations emanating from the model.

What's Next

Getting out there and doin' it! The time has come to take what you've learned and use it in the world to construct better mental models, simulate them more reliably, and communicate them more effectively. We'll be looking for your "short stories" on the NY Times Best Models list!

List of Figures

Chapter 1

Chapter 2

Chapter 3

Chapter 4

Chapter 5

Chapter 6

Chapter 7

Chapter 8

Chapter 9

Chapter 10

Chapter 11

Index

G

H

I

J

K

L

M

N

O